habnf   HEB

636.9322 S

Smith, Caleb, author
Peacebunny Island
33410017091473   4-08-2021

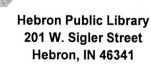

Hebron Public Library
201 W. Sigler Street
Hebron, IN 46341

Advance Praise for *Peacebunny Island*

This is the story of a boy with a vision to make the world a better place through the power of bunnies. Caleb's rabbits are fully alive and brimming with their own unique thoughts, opinions, and personalities. Most of all, however, they are curious and empathetic beings that generously offer unconditional love and affection to those who need it. There are big dreams on every page of this unique and joyful story, written by an unstoppable young man who cares deeply about others and offers himself, his bunnies, and now his island as an oasis brimming with hope, hops, and heart.

SUSY FLORY
New York Times bestselling author and coauthor, writers' conference director, mom of a rescued racehorse, and part-time squirrel nursery attendant

Peacebunny Island is an absolutely delightful and deeply insightful book. Caleb Smith writes with the optimism and authenticity of the young man he is and with the hard-earned wisdom and insight of the old soul that lies within. If you find yourself in need of comfort—or of a reminder of the good that still exists in this world—the precious bunnies of Peacebunny Island stand ready to hop into your heart and fill your soul with peace.

JENNIFER MARSHALL BLEAKLEY
Author of *Joey* and *Pawverbs*

Peacebunny Island is a heartwarming story that will encourage your soul. Enjoy the improbable tale of a young boy parlaying his love for rescued rabbits to make a real difference. I love the sweet reminder of how God uses the childlike faith of Caleb Smith to accomplish His purpose.

DAVE BURCHETT
Author of *Stay: Lessons My Dogs Taught Me about Life, Loss, and Grace*

Caleb's skill at describing his experience after the tragedy at Sandy Hook is such a beautiful tribute to the gift of presence that was provided to the Newtown community and especially to me. Our emotional response to the story tells us that he captured the essence through his observations and reflections. The clarity of language, precise word choice, and heartfelt honesty come shining through!

DR. ANTHONY J. SALVATORE
Retired public school administrator of Newtown Public Schools in Connecticut

You don't need to be an animal lover to fall in love with this tale of one boy's dream of rescuing rabbits, training them as comfort animals, and then buying them their very own island. Encouraged by parents who met his dreams with a healthy balance of support and reality-checking, Caleb is a relatable hero whose youthful wisdom applies to anyone with an entrepreneur's spirit. I read this book in two days simply because it is a delight and I could not stop. If your soul, like mine, could stand a good dousing of sheer joy, read this book. And if you need a little inspiration to follow your own dreams, pandemic and beyond, look no further. You've arrived.

SEPTEMBER VAUDREY
Author of *Colors of Goodbye*

Deeply moving and profoundly hopeful, the story of *Peacebunny Island* is an inspiring reminder that we can all make the world better for the people (and animals) around us. Highly recommended.

MATT MIKALATOS
Author of The Sunlit Lands trilogy

In *Peacebunny Island*, Caleb Smith walks through his journey of fulfilling his dream with business savvy and prayer. Readers of this book will be inspired to persevere, trusting God's guidance along the way. We can all make a difference and show kindness and compassion. I love animals and have written many books about God's creatures. But from now on, I'll have more appreciation and affection for the bunnies, especially those on Peacebunny Island.

DANDI DALEY MACKALL
Author of the Winnie the Horse Gentler series and *The One Year Devos for Animal Lovers*

PEACEBUNNY ISLAND

CALEB SMITH

Peacebunny Island

the *EXTRAORDINARY JOURNEY* of
A BOY AND HIS COMFORT RABBITS,
and HOW THEY'RE TEACHING US
about HOPE & KINDNESS

TYNDALE
MOMENTUM®

The Tyndale nonfiction imprint

Visit Tyndale online at tyndale.com.

Visit Tyndale Momentum online at tyndalemomentum.com.

Visit the author's website at peacebunnyisland.com.

TYNDALE, Tyndale's quill logo, *Tyndale Momentum*, and the Tyndale Momentum logo are registered trademarks of Tyndale House Ministries. Tyndale Momentum is the nonfiction imprint of Tyndale House Publishers, Carol Stream, Illinois.

Peacebunny Island: The Extraordinary Journey of a Boy and His Comfort Rabbits, and How They're Teaching Us about Hope and Kindness

Copyright © 2021 by Peacebunny Islands, Inc. All rights reserved.

Cover photograph of rabbit copyright © Life On White/Getty Images. All rights reserved.

Cover photograph of sky by Thomas Willmott on Unsplash.

Unless otherwise noted, back cover and interior photographs are from the Smith family personal collection and used with permission.

Photographs of bunnies by Henry Schneider/Open Window Production. Copyright © Peacebunny Islands, Inc. All rights reserved and used with permission.

Back cover photograph of bunny hopping away by Barbara O'Brien.

Author photograph by Henry Schneider. Copyright © 2020 by Peacebunny Islands, Inc. All rights reserved.

Designed by Dean H. Renninger

Edited by Stephanie Rische

Published in association with Trident Media Group, LLC, 41 Madison Avenue, Floor 36, New York, NY 10010.

For information about special discounts for bulk purchases, please contact Tyndale House Publishers at csresponse@tyndale.com, or call 1-855-277-9400.

ISBN 978-1-4964-5247-4

Printed in the United States of America

27   26   25   24   23   22   21
7   6   5   4   3   2   1

To my family, some furrier than others

Author's Note

This is a true story of how I started a bunny business as a little kid and how within a very short time it inspired my dream to acquire a private island where I could raise rescued and endangered breeds of rabbits and train them as comfort animals for people in need of hugs, hope, and hoppiness. There were lots of things that needed to happen before I could log on to Google Earth and begin searching for a place I could call Peacebunny Island.

Along the way, I became the guardian for a bunch of rabbits (some of which became valued friends and mentors), conducted hundreds of classes, fostered rabbits to families wanting their own bunny experience, and shared rabbits with people who were dealing with loneliness, trauma, and grief. With a bunny snuggling up close, everything in the world can stop for a few moments and just be about love.

For me, rabbits have been a way to learn about people and how we relate to each other—and how we can do it better. Countless times, I have seen the way these furry creatures help people become more human. They change people's lives. They have changed mine.

Peacebunny Island is my special place to get away from everything, sharing extended time with family, friends, and my rabbits. It's a place where we ask God to calm our hearts while we wait for answers to life's big questions.

Everyone has their own Peacebunny Island. It may only live in your head and your heart. That's okay. I hope this book inspires you to journey there, just as I did.

Caleb Smith

MARCH 2021

PART ONE

The Peacebunnies

My Portfolio

So, the first thing you're going to want to know is what a kid from Minneapolis was doing onstage in a Philadelphia bar when I was still two years shy of becoming a teenager. Your next question will likely be where my parents were. And if you're interested in every little detail, you will want to know what song I sang.

To start, I was belting out the chorus of "Don't Stop Believin'" by the band Journey, which I learned at our hometown ice arena, where I grew up watching hockey games and singing all the songs they played to rev up the crowd.

Getting onstage wasn't my idea necessarily, but I was already entertaining those around me in a spirited sing-along with the band when the guitarist pointed his finger at me and invited me up. I gave him one of those *You mean me?* looks, and quicker than you can say "up and down the boulevard," I was in front of the microphone—and loving it.

As for being in a bar, it was part of a pub crawl, which makes the scene sound even worse, but I promise nothing sketchy was going on. I was in the second-largest city on the East Coast to attend a *Forbes* magazine–sponsored conference for entrepreneurs under thirty years old. The organizers scheduled the pub crawl as a networking event without considering that one of the attendees would be in fifth grade. Before anyone gets worked up, I was with my mom and my very tall uncle Kris. My dad was back home, working and tending to my chores at the farm.

I had one other traveling companion, a pet named Whatchamacallit. An Angora rabbit with long, luxurious wool in various tones of gray and black, Whatchi was with me because we were, and still are, friends and business associates. My portfolio at the time included raising rare heritage breeds of rabbits, hosting Easter events and birthday parties, creating a STEM-based learning program for schools and libraries, and facilitating a bunny foster program involving nearly three hundred families, many of which included children with autism, critical health conditions, or special needs who connected with my rabbits in a way they couldn't with us two-leggeds. What had started as something of a whimsical quest for a new best friend years earlier had ballooned into a multilayered business that now engaged my whole family, a bunch of friends, and even more bunny enthusiasts and volunteers.

I'm not saying bunnies are smarter than people. It's just that emotionally they seem to be a little better at certain things, like listening and being patient.

The conference took place shortly after I had started to realize that one of my purposes in life was to be a guardian for sweet, furry creatures that bring comfort, joy, and much silliness. Among my fellow entrepreneurs, my perspective was unique. I did not own the rabbits. God did. I just helped take care of them.

As focused and busy as the bunny business kept me, I had plenty of time for being a kid. Why rush through the best part of life? To me, that meant playing with my neighbors, creating forts in my room, going to school, and participating in baseball, church, and scouts. When I was in fourth grade, a local bank president said, "This kid is a bunny farmer for now. But I can't wait to see what he's doing after college." Before I picked a career, though, I had to pick my Little League uniform number, classes for middle school, and which merit badge would be my first as I crossed over from Cub Scouts to Boy Scouts.

Even when pursuing adult-size dreams, I still enjoyed being a kid, and that included just relaxing with my rabbits. When that wasn't possible, I brought them along to whatever else was scheduled. Having a bunny around makes almost anything more fun.

No more proof was needed than the crowd in Philadelphia. After going offstage to rousing applause, I picked up Whatchi, whose long wool locks attracted the kind of attention the Beatles did when they were known as the mop top lads from Liverpool. Only I think Whatchi was cuter than Paul, John, George, or Ringo. People surged close with their cell phones out, taking pictures and videos. Then the group migrated to the next bar, and Whatchi, my mom, Uncle Kris, and I rode the wave of people down the street.

I'd never surfed the sidewalk amid such energy and spirit. Whatchi sat in his wagon like he was part of a parade organized just for him. At the next stop, someone introduced me and Whatchamacallit to a little woman who looked like a great-grandma. She watched me hand the bunny to my uncle and invited me to sit down next to her on the outdoor patio.

"Your rabbit is beautiful," she said.

"Thank you." I smiled.

"What can you tell me about rabbits?" she asked.

Initially, I had some trouble understanding this inquisitive woman because she spoke with a thick German accent that made her voice both choppy and sweet. We were surrounded by people leaning in to hear us and recording the conversation with their cell phones. There was also traffic in the nearby street. So the environment wasn't perfectly suited to my Rabbits 101 talk, but I recounted the basic facts that I normally share at birthday parties, bunny camps, and other events. I told her that all mammals with eyes on the side of their heads are vegetarians, and that mammals with eyes on the front hunt and eat meat.

"Very good." She smiled. "Keep going."

"Because rabbits have eyes on the side of their heads, you shouldn't approach them from the front," I continued. "It's also important to be gentle and not overcuddle them immediately, like that one relative we all have who smothers you as soon as you walk into the room."

People nodded and chuckled. I guess everyone really does have that relative.

"And Angora rabbits," I said, pointing to Whatchi, who was being held up by my uncle Kris, "need haircuts three to four times a year because their wool grows extremely fast, about an inch a month. Their hair can be spun into yarn and is highly prized for being super soft and warm."

I reached into my backpack and showed her a gallon-size baggie with several Angora yarn samples. Some of the people around the table asked for a closer look, and the bag was passed around the group of enthusiastic onlookers. I thought our chat was winding down when the baggie got back to me. But then the woman started asking about the reproductive habits of rabbits, which caused those closest to us to smile and jab each other as if this were a funny question.

And who knows—maybe it was funny to them, or a little embarrassing. It wasn't to me. I'm asked those questions all the time. I know the jokes about rabbits. I was ready with answers, and my sincerity and seriousness seemed to amuse the older woman. As her smirk turned into an audible chuckle, people lost it. They started laughing quite loudly, enough that my flow was interrupted. I felt myself snickering too, wanting to be in on the joke, although, quite frankly, I didn't see what was so funny about a rabbit's reproductive cycle.

Eventually someone who was standing nearby—a woman I saw later in the week at the conference—leaned in and told me that I was explaining the sex life of rabbits to Dr. Ruth Westheimer. I turned to my mom and mouthed, "Dr. Who?"

It was an interesting topic on the ride back home.

A Wrinkled Dollar

As the conference got underway, I attended multiple lectures and breakout discussion groups. Mindful that I was there to practice my business pitch and explore the demand for Angora wool that could be made into yarn, I signed up for the fashion-focused Art & Style track. That seemed the closest fit to my business interests, compared to courses focused on venture capital, consumer tech, entertainment, and gaming.

Angora fur is used to make high-end hats, gloves, scarves, and sweaters. I'd read everything I could find about Angora rabbit fiber, but I had no clue about the fashion world except that the industry as a whole had pulled products with Angora wool off their lines, denouncing farms that had been filmed torturing rabbits to get their fur, which could be acquired (and which I did acquire) with gentle haircuts. I saw a video clip illustrating the mistreatment, and it destroyed me. Within three minutes, I grew up and almost threw up.

I found it ironic that the boycott was gaining momentum just as I took in my first few Angora rabbits. I acquired mine because they were rabbits in need of a home, not because of their wool. But this well-motivated boycott had accomplished its goal to shut down inhumane sources of Angora wool in the industry worldwide. As I sat in the workshops, I wondered if the already-existing humane sources in North America could be ramped up in a way that addressed concerns about animal welfare and the welfare of the workers.

I made a note to my future self. The way we care for each other and our animals is a reflection of what's in our hearts, and over the long term, what's in our hearts has more of an impact than what's in our bank accounts.

Over the four days of the conference, I handed out all my home-printed business cards and collected way more than that in return. I underestimated the number of business cards I should have brought along. Such was the drawing power of Whatchamacallit, who perched contentedly in his wagon with his front paws resting on the edge, eagerly greeting each person who came over to say hi.

Whatchi listened as I explained that my rabbits lived on a small farm, where they were given regular, gentle grooming, lived in small colonies, and had playtime in a protected pasture during the warmer months. People were entranced by Whatchi's cuteness. I enjoyed observing as people stared, gave him a gentle pet, commented on his soft fur, and attempted to describe him.

"Look at his angel-wing ears!"

"It's like a tiny Ewok!"

"No, he's like a cross between a Lhasa apso, a Maltese, a puli, and a shih tzu!"

I understood the Star Wars reference, but I had no idea the last commenter was referring to breeds of dogs. What I heard instead was "a lasso opso, a malt, a pulley," and a bad word. A refined and elegantly dressed woman stepped through the small crowd and immediately ran her fingers through Whatchi's fur. As she put her face close to his, she started talking in a sweet, babylike voice.

"Oh, you're just sweetness overload, just like a little puppy sitting here," she said. "I could just give you kisses all day. Yes, I could. Yes, I could!"

Then, standing upright, she switched back to business mode and handed me her card.

"This fur is amazing," she said. "I would buy twenty thousand pounds a year. How much can you provide?"

I turned to the ten-pound cotton puff with a black nose and eyes that were nearly covered by a long flop of hair, two ears decorated with gray tassels, and four legs tucked so deep beneath the huge ball of fur that they were invisible. I did some fast calculations based on the ratio of one and a half pounds of wool per rabbit per year.

"I have six Angora rabbits," I said. "Right now, I can probably sell a little less than ten pounds of Angora wool a year."

"When you scale up, keep me in mind," she said. "This is awesome. Seriously, young man. Do this."

After sharing a laugh, we shook hands, and for a moment I imagined the future and tried to picture how many families and farms it would take to house that many fuzzy bunnies humanely.

I noticed it was nearly time for the next presentation I was scheduled to attend, so I slung my backpack over my suit, grabbed the handle of Whatchi's wagon, and headed outside. A gust of wind rippled through Whatchi's fur, a stunning display of natural beauty.

Outside, as we made our way to another building, we passed a gentleman pushing a rickety cart full of personal possessions. He did a double take when he saw the striking figure in my wagon and called out to me, asking for a short visit with my rabbit. This isn't unusual—I regularly get stopped on the street when I'm out with one of my bunnies. People often reach out to touch them or take a picture of us; I just wish they'd ask first. This man, huddled over his cart, was incredibly polite. I was struck by his courteous manner and how he treated me with genuine respect, not like a kid.

Still, I almost dismissed his request because I had traveled a long way to be at this conference and was in a hurry to get to my next appointment. But something nudged me to slow down and be in the moment. It's hard to explain the idea of Providence, but you know it when you feel it. So I stopped and witnessed something I'd never seen before: the man bent down until he was eye to eye with Whatchamacallit, and then he tilted his head to the side and waited for Whatchi to acknowledge him. They looked at each other for a while. Then he asked my rabbit if it was okay to have a visit together. Only after Whatchi came over to the edge and engaged with the man did he reach out to pet Whatchi's fur. Despite the bustle around us, it was like time stopped.

The man sat down on a nearby bench. I pulled Whatchi's wagon next to him, and the two of them had a lengthy heart-to-heart talk. I stepped back to give them space.

Maybe it wasn't just any bunny this man needed to be with, but with Whatchamacallit in particular. They clearly connected. Whatchi was especially patient and willing to let people stroke his fur for extended periods anyway, but he genuinely warmed up to this man on the street, and the connection was mutual. It felt like I'd come to Philly so Whatchi could spend time with this man and so he could spend time with Whatchi. They seemed to understand each other.

Only recently did I wonder if the two bonded because Whatchi came to our house with his own hard past. His mom was one of four Angoras who survived a barn fire in northern Minnesota. Because of the smoke, they all died soon after, but not before one gave birth to a small litter that included Whatchi.

Whatchi was the smallest and was different from the others in both looks and personality. It seemed to me like he truly grieved when his mother died, and although I'd never seen a rabbit act sad before, it made sense because he lost his appetite, stared off at nothing, and was no longer interested in playing. Over time he opened up again, and he let me in. People talk about dogs and other animals being able to sense things. I think the same is true for rabbits; it certainly was for Whatchi. Who knows—maybe his past had given him a special kind of empathy.

I don't know exactly how long Whatchi's visit with the man lasted—it's not like I checked the time. Finally he nodded toward me, motioning me to come closer. As I did, he stood up, reached into his pocket, and pulled out a wrinkled dollar bill, which he handed to me without an explanation. Knowing he had a sign on top of his cart asking for donations, I didn't feel right taking money from him.

"Thank you for your time," I said. "That's enough of a gift."

He shook his head and pressed the bill firmly into my hand.

"Young man, this dollar isn't for you," he said. "It's for my friend here who has done more for me in the past fifteen minutes than any human has done for me in years. Do you understand?"

Our eyes met and I nodded my head. Yes, I understood.

Here My Yam

After I returned from the conference, I kept busy with bunny events and business responsibilities, chores, and finishing elementary school.

Not that I have other personal experience to compare it to, but I've had one of the coolest backdrops for growing up that a kid could hope for. I'm the only child born to hardworking Midwestern college sweethearts who managed a junior hockey team for ten years, which made me a lifelong hockey fan even though I don't play. I loved attending the team's practices and games, and going on road trips across the United States to recruit players. We traveled as far as Italy and even went to Vancouver for the 2010 Olympics, where our team served as peace ambassadors and I lost my first tooth.

I was young enough to be treated like a mascot, and for me, it was like having a whole bunch of big brothers. At games, I helped my grandmother in the merchandise stand between periods and had fun singing along to the '80s rock anthems that blasted out over the PA during intermissions. If you want to hear music that pumps you up with energy, I suggest going to a hockey game.

My best friend in the world is Noah Bachman. His family lives across the street. We've played together almost since the day he was brought home for the first time. Although I'm a year and a half older, he had a major growth spurt this past year and now towers over me. I've given up hope of catching him. His whole family acts as if the extra chair at their dinner table has my name on it, with me fitting between Noah and his brother, Markus, who is five years older than I am. Markus was born with health challenges that have kept him closer to our speed, and I'm thankful he has always been one of my closest pals too.

Our parents met at church, but their friendship blossomed through softball league on Friday nights. The Bachman family moved into the neighborhood first and picked the house with a detached garage where all the neighborhood kids' heights, starting with Noah's big sister, Heather, would someday be recorded. My newlywed parents followed soon after, and with four houses for sale on the suburban street, they had their pick. We ended up in the blue house across the street after my mom fell in love with the historic elm tree in the front yard. Then Noah's mom, Ms. Deb, continued filling the other houses with friends she met at nursing school.

My mom and Noah's mom pinkie-promised that neither family would move until all the kids graduated high school unless one family received the other's blessing or if they both moved somewhere together. The day after my parents finalized the purchase, the majestic tree in front was struck by lightning. Thankfully, it didn't hit the house when it came down. Although they were disappointed about the loss, my parents later explained that you can add a new tree to your yard, but good friends are irreplaceable.

The Dutch elms along the street matured into stately shade trees, as did a maple tree in our front yard that my parents planted the day they brought me home from the hospital (the reason we call it "the celebration tree"). Eventually the houses on both sides of ours and down the block filled with young couples with kids, mostly boys. For me, that meant more friends. In the house to my right lived Alexander and Diego, whose father was from Mexico and was still working on his citizenship. Jamaal and his brother, Qiandre, lived at the far end of the street for a few years. Evangel and Bishop, who were next door on my left, were several years older, and next door to the Bachmans were three brothers who my dad affectionately called "the

Troubles" after they climbed up their stacked trash cans to conduct so-called gravity experiments from their roof.

The homes on our street have contiguous grassy front yards but four-foot chain-link fences enclosing most of the backyards. Someone always seemed to be climbing over one of these fences to chase after a ball, but generally we shuffled between basketball hoops in each other's driveways or played on our street, which never had much traffic. It seemed like there was always a game to join the moment I stepped outside.

When I was still too young to cross the street by myself, I began each day by requesting an escort to the fun in their yards. I'd put on my blue sneakers that lit up with each step, preparing for liftoff. I opened our front door, stepped outside, and shouted, "Here my yam! Let's play!"

We Hug and Then We Play

I know it sounds like a pretty great place to grow up, and it was—and still is—but occasionally there were problems, as is typical with kids who have good and bad days, just like everybody else. Someone would get angry and throw the kickball into the neighbor's yard. Or someone would get kicked while on a swing. Or poked for no reason. We were kids, and we got mad at each other. But after one memorable incident, I introduced the gang to our family rule, which made so much sense that the younger kids adopted it as a neighborhood rule.

If anyone cried or got physically hurt, we took a break and talked it out. Eventually we came to a place where the offending party said, "I'm sorry. Will you forgive me?" Then we hugged and play resumed. The rule morphed as we all grew up, but it was important that we knew how things worked in our neighborhood, and all of us returned the next day to play. It became the expectation that if anyone yelled or cried, we immediately stopped to talk until we could forgive and hug, and then play would resume. I know it sounds too good to be true, but all of us really did get to a place where we agreed that play was more important than fighting. If an argument broke out or another problem arose, someone shouted our rule: "Say you're sorry. Then we hug and then we play."

I learned that these rules didn't extend beyond the neighborhood when

I was watching baseball practice at the local private high school where my mom worked part-time in sports medicine. At nearly six years old, I was quite happy to watch the team working out on a spring afternoon, especially if warm pretzels with cheese were involved.

That day someone from the team borrowed my little foam bat and Wiffle ball without asking my permission. Then my equipment was gone. A few guys helped me look for them, and one of them found my bat sticking out of a metal trash can by the locker room door. The bat was bent in half.

Upset but willing to forgive, I asked the baseball coach if I could talk to the team. I knew all of them by name from hanging out in the dugout and giving them fist bumps when they went onto the field. The players were warming up and stretching inside the gym when the coach walked me to the front and commanded their attention. I held up my broken bat.

"I don't know who did this," I said to the team. "But this isn't how it works. Let me tell you how it works. You ask me for permission to borrow my stuff, and because you're my friends, I say okay. If the bat gets broken, you come and tell me it's broken. You say you're sorry. Then I say I forgive you. Then we hug. Then we play. That's how it works." I paused.

"Any questions?" I asked.

Let's just say I got a lot of hugs before the guys ran out to the field.

Snickers

I quickly learned this hug rule also did not work in the pet world. After this bunny came to live with us, the woman who lived in the house behind ours complained repeatedly that our rabbit was taunting her dogs. We had no reason to doubt her word, but it was still hard to believe. Her fox terriers weighed at least fifteen pounds and Snickers was six pounds if he took a bath, which he didn't. However, Snickers did seem to think he was a cat, not a rabbit, and given the way most cats and dogs get along, she may have had a point.

The fact that Snickers was at our house was probably the most remarkable thing about him. He was my first long-term pet with fur, and I had much to learn. My initial appreciation for animals may have been influenced by my grandpa on my mom's side, whom I called Grandpa Tractor. He came from a long line of farmers and was the first in his family to leave the country and get a job in a large city. After retiring, though, he bought land back from distant relatives, and we visited him and my grandma there several times a year. My favorite part about going to visit was sitting next to him on his giant tractor, stretching up high on his shoulders to pick monster-sized blackberries, and walking through *his* grandpa's old blacksmith shop.

Hearing my grandpa tell stories about our family's long history of working the farm lit up my imagination and connected me to the past in a way that I could feel in my bones. I laughed whenever he spoke about animals and pets, because he was very definite in his opinion that cows and horses lived in barns and stables, rabbits either shared space in the barn or were housed in smaller hutches nearby, and cats belonged outside, where they could earn their keep by catching rats and mice. As for dogs, he believed they were generally too large and too dirty to be allowed indoors, except when the weather turned bitter.

"It's a luxury to have a pet when you need to feed your family," he once said, "especially when times are uncertain."

Mom generally agreed with that worldview but had more grace when it came to pets. She admittedly married someone who was like her father in many ways—mostly good ways, she always says—but that includes his opinion about pets. My dad prefers animals that are in someone else's yard.

Goldfish were apparently an exception to the rule. When I was five years old, several took up residence in my bedroom. The first three were named Flaggada 1, Flaggada 2, and Flaggada 3. The new one with red spots that came home on February 14 was appropriately named Valentine. They were easy pets to maintain and caused no trouble for gracious neighbors who cared for them when we were on the road with the hockey team. They swam around a tank I got from Noah's big sister, which we set up next to my moon-shaped night-light. The fish swam contentedly, sometimes with a look of curiosity as they watched me play with my Legos or organize the hand-me-down collection of Smurf figures that built up thanks to my grandpa, who brought one home from each of his business trips.

But after a few months, there came the fateful moment for each of them when I assumed they grew tired of swimming and decided to float.

I learned otherwise.

My parents talked to me about what happens after you die, and following a brief prayer and some words of thanks for being such a good fish, we ceremoniously flushed the deceased down the toilet. I put my shoes back on and joined Noah, who was using chalk to create a road for our Matchbox cars all the way into their garage.

I was never lonely, but I did miss the companionship, and at seven years old, I decided I wanted to invite a bunny into our home. I thought briefly about a dog or a cat, but neither felt right. Other typical pets like a hamster, a bird, or a lizard didn't even cross my mind. With me, it was always a rabbit, and given the way things developed, I'd say that maybe it was just meant to be.

My mom eventually sold the idea to my dad. Ordinarily he's quicker to say yes than my mom, but he had concerns about what would happen once the novelty wore off. His instincts weren't wrong, but I was putting my hopes on the lucky fact that when my mom was a kid, she had a little white rabbit named Clover. This pet evoked nothing but good memories and cute pictures, which I hoped would tip the decision my way.

Several days passed before I heard any feedback from my parents. I tried not to overthink things or mess up my chances by bugging them for an answer. I hoped they would see how respectful and responsible I was being by not badgering them. At the same time, I wanted to make sure they knew I *really* wanted a rabbit. I hoped they also understood they would be the best parents ever if they gave me permission to adopt a furry friend.

The wait felt like torture. But I knew things were looking hopeful when my mom sat down in front of the desktop computer and invited me to help her research available rabbits. I didn't want to get my hopes up, but I could tell from the banter that we just needed to find a good fit. I hung on the back of her chair and read over her shoulder while we searched various rescues and then checked Craigslist for another half hour before we came to an ad for a brown-and-white bunny with a description that said, "Older, friendly, trained."

Grinning like we'd found a map to buried treasure, we turned to each other and said, "I think this is the one."

Then my mom scrunched up her face with a silly question.

"What do you think it's trained to do?" she asked.

I shrugged. "I don't know. But a trained rabbit would be the coolest pet ever."

The people selling the rabbit lived forty-five minutes north of our house. I packed a water bottle, a snack, and something to do in the car, a habit from traveling with the sports team and our family adventures. It also distracted me. From the moment we arranged to meet the family with the rabbit, I could barely concentrate on anything else. Full of nervous energy, I spent the entire drive fidgeting in the backseat and singing along to CDs with my dad and the band Tenth Avenue North.

"Caleb, how old are you now?" my dad asked in a way that I knew was leading to a lesson.

"You know," I said.

"Come on now, how old are you?" he repeated.

"Almost eight," I said, feeling my eyes roll a little.

"If rabbits can live ten years, have you thought that, depending on this rabbit's age, he might still be at our house when you get your driver's license?"

My dad's eyes met mine in the rearview mirror, and I shook my head.

"That seems light-years away," I said.

High school might as well have been in another solar system. The only thing I'd planned out that far on my life map was becoming an Eagle Scout by the time I finished high school.

"Maybe this rabbit will help you celebrate that big day," Mom chimed in.

But first we needed to find the house, and it was an unexpected challenge on the unlit street. None of us could see the house numbers very well, and Dad drove up and down the street and turned around a few times, muttering, "The house has to be in here somewhere."

Mom suggested we call and ask for directions, but the phone number wasn't on our note sheet. In the meantime, my heart was beating so loudly I probably wouldn't need to knock on the door once we found it.

When we finally pulled into the driveway, the porch light was on, but the curtains were drawn tight, and it looked like no one was home at all. I wondered if they forgot we were coming to meet the rabbit. I heard my parents speaking under their breath about the craziness of meeting complete strangers at their home well after dark to select a pet they hadn't even been looking for in the first place. My mom said they wouldn't even buy a sofa this way.

That's when the door opened, and an older man invited us inside. A moment later, I met Snickers for the first time, a rabbit named after the man's favorite chocolate bar. I thought that was funny and tried not to laugh.

Snickers was a brown-and-white Dutch rabbit with traditional markings, including a white wedge-shaped blaze coming down the bridge of his nose, and round cheeks. My dad stood along the wall and observed while I sat on the floor and said hello to the bunny. My mom and I had hardly met him before Snickers bonked my leg with his nose and then made himself at home in my lap. He took a long, warm lick on the back of my hand with his rough tongue and looked up with big eyes and long lashes. It seemed like Snickers chose me before I even chose him.

Nothing needed to be said. I stood up and took the fifteen dollars I knew was in my mom's pocket, handed it to the man, and shook his soft hand.

"Thanks for taking care of my bunny," I said, and from that moment on, Snickers and I were best buds and pretty much inseparable.

The people selling Snickers had cats and a dog, but they only wanted to keep the cats. They were done with all the others, the man explained. The way he used the word *done* struck me as gruff, and I felt bad for the animals that were stuck there unwanted. His Craigslist ad had said he would provide everything we needed to get started, which I assumed meant a decent carrier and food enough for a few days. But as he handed me a tiny cat carrier and wished me luck, I realized he meant "everything to get started to the car."

That is why I like to say Snickers came to us with nothing more than his big heart, which was more than enough.

As soon as my dad pulled the car into our driveway and turned off the engine, I took Snickers out of his carrier and welcomed him home.

"Come on in, little buddy," I said, eager to give him a tour of the house.

I stood in the middle of the living room and spun around. "This room is where my family hangs out at night," I told Snickers. "You can share my blanket when we're on the sofa."

Then I put him on the floor in the hallway and coaxed him to hop behind me into my bedroom. "This is my new bunk bed, which is how you can tell it's my room. My mom and dad don't have a bunk bed. Come in anytime—except when I'm sleeping. But you'll be in your area then, so don't worry about it."

We went back into the hallway, and then I showed him the office. "This room is off-limits. My parents didn't bunny-proof it, and you'll be in big trouble if you nibble on any work stuff. And if you're in big trouble, it means I'm probably in big trouble too. So off-limits, understand?"

He seemed to get it. Just to make sure, I let him explore the baby gate that had kept me out of that room years ago. He stood up on his back feet and looked into the room.

"Seriously, don't even think about it."

I closed the door, which allowed him to catch a glimpse of his reflection in the full-length mirror. He must have thought there was another rabbit in the house. He spun around and bolted down the hall and didn't stop until he stood at the next open door, poking his head inside.

"That's our bathroom," I said. "Sometimes we run there too. It's where we . . ." I caught myself. He was a rabbit. How would he know what we did in there? Then I remembered his former family had told us that he'd grown up with cats and trained himself to use a litter box. I didn't believe it was true. A rabbit?

"Well, you've got a box of your own in there to . . . you know . . ."

It turned out Snickers did know!

He was, indeed, housebroken, if that's even the right term. As a result, I was permitted to play with Snickers in my bedroom and didn't need to worry about him messing up the carpet or my comforter. Before long, he roamed freely through the house during the day. He was extremely social, something that could not be attributed to growing up with cats. If he were a human being, I would call him a people person. He liked being in the middle of the action and interacting with everyone. If I was building something, he sat next to me and watched. If I was reading, he crawled under my legs. If I was making up a story with my Smurfs figures or Rescue Heroes, he hopped in the center and made himself part of the story.

He also liked meeting all the kids on the street.

"Welcome to your new home, Snickers." Noah beamed as I conducted introductions under the shade of our celebration tree, which was now also third base for street ball.

"That's a cool name, for a rabbit," said Trouble 2. He spoke with greater enthusiasm than I'd heard in months. Something about being a middle schooler made him slower to get excited than everyone else, but they all ran off to grab dandelions or clumps of grass and clover. What a lucky bunny! Snickers was the first rabbit my friends had played with, and they were eager to find out what he liked and how to include him. That's when I started realizing they were asking the same kinds of questions I was. It was like we were doing scientific observation studies and making all sorts of discoveries along the way.

Snickers wasted no time showing that he was smart too and that he was studying us as much as we were studying him. When he was in our backyard, he sat on the side of the swing set so he wouldn't get smooshed when someone jumped off. He also figured out where he could safely hop when we played kickball. If someone launched the ball into a neighbor's yard for a home run, I scratched Snickers's back the way he liked while the rest of us waited for someone to retrieve the ball. If we stopped playing and took a break for ice cream sandwiches, I made sure to give Snickers a special treat too. He was one of the guys.

Not long after, my parents gave me permission to build a play area in the backyard for him. I wanted him to have his own place to relax and play while we were outside. With a curiosity that I had begun to take for granted, he watched me hammer nails into long plywood boards that became the sides of a mini fort in the purple lilac bush. As soon as I finished attaching the boards, I draped a blanket over them to create a roof, and Snickers hopped inside. He let me drive trucks around him and surround him with plastic army men that were on a mission to climb up Snickers Mountain if they didn't want to get wiped out by a tidal wave of loose dirt.

That summer, I painted a lot of pictures of Snickers, mostly in the evening after all the other kids went back to their houses. He was both an excellent muse and model. On warm nights, we slept outside in the pup tent I'd won the year before as the second-place prize in a back-to-school bingo game. Each time Snickers and I climbed inside, I couldn't believe the kid who won first place chose that bright-yellow SpongeBob figurine instead of the tent.

In no time at all, Snickers was part of my family. Whether we were going out to play, getting up in the morning, or waking from a nap in the lilac bush, I only had to say, "Let's go," and he was on his feet, often up on his hind legs, looking at me with shiny eyes. He wasn't merely trained. He was amazing.

Later that summer, though, I noticed that Snickers was moving slower, with less than his usual excitement. Now when I said, "Let's go," he wasn't as quick to respond. He seemed to think about it for a while first. He still looked up at me with the same big eyes that had first greeted me, only they weren't as bright. He seemed to be sending me a message.

One Last Cuddle

Several weeks after the school year ended, Snickers came on our family vacation to my grandparents' cabin. He was his normal, inquisitive, playful self as I introduced him to Grandpa Tractor and Grandma Deer, whose name came to me after seeing a photo of her posed with a deer on the bluff overlooking their forty acres. After my grandpa retired from the same company he'd worked at since he was eighteen years old, he and my grandmother followed their lifelong dream of building a wooden home in the middle of nowhere on land that had generations of our family's history tied to it.

Moving in was like a homecoming for my grandparents. Names for surrounding roads match the names in my family tree. From the front-porch swing, you can see over the distant ridgeline where his grandfather raised Angora goats. Several hollers past that is the site of my great-great-grandpa's blacksmith shop. And in the middle of the woods is the one-room church with a steeple by the creek where his grandparents first fell in love—and where my grandparents still go for Sunday worship, as I do when I visit.

Snickers joined all my adventures on the trip, except church on Sundays and jaunts to the river, where I fished for perch to add to a huge fish fry. But he was content to relax in the air-conditioning before all of us men headed outside to hand-crank the ice cream. I loved hiking in the deep woods, and although I could just follow the fence line to find my way back, it was fun to make rock piles as markers along the way.

One night, as I sat on the porch swing rocking back and forth with Snickers in my lap and watching the fireflies, I had a strong sense that I belonged there. It radiated up from the ground and into the core of my being. Family roots there ran deep.

Most people out there in the country live on a small plot of land, and something about crops growing and animals feeding gives a person the sense of new life and possibility. Snickers especially liked playing in Grandma's flower beds that surrounded the cabin, chasing butterflies and nibbling a little here and there. He touched his paws in the rainwater collection pond lined with a rock garden and purple coneflowers, and I could tell he felt the same connection I did.

We had been back home for a few weeks when I noticed a subtle change in Snickers. This was right before his decline became obvious. Several times he had rebounded, like he'd just been feeling under the weather, and he was nearly back to himself. Then one evening his health suddenly took a dive, and it was apparent he couldn't get comfortable. Rabbits don't say anything vocally, but I saw it in his eyes. The reality of what was happening was hard because I didn't want to see him hurting at all. I hadn't even contemplated what life would feel like without him.

Although we did not know Snickers's age, my mom figured he might be getting up there in years because he'd been raised with the former family's cats and the cats were pretty old. She wondered if part of the motivation to move him out had been to avoid paying veterinary bills and dealing with the situation we were about to face. We would never know, and frankly it didn't really matter. As I kissed his ears, my little buddy taught me an important lesson: if you worry too much about what might happen in the future, you miss out on what's happening right in front of you.

For me and Snickers, it was one last cuddle as the summer sun dipped behind the Bachmans' house. My parents arranged to take Snickers to the veterinarian in the morning because it was important to all of us that he didn't suffer. Before I went to sleep that night, I was sitting on the floor, propped up by my bed while I read a book. Snickers scooted over to me and tunneled under my legs, as he'd done since the first day we brought him home. I figured the time had come to tell each other goodbye, because I had a feeling it might be too hard the next day at the vet's office.

I put down my book, crossed my legs, and settled Snickers into my lap so I could stroke his back and rub him behind his ears. This is something most rabbits enjoy, and Snickers was no exception—especially right then.

After a while I crawled into bed and said good night without putting him back in his normal sleeping area down the hall. If this was going to be his last night, I wanted us to spend it together. I fell asleep pretty quickly, and I later found out that Snickers ambled out of my bedroom and made his way down the hall until he found my mom sitting in the chair in the living room. She picked him up and held him in her arms, where he died a few minutes later. Mom said it was like Snickers knew it was time and he wanted to be held by someone.

She cried in a way I hadn't seen before. Dad said it was because my mom is a fixer and she wasn't able to fix Snickers—or me.

For some reason I woke up shortly after Snickers died. I must have heard my mom crying or my dad consoling her in the living room, which is relatively close to my bedroom. Mom was still holding Snickers in her arms when I entered the room. Her eyes were red as she looked at me from across the room, and I saw that her face was wet with tears. With the way she was cradling him, Snickers was barely visible. I walked over and stroked his fur. Still soft and warm, Snickers looked like he was asleep.

As the reality sunk in, I was hit by a wave of sadness, knowing that Snickers would never wake up, and then suddenly I was free-falling with a sense of loss and emptiness. I was going to miss him so much.

I cried quietly for a long time.

My parents had spoken to me about death the first time after I found Flaggada 1 floating in the tall rectangular aquarium. Death didn't make total sense to me at any of the fish memorial services, but somehow seeing Snickers cradled in my mom's arms made it clearer that, while the physical body remained, the spark that created life was gone.

Eventually, I took Snickers from my mom and held him close. With my eyes closed, I thought of all the time we'd spent together, and I knew this would be the last time. I remembered my parents once telling me that our love for a person or pet doesn't stop just because they're no longer alive, and I knew this would be true with Snickers.

We'd done the absolute best we could to take care of Snickers, so I didn't feel any remorse. We lived each day the best we could, spending plenty of time together, even up to the very end. Plus, I was comforted in my simple belief that pets went to heaven and were welcomed there by family.

"We'll have a funeral tomorrow," I informed my parents.

"How are you going to tell everyone?" my mom asked.

"Don't know. It's going to be hard."

Dang, I'll Miss You

Eventually I put Snickers down in his cage and crawled back under the comforter. Worn out from crying, I fell asleep quickly, and the rest of the night flew past in the blink of an eye. Literally. I felt as if I shut my eyes, and when I opened them again, it was morning. I checked in on Snickers on my way to the kitchen. He was still dead but seemed to be in a deep, peaceful sleep. My appetite was pretty much gone. I didn't want to play either.

I hesitated to share the news with the neighborhood pack. Going outside and telling people would make everything real.

As I stared at the doorknob, I confirmed the day's to-do list and timeline with my parents. I was committed to giving Snickers a funeral. And it was important that all the neighborhood kids be invited, along with their families if they wanted to come.

Thoughts weighed heavily on my mind. Some people have described me as sensitive and thoughtful; others call me a deep thinker. I suppose I do spend time trying to figure things out. It's one of the reasons the Boy Scouts and science and church appeal to me—all are about exactly that.

Both my parents were raised in homes rooted in deep, personal faith in the God who created everything, who is still engaged with us in our day-to-day lives, and who even cares about the little things. Early on they began answering my questions as they came up, but they always gave me room to figure out my own views about God and my place in the world. I remember chatting on one of our long family road trips, and Mom said something that stuck with me, even though she said it wasn't original: "At some point you must decide for yourself, because God only has children. God doesn't have any grandchildren."

I had already concluded that there was a God and I was not Him, and that both truths were good. Around the same time Mom and I had that discussion, I needed to decorate a school poster titled "All about Me," which made me start thinking about where I fit and what set me apart from anyone else—what made me different or special. I really struggled with the assignment. I wanted this to be about more than just narrowing down my favorite songs and colors.

How could I explain that I hear music in my head wherever I go, as if it's my own personal soundtrack? How could I explain that I love every little step related to getting ready for a baseball game, not just playing baseball? As for a favorite food, I simply like eating. After school, I'll often come home and heat up a tortilla with cheese and salsa, but nothing is better than church potlucks. A bite of a chicken enchilada followed by a forkful of some cheesy hot dish and a sip of ice-cold lemonade is my idea of a perfect meal—and proof that God is good.

I had no idea how to put all that on a poster. Now that I was older, I realized it was unlikely that I would someday become a goalie astronaut on the moon who was a news reporter on the weekend. All I knew was that Snickers was my favorite.

The idea that helped me process losing Snickers was intentional stewardship, a concept my parents modeled for me. Basically it means that everything belongs to God, not to us, and what we have has been entrusted to us. We are caretakers. That's why I still see myself as a bunny guardian rather than an owner. I'm a steward. The neighborhood kids come to play in our yard, but it's not really our yard. The farm is God's farm; we just get to use it. I have food to eat, but it's not really *my* food, so I should share when I can. And while Snickers was our family's pet bunny, he was really God's bunny. Also, in a sense, the whole neighborhood had adopted Snickers.

"I'm concerned about how Noah is going to take the news," I told my mom as I sat at the kitchen table making invitations to the funeral. "He's going to have a hard time. And I hope Markus is feeling well enough to come. That would be nice, but I understand if he can't, and obviously Snickers would understand too."

"Well, why don't you go talk to Ms. Deb?" my mom said, which is what all the neighborhood kids call Noah's mom. After I made the last invitation, I laced up my shoes and crossed the street to the Bachmans'. My mom stayed behind while I knocked on the door and delivered the news, followed by the invitation. Both Noah and Markus said they would come and help say good-bye. Then I went to all the other houses on the street. I saw my mom nod or give a thumbs-up to the other parents as they opened the door. We were surprised everybody was home—that was rare with all the kids' busy schedules.

Back at our house, we had about two hours before the funeral. Noah and Markus came over early to see Snickers before I wrapped him up in a blanket and put him in the decorated cardboard box. They just sat with me while the clouds moved, but it felt like nothing else did. Noah seemed pretty lost, which was understandable. Markus helped supervise as I dug a hole next to the purple lilacs that Snickers liked to sniff and nibble.

Before this I'd had two other experiences with funerals. One was for an older lady who served cookies to our Sunday school class, and the other was an extremely sad occasion, when a young mother sang a hymn through tears for her baby girl. Both days were bleak, gray, and chilly, the weather seeming to reflect the somber mood. But this afternoon was bright and sunny, and once all my friends and I gathered in the backyard, it almost felt like a normal playdate. Except we knew better.

My mom and dad welcomed everyone, said a brief prayer, and then backed away and let me take over. I set Snickers's box in the hole and added a scoop of dirt before I said my own goodbye. I hadn't written anything down, and I didn't know if I'd be able to choke out the words, but when the time came, my gut told me to step forward, and I did. My mom pointed the camera to the ground just like I'd requested. I wanted to save this incredibly special moment but instructed her to record only the voices so I could remember what I saw in my mind's eye.

"I am grateful to have had a friend like Snickers," I said. "He was special. I don't think my heart can ever love like this again."

After I pitched a shovelful of dirt into the hole, one of the other guys took it from me and said a few words of his own. And so it went until everyone had spoken.

"Dang, I'll miss you. You're the best pet on our street. Sorry. No offense to Champagne." I didn't think the Bachmans' dog would mind.

"I'll miss you, Mr. Fuzzy Fuzzy. Hope death didn't hurt. This stinks."

"I just saw you yesterday. I'm sorry I didn't say goodbye then. So goodbye, Snickers."

"I don't know what to say. Sorry, bunny, you got dead. I'm glad you knew me. We had good times, didn't we?"

"Snickers, you deserve a golden carrot. Hope you have teeth in heaven. You were the best rabbit I ever knew."

"We wish you the best. Hope you stay warm. We put you in a blanket."

"I'm glad you were here. See you later. Um, sorry. Guess not. But maybe."

I had Snickers less than a year, and when I think about how we first came together, it seemed like chance. But I don't know. Are the stars in the night sky total chance? Is life on this planet chance? It depends what you believe. What I know for sure is that Snickers came from a family that was eager to rehome him and he was the perfect pet for as long as he lived with us. In return, he changed the rest of my life.

2

Grandma Deer's Pies

The usual summer activities resumed—baseball, neighborhood kickball, and backyard campouts—but I still felt like there was a Snickers-size hole. Several times early that summer I caught myself laughing, and I felt a little guilty for having a good time without Snickers being there too. My pastor said that was normal and healthy. I figured Snickers would have wanted me to keep having fun: rabbits are, for the most part, unselfish creatures.

Every so often my parents asked if I wanted to foster another pet. I was not remotely interested. I didn't even want to go to the zoo. Our home belonged to Snickers, and I was not going to open the door for any other animals.

My parents gave me permission to express a full range of emotions and continued to answer my questions about what happens to a body when a person dies. To my surprise, most of those conversations ended up focusing on how the person lived before they died. One day they said they understood the struggle I was having with this loss. They said others experienced it in their own ways too. I learned to put a name to what I felt—it was called *grief.*

"You won't get over losing Snickers as much as you will move through it," my mom said.

"He was such a perfect bunny," I said.

"I won't argue that."

"What's the point of trying something new?" I asked. "I can't ever replace the irreplaceable."

"Don't think of it as replacing Snickers," she said.

"I won't," I said. "There's a hole in my heart, and I wouldn't want to fill it, even if I could. I've already known perfection."

Over the next few weeks, I filled my journal with things people said to make me feel better.

"Everyone needs to find their own way to keep moving forward," said Noah's dad, Mr. Mike. "You'll find your place, though it might take a while."

Ms. Deb said, "Breathe in and out. Repeat. Breathe in and out."

My two grandpas said things like "God's got this." "Take care of what you can take care of." They also said, "Make your bed."

Someone else added, "Keep your heart open." I have a feeling that was my mom, who also said, "Remember everything."

The more time passed after the funeral, the harder it was to remember all the details of everything that Snickers and I did together, but I had no problem remembering the way he made me feel. He opened my heart. Looking back, I can see that I wanted to keep that feeling Snickers gave me, and my wounded heart was struggling to protect itself.

Dad knew just what to say. "You know how Grandma Deer takes a freshly baked pie out of the oven, and we all savor that final bite while at the same time hating that it's the last one?"

I nodded.

My mouth started to water as I thought of the delicious aroma of her homemade cinnamon-apple pies filling not just the kitchen but every square inch of their cabin, and then tasting the way the flaky crust melted on my tongue.

"When it's all gone, you wish you could savor the taste forever," my dad continued. "But then Grandma says she'll make another pie later in the week, and you start anticipating that next time."

His analogy made sense. Maybe Snickers was like a piece of Grandma's pie. I would always remember it as a favorite and be sad it was gone. But I could also look forward to enjoying apple pie or cherry cheesecake in the future.

Something Tells Me We Should Help

As summer began to give way to shorter nights and cooler weather, I heard about an elderly woman living in a trailer park who had stopped buying food for herself and her husband of over fifty years and was instead using her meager income to buy food for her cats. I told the sad story to my parents and said, "I think we can help." Then I added, "I want to help."

I thought about how at church we are often challenged to consider our responsibility to help those who are struggling. Our family devotional prayer concluded by reciting, "Help me see people like You see them. Help me find ways to help when I have the power to help. And give me courage to act." What was the use of saying that every day if I didn't actually do it when I saw a need and felt the urge to act?

The elderly couple needed to be out of their mobile home for several weeks—something to do with social services and cleaning. They were making plans to stay someplace temporarily that did not allow them to bring their cats, so they needed a kitty camp for their pets. But they were genuinely concerned about the cost of boarding them in a facility and consumed by fear that somehow the cats would be euthanized if they took them to a shelter.

Due to some bad experiences in the past, the woman didn't trust any system or agency. Her deepest fear was that if they were separated, they would never get back together. The cats were their family, and by the time we contacted them about their situation, they were desperate enough to do anything, including let the cats stay with people they'd never met.

"It's short-term, so it's just a foster situation," I told my parents. "And because they're cats, I won't get attached to them and they will probably feel the same way about me."

"You think?" my dad said.

"It'll be fun," I said.

"Really?" My mom didn't sound convinced.

We had taken time the night before to decide how to decide, which was how we approached most big choices. In the car on the way to meet up with the couple, we reviewed our plan—a simple green, yellow, and red light criteria we applied to ensure we didn't rely on emotions. We needed it—we were a family of softies.

"Let's make sure we're on the same page," Mom said.

"Ready," I said from the backseat.

"Green light?" she said.

"We help the family, and up to two cats come home with us for a visit," I replied.

"Yellow light?"

"If the cats look sick or hurt, we say no thank you because we aren't in a position to deal with vet visits and bills."

"Any red lights?"

"Yep," I said. "If anyone feels unsafe, it's red lights, sirens, and we're outta there!"

"Roger that," my mom said.

I looked out the window at the road in front of us and hoped for green lights.

The couple seemed to be the same age as my great-grandma, but they were weaker and feebler than I'd imagined. Their cats, though well-loved and healthy, looked a little thin. There were six altogether. Two of their neighbors in the mobile home court had agreed to take two cats each, leaving them begging everyone they could think of to take the last two, a mama and her young son.

After we showed up, they couldn't stop expressing their gratitude and appreciation for just meeting them. We listened to their story, which was a blur for me, because all I could see was this concerned grandma with no family to call on.

The man gently packed up the cats, and she hugged me like she didn't want to let go of either me or the cats. After she finally pulled away, she hugged me again. Then, as if remembering something, she reached into a worn shopping bag on her kitchen counter and handed me two cans of cat food.

"Take these," she said. "I'm sorry I don't have any money to give you for their food."

I told her not to worry, but I was glad to accept the cans of food so I would know what to look for the next time we went to the store. I had no clue what her cats liked. These cats were going to a strange house; the least we could do was feed them something familiar.

Once we were back at our house, the excitement of picking up the two cats was replaced by the more practical matters of how to care for them. Did they like to eat in the morning or at night? How much food should they get? Did they get a bowl of water or milk? What kind of milk? Would they be afraid of new noises? Of me? Were they sad or lonely? Did they miss their owners? Should I give them a blanket?

As houseguests, the cats turned out to be relatively easy. The two of them stuck together and did their own thing. They rubbed up against my legs every once in a while and let me stroke their backs, but it was always on their terms. They licked my fingers a few times with their rough tongues and purred as they settled down for a nap, sometimes next to me, though I couldn't figure out how they determined when they were in the mood for a visit. Snickers was always up for a cuddle. Thankfully, they began to use his litter box right away and settle in.

The only downside was that Noah found out he was allergic. He rubbed his eyes when he came over, so we started playing at his house more, and the cats stayed inside at my house.

"Do you like the cats?" he asked one day.

I shrugged.

"I'm still more of a bunny guy," I said.

We were a few weeks into this fostering arrangement when my dad paused the conversation at the dinner table and asked about our backup plan with winter on its way. Both my mom and I were confused. A backup plan for what?

"What if the couple doesn't call us?" he said. "What if they're never ready to take the cats back?"

His point, though a valid concern, sat on the table like a bowl of over-cooked veggies that no one wanted to acknowledge. We didn't know where the older couple was staying while their home was being cleaned. We didn't have a cell phone number for them. We didn't even know if they had a cell phone. After several weeks of silence, we drove out to their mobile home to check on them, hoping they were okay even if they weren't quite ready for their cats yet. An eviction note was taped to the front door of the mobile home they rented. I knocked on the front door. No one answered, and none of the neighbors knew anything.

"This is not good," my mom said.

We prayed for the couple, and I felt a lump in my throat as I thought about them. I hoped they were okay and asked God to watch over them.

We returned home and fell back into our normal routines as more weeks passed. Halloween came and went, and I took Jasper, the boy kitten, with me trick-or-treating. I dressed up as a football player with a cat. Cole, the other cat, never wanted to go anywhere. Winter sports started, and I occasionally brought Jasper with me. Although my parents must have discussed options, they never spoke about them with me. We simply mentioned the couple in our prayers and kept on the same course.

Then, shortly before Thanksgiving, the phone rang. It was the elderly man, excited to share good news. They were resettled and getting some additional income social services had helped them apply for. Soon after the call, we returned Jasper and Cole, and we all had a warm reunion. Though the elderly couple appeared to have lost some weight, they looked to be in a better place. The woman assured us they could now afford to feed themselves and their cats, and they were moving to a new place up north.

I no longer saw fear and helplessness in her eyes the way I had the last time we were together, and I sensed she was telling the truth to us—and to herself.

I said goodbye to the cats. It was harder than I thought, but I didn't have a deep feeling of sadness or strings of attachment, which was the plan. I received one final snuggle from Jasper, got an ambivalent head flick from Cole, and took in a long, appreciative hug from the woman. Her husband shook my hand as he thanked me for helping them out. He shared that the whole time they were living in their car, they took comfort in knowing that the cats were okay.

In their car? What happened to their housing? I thought about how cold

November had been, and my heart sank. How did they stay warm? Did they have blankets? Where did they park at night, and did they feel safe? What about a bathroom? What did they eat? I was so glad we could help them by caring for their cats, but who had cared for the couple when they needed it most? Didn't anyone know they were living in their car? If someone knew, why didn't they invite them inside?

The whole situation gripped my heart and twisted it in ways I'd never felt before. I had so many questions about how the world works. How was it possible that they had no family or neighbors to help? Did their loved ones not know the situation? And if they did, why didn't they do something? If someone like them asked us, would I be willing to give up my bedroom to help strangers or use my money to support them? It all boiled down to a few questions in my mind: Even though pets are easier to take care of than people, how can we do a better job being kind to the people who cross our paths? How can we care for those who really need it?

In the car on our way back home, as I sat next to the empty pet carrier, my dad summed up our fostering experiment by saying it had been good for the cats, the couple, and our family. Hearing him say that made my chest swell with satisfaction. It was true. The cats had bonded our family through a completely new experience. We could check the box on the cat thing and move on. Dad was glad it wasn't a super long commitment, but we all wished we'd had more of a specific timeline from the start, including an exit plan. A phone number where we could have learned a few basics also would have been nice. But we survived, and so did the cats. In fact, I think we did much better than that.

"I'll tell you one more thing I learned, kiddo," my dad said.

"What's that?" I asked.

"I learned that it would still take an awful lot to turn me into a pet person."

Go Get Frosty

One evening, I overheard my mom and dad talking about me in the kitchen.

"I believe the cats broke the spell," Mom said, with what sounded like relief in her voice.

She was right. Earlier, I had told her that I would be open to fostering another animal, depending on the situation. But I don't want to give more credit to the cats than they deserve, for obvious reasons—not the least of which was the fact we barely knew each other. The real catalyst (no pun intended, but I'll take it) was the thought of helping someone when they really needed it. That was a win-win.

After my parents moved to the living room, I took a gob of yarn that Jasper had pulled out of our craft box the week before and tossed it into my mom's lap. That got her attention.

"The couple was so nice," I said. "I'm glad that we could help them and the cats."

"It's crazy how once things started to go bad for them, everything tipped the wrong way and then kept getting worse," she said.

I looked at the mess of yarn. "Should we try to untangle this or pitch it?"

She shrugged. "Let's try. Here, grab an end. Think about if someone gets hurt in a car wreck. The medical staff arrive and start to help right away. They don't stand back and try to figure out who caused the problem."

I kept looping and unlooping the end, trying to untie the knots.

"An emergency is the time to choose mercy and help if you can," Mom continued. "Your grandparents taught me that grace is when you get good stuff you don't deserve. And mercy is not getting the bad stuff you do deserve." She paused and looked at me. "I hope your heart always stays soft," she said. "Time causes most people to look the other way instead."

"I feel like I got back more than I gave," I said, and then added, "I think Dad feels the same way."

But we didn't fire up the computer and start looking for more pets to foster. Nor did we run to the pet store or our local animal shelter. When my mom suggested a trip to the nature center or an outing to the Como Zoo, I responded with an appreciative but firm "No, thank you." Although I was an animal person, I wasn't ready to reopen my heart fully. If anything, I was glad the relationship with the cats had been short-term. Snickers was still my forever pal, and I wasn't looking to fill that space.

Months later, I was tested. Some missionaries who had been home for a few months after a lengthy stint overseas discovered that their pet sitters had not kept their dogs apart. While they fully enjoyed the miracle of birth, they also needed to find homes for their five new Labrador retriever puppies before they left the country again. It wasn't anything they'd planned, but they accepted the responsibility, and by that point, they'd been able to place all the pups in the litter except for one little guy.

By the time we heard about their situation, they were desperate because their flights were the following week. Still, they were hopeful that someone would take in the puppy who was almost too cute to resist: he was all black except for white around his nose and ears and the tips of each paw. The puppy looked like he'd dipped his paws into a bowl of white frosting, then batted his nose and scratched his ears, leaving the sugary patches behind.

Hence his name, Frosty, suggested by Mr. Mike on the day we began puppy training. While other people continued to look for a permanent home, we were glad to alleviate some of the family's anxiety about placing him before they left town. Before bringing Frosty home, we plied them with questions and were as prepared as we could be to foster a puppy. We knew plenty of people who could help if we needed it. The clincher was knowing the arrangement was a temporary one.

Frosty was a bundle of energy and joy, filling our house with play and love and, as we noticed repeatedly, pee and poop. House-training him was difficult, and there seemed no end in sight. Every time I thought he was catching on, we found yet another new spot.

Being an inquisitive puppy, Frosty constantly looked for a way to explore the world beyond our backyard. I could tell he was plotting an escape by the way he sniffed and tested the fence corners in search of a way out. I gave up saying hello to friends who came over to play and instead shouted, "Close the gate!" Not that it mattered. He was poised and ready for escape the first chance he got. Inevitably one of my friends would come over and open the side fence too wide, and I'd find myself sounding the alarm: "Oh no! Go get Frosty!"

He never ran any place specific so much as he simply ran because he seemed to enjoy running—and even better if we chased him. For him, it was a game. Eventually he'd let us catch him. I think he just got tuckered out. He was a puppy, after all. Indeed, after a short nap, he'd go back to waiting for someone to open the side gate again so he could try to scamper outside.

One day I noticed he had stopped peeing inside the house. To be more precise, I woke up and noticed there was nothing to clean up and Frosty himself was sniffing at the back door, signaling that he wanted to go outside. He repeated this again and again until we got the message. He was finally trained. And so were we.

Two or three days later, neighbors a block over said they had good news for us. They had found a permanent home for Frosty with friends from work. I shared in the joy, of course, because Frosty deserved a forever home. It seemed slightly unfair that this next family would get all the benefit of my hard work, though.

"What did you think?" my mom asked my dad the first dinner we had without Frosty's yippy voice serenading us.

My dad took a drink of water before he said anything. "It's not that I'm against dogs," he said. "But—"

I cut him off.

"But you're just not a pet person," I said.

"Exactly."

Put Me In, Coach

I was getting eager to play baseball when out of left field my dad presented a list of conditions that must be met if we were to bring another animal into our life. My mom and I stopped what we were doing and stared at him, trying to figure out what had triggered him and if this avowed non–pet person was of his right mind.

"For instance, I don't want to deal with manure," he said.

My mom stifled a laugh as she nodded in agreement. "Nobody wants to deal with manure," she said.

I was still perplexed. My dad went on to state that we could not get a cow or a horse, which struck me as kind of ridiculous, since we lived in a house in the suburbs and the appearance of either a cow or a horse would have really caused a commotion among the neighborhood dogs and cats. But he was making a point.

"I don't want to be the one who cleans the pet cage," he said.

We nodded in agreement.

"And no more animals doing their business on the floor."

"Never again," I said.

"And definitely, absolutely what?"

"No puppies," my mom and I said at the same time.

"Good," he said with a nod of finality. "Just making sure we're still all on the same page even though none of us is interested in getting another animal right now, right?"

"Right," we said.

Somehow he knew this wasn't the end. As the calendar neared Easter and this conversation had long since disappeared in the cracks between the sofa cushions, I walked into the living room as if taking center stage, which I suppose I was. Standing between the couch and the TV, I made it clear that I had something to say. Something important.

"I would like to have a family meeting about providing another forever home for a pet," I said.

My dad turned toward my mom and raised an I-told-you-so eyebrow.

"Well, let's talk to Markus," he said. "I'm sure you could help take care of their dog, Champagne, or their guinea pig, what's-his-name."

"His name is Boo," I said. "But that's not the same."

"What about helping feed Simon down at the end of the street?" my mom said, referring to an elderly couple's cat. "He has wandered into our yard often enough looking for a mouse to eat or play with, and he seems nice. Plus, the couple he belongs to could use some company."

I shook my head no. I didn't want a temporary pet. I didn't quite know how to articulate it, but at the end of the afternoon when everyone went home to eat dinner or do homework, or on the days no one was available to play, I wanted a pal—and I wanted to be a pal to someone. Someone who was always present, a full-time resident of our house, like me. I heard Mom talking to Grandma Deer on the phone about me, and she used the words "hint of loneliness" to describe my mood. I had a hard time wrapping my mind around that term as it related to me because I had my parents and plenty of neighbors and cousins, and of course the kids from scouts, school, and my Purple Pirates baseball team. It didn't make sense that I could be lonely with so many people in my life. I also genuinely loved to play alone, especially when I was busy building or creating things.

But she was probably right. I might have been suffering a hint of loneliness. It described the feeling I had when it was too early on a Saturday morning for the neighbor kids to play but I'd been up and ready for over an hour. Or when the wind was biting cold and I found myself sighing at the mere thought of putting on all the layers of clothes plus my snowsuit and gloves and scarf along with heavy boots to go outside and try to convince someone to hang out. Or when Noah's family was at their cabin for the week and it was still only day four. Or when I felt like cuddling with Snickers, which I did a lot, only he wasn't there.

"It's clear that you're missing out on all the creative torture of having a brother or sister," my mom joked. "What if one of your uncles came for a visit?"

"That would be awesome," I said. "Uncle Paul sent a diagram for building a potato launcher that we could try. Or Uncle Kris could help me build a trebuchet in the backyard."

"Or we could look into getting another family pet," she said.

I wrinkled my face as if weighing the choices.

"Uncle or pet? Is that what you're asking?"

"What kind of animal do you think would want to live with us?" Mom asked.

I scratched my head. "I'm thinking about another rabbit."

I hadn't uttered a word about wanting another rabbit. But somehow my parents knew. They were sneaky that way.

Later that night, after I got into bed, I overheard the two of them talking down the hall. The sound of their voices carried just far enough for me to hear my dad express concern over me getting attached to another pet and then something happening that would make me sad again. My mom said the rewards outweighed the risk.

"He's grown up so much this year, and he wants to open his heart again," she said. "Sure, you can get hurt with love. But is that a reason for us to say no?"

I remember wondering if I should run into their room with my answer. It seemed like a good idea. However, before I could get out of bed, I drifted off to sleep.

How Do You Pick a Friend?

The spring air was fresh and crisp. Easter was a few weeks away, and the timing aligned with the nation's annual obsession with bunnies. We agreed to wait until the hockey season ended and Easter passed to think more seriously about getting another rabbit, making sure we weren't just caught up in the moment either. We also wanted to take a spring break trek to visit my grandparents' cabin first. But the more I tried not to think about rabbits, the more I thought about rabbits.

In a change of policy, my parents gave me permission to search the internet on preapproved sites like the Humane Society and several local rabbit rescues they knew about, as well as the Craigslist pet pages. This was a noticeably big step. Every so often, one of them popped their head in the room and asked if I was making progress. I suppose I was, though in reality I think I was overwhelmed—and not just by the number of rabbits there were to look at and consider. I was also swimming in thoughts I hadn't anticipated, starting with the most obvious: How do you find a pet soul mate?

Since I considered Snickers the perfect rabbit, I made a list of his characteristics so I could compare the available options. Could I find another rabbit that awesome? Was it even possible? What *was* a perfect rabbit? What's perfect to one person might be quite imperfect to someone else. I knew there were plenty of things about me that wouldn't be on someone's ideal list for a neighbor, but I was sure glad that Noah put up with me anyway. Sure, we drove each other crazy sometimes, but we had a ton of history together. And there's one definite perk of being my friend: you're guaranteed to look like the normal one.

Seriously, though, as I scrolled through the listings, I saw that what some people consider deal breakers or imperfections are the very traits that other people like. The variety of pets available online for rehoming made me realize the world is composed of people with their own unique, highly subjective perceptions of what is cute and what is the perfect fit. Similarly, all of them probably had as many reasons for acquiring a pet as they had for getting rid of that same pet later.

Was I any different? I was spending all this time researching a new forever pet when I'd been ready to adopt Snickers after reading three words in an ad.

And look how amazing that turned out! Yet this time, I didn't want to leave anything to chance. I became comfortably uncomfortable with deciding how to decide. That was when my parents threw me a curveball by reminding me that they were proof that sometimes you find something even better than what you write down on your list.

"Are you talking about how you met in college and fell in love?" I asked.

My mom turned to my dad and gave him *that* look, the one that answered my question.

"Yeah, thanks, I'll just stick to my process anyway."

There were so many ads on Craigslist, with new ones being added all the time. I wondered what made so many people want to rehome their bunnies. Was there something wrong with the rabbits? Or was there something wrong with the people? What traits should I be looking for? What was going to make one right for me? How would I know?

My dad came and sat down next to me and started to help me process out loud. "Do you know what you're looking for so you'll know when you find it?"

"Rabbits hopefully live a long time," I said. "So I want a good one."

"How are you defining 'a good one'?" he asked.

"Healthy, I guess. But personality is the biggest piece," I said. "In the end, I don't care what the rabbit looks like. They're all cute in their own way. It's mostly about how the rabbit interacts with me and if I feel like it's a good fit, and you can't tell that from a picture."

"Maybe you need to meet up and spend some time together," my dad said.

My mom called out from down the hall, inviting herself into the conversation. "Aha! I think you just described how you go about finding a friend."

But I didn't have time to spend with each rabbit. Acknowledging the overwhelming number of available rabbits, my mom showed me how to make a spreadsheet. Soon I'd created a fairly sophisticated tracker with columns and rows of features and details I could easily refer back to, including color, gender, age, breed type (if available), location, the family's reason for getting rid of it, and a photograph (if provided). I worked slowly and methodically, copying and pasting the pertinent information and studying it at night, as if it were a treasure hunt, with the prize being the perfect rabbit somewhere in the Minneapolis–Saint Paul metropolitan area.

Doing the research gave me confidence that I was exploring all my options and I would ultimately make an informed decision. I didn't want to be impulsive. After I was a month into my search, though, no one was going to accuse me of making a rash decision.

In May, I finally reached the end of my quest after one little bunny caught my eye. I also didn't want to look any more and figured I would print off the spreadsheet and choose one from the options. I restocked the printer with paper and clicked Print while I ran off to the living room and did a little reading with my mom. When I heard the printer stop, I rushed into the spare bedroom my parents had converted into a home office and saw that the paper tray needed to be refilled. This happened one more time before the spreadsheet printed in its entirety.

After carefully straightening the stack of paper, I started back out to the living room, but I only got halfway down the hall before my legs stopped working. I couldn't move. Those three pounds of paper in my hands felt like three hundred pounds as I dropped to the floor and the pages spilled all over the carpet. I buried my head in my hands and began to cry. I couldn't explain it at first, but I came to understand it was because I suddenly realized that all those entries I'd neatly organized were real live bunnies that nobody wanted anymore. It was terribly, overwhelmingly sad.

I had every reason to believe that these pet owners had started with the best intentions. People had fallen in love when they brought the bunny home, but then something changed. Life happened. But perhaps in some cases they were more in love with the *idea* of having a rabbit, because many of them fell out of love with the reality. I was so busy on my treasure hunt over several weeks that I hadn't paid attention to how many entries I'd filled in until that moment, when I saw the total was 362. That was in the Twin Cities area alone—and the number didn't include the pages from the actual rescue organizations.

I picked myself up and fell onto my mom's lap, where I sobbed. She ran her fingers through my hair, sensing that I didn't want her or my dad to ask any questions or talk or try to fix anything, like parents tend to do when their kids are upset. I just needed them to listen to me cry as I asked questions with no easy answers. Why are people like this? How can they love a pet one day and get rid of it the next? Is this the way the world works? If it is, why is that?

I believed we could do better—and whether I realized it or not, this was probably the moment I decided *I* would do better.

I Want to Save the Rabbits

My tears that day had the effect of washing away another layer of rosy protection from my eyes and opening me up to a more realistic view of the world. I wasn't deterred from finding a new forever pet; the next steps were merely delayed as I processed the tidal wave of emotions. My parents waited for me to start the conversation. They weren't in a hurry, and neither was I.

After a week, I was ready. I presented Mom and Dad with the photo of the specific rabbit I had in mind. He was a larger breed with noble blue fur, and he had an expression that set him apart. After some research, I learned he was a pedigreed rabbit, a rare heritage breed, and it felt like my future had tapped me on the shoulder.

"He seems like a good fit for our family," I said.

"How do you know?" my mom asked.

"I can't explain it," I said. "I just know."

Although there were a few other contenders, none approached this guy. He was different from all 361 other rabbits. If this were a baseball game, I'd call finding him a walk-off home run.

There was a reason for his special look. He was an American Blue rabbit, known as a German Blue Vienna rabbit prior to World War I. Eager to learn more about his breed, I scoured the American Rabbit Breeders Association website. I learned there was also an albino variety, with white fur and red eyes. On the Livestock Conservancy website, I found out American Blues were one of nine breeds considered endangered, meaning there were fewer than two thousand registered in the United States. Their numbers were declining at a rate that meant extinction was a serious concern if an intentional plan and a new demand for the breed weren't created.

Historically this breed was raised for meat and fur, but when demand for those products dwindled, all the larger breeds—including American rabbits—declined too. It's not like all the breeders met up in the 1950s and decided to stop raising big rabbits anymore. It just happened, apparently without anyone paying attention, while the main demands for rabbits in North America shifted to smaller, more petite breeds that were known more for being pets. By the time the census was taken a few years back, the American breed was listed as "critical."

I never anticipated that picking a forever pet would expose me to issues like abandonment and extinction. Seeing how heavily this was weighing on me, my parents helped me talk through some harsh realities and challenged me to think about what I could do to make a difference. They didn't need to convince me, because I was already diving deep to find a solution.

"I want to figure out a way to save the rabbits," I said.

"Honey, if you can figure out a way, we'll support you," my mom said.

My dad agreed. Now, looking back, my parents laughingly warn people to be careful what you promise your kids. But that's a family joke. They never wavered in their support of my dream. They took me seriously. They saw the gravity in my eyes and felt the weight of it on my heart.

A few weeks later, when I said I was finally ready to discuss a final decision, we scheduled a family meeting. I walked into the living room dressed in the suit I usually wore to church on Sundays because it seemed appropriate for all that was on my mind. I had a business proposition to pitch, and as a fan of the TV series *Shark Tank*, I knew it was important to have a good presentation—and to get right to the point.

Good evening, sharks. I want to help stop the pet-abandonment cycle, one bunny at a time.

Rabbits are undeniably cute. It makes sense that they are very popular pets. However, because they're so cute, many people just can't fight the urge to bring one home on impulse, especially in the spring. But when the family gets busy or find out they are allergic or the kids don't want to help out or they have a baby or plan to move, they often want to just get rid of it. Boo! Rescue shelters are awesome, but they're already quite full of bunnies ready for adoption. On my spreadsheet, there were 362 rabbits available right after Easter in Minneapolis and St. Paul alone, and that doesn't even include the lists from the rescues!

So, what's the solution?

Our program will focus on education and prevention rather than creating another place to put unwanted animals. We'll aim to stop people from buying pets on impulse by giving them information and experiences where they can learn what they're getting into.

How would it work?

1. Our program will take in rare breeds like the American Blue to help save these awesome rabbits and to create a demand for them. And we'll start with one at our house.

2. We will take the bunnies everywhere, such as egg hunts, scout meetings, and community events. As people spend time with the bunnies, they'll learn about them and have more realistic expectations, like that rabbits poop—because, well, all animals poop. Did you know that almost one-fourth of the bunnies on my list were surrendered because of poop issues? At the events, we will accept donations, and then, when we have enough money, we can pay for the rabbits' food and eventually take in more bunnies.

3. We will create a formal foster program so families can take bunnies home for short-term stays. Then, if they fall in love for real and they don't have allergies, they can buy the rabbit. We will provide the cage and supplies and everything else they need. We will give them educational worksheets and ideas of how to play with their bunny. We will set them up for success from the start. And we will offer an exit strategy—they can return the bunny at any time. The bunnies are guaranteed a forever home once they come to us.

4. We will grow the program by using the money we get from donations to buy bunny food, hay, and supplies so we can save more unwanted rabbits and place more of the rare heritage breeds with families. Maybe people will donate cages and other supplies.

How would we pay for it?

As you know, parents are willing to pay for educational stuff. So the fostering program will involve life science and math. It's more than just a family bunny experience. We'll offer it as a learning program called STEMbunnies. The STEM part stands for science, technology, engineering, and math, just like at my school. Families will be charged for classes and worksheets, and they'll pay us ten dollars a week for the fostering experience, so the program will pay for itself. It's not about us getting the money, but when kids pay for a pet, they place more value on it.

The staff will be volunteer kids who teach other kids. We just need parents to drive us and help us work out stuff with the other parents. We'll contact teachers, and they'll help us find more kids who want to foster or volunteer. Together the kids will save the bunnies.

So what do you say, sharks? Will you help me?

My parents sat in stunned silence on the sofa. I think I saw Dad blink. Apparently when they told me to "figure it out," they weren't expecting charts and a formal pitch.

Knowing a successful pitch needed a strong close, I paused to make eye contact with my parents, first my mom and then my dad. Then I said, "The best way to start is by becoming my first example. Just think of all the cool adventures we'll have together. So who's ready to join the bunny crew?"

"I'm super proud of you, Caleb." My dad came over and started to ruffle my hair but paused and shook my hand instead. "You've really thought things through. Now which bunny were you thinking about to start your business?"

Eight Pounds of Cuddle

A few days later, we drove about thirty minutes south to meet the family selling the rabbit that I'd identified as the best option. The family's daughter, who looked to be in her early twenties, showed us into their backyard, where the rabbits were playing in a pen. She noticed my intense scrutiny of the rabbits as I searched for "the one," and she motioned me forward.

"Come take a closer look," she said.

Sitting off to the side of the pen, near the wall and in the comfort of a shade tree, was the rabbit from the photo. He was even more beautiful in person. The blue of his fur was richer in color, and the curve of his back made him look sleek and fast, like a sports car. When I ran my hands over his back, I felt some squishy baby fat under his fur. It was just a hunch on my part, but I guessed his muscles weren't fully grown yet. She showed me the pedigree; it confirmed he was only four months old and therefore not quite fully grown. Two months to go until he'd be full-size and could reproduce, although she informed me that he was already interested.

"How much does he weigh?" I asked.

"About eight pounds so far," she said.

My mom's face lit up. She squeezed my shoulder and leaned down to whisper in my ear. "You realize this rabbit weighs about the same as you did when we brought you home from the hospital?" she asked.

"Wow. Really?" I let that sink in.

It was kind of mind-blowing to think of myself as the same size as this rabbit. "This is going to be one big rabbit!" I exclaimed.

As I studied him more closely, I decided he looked like the rabbit pictured in the ARBA *Standard of Perfection* book, with the distinctive semi-arch from his neck to his back end, something called a mandolin shape.

"He hasn't molted yet," the daughter said. "He still has his first coat. It's a lot softer than judges like if you were to ever show him at the county fair."

I kept running my fingers through his fur.

"I wonder how he'll change over the next few years," I said, trying to picture him in the future, which led me to look at my parents and add, "That will mean taking lots of pictures."

What would the more mature fur feel like? Would it feel coarser, like the rough whiskers on Dad's chin? Rabbits grow up so fast, and I didn't want to miss any more of this guy's development than I already had.

We spent a few minutes sitting on the grass together. The rabbit seemed as interested in getting to know me as I was to know him. Then he settled in my lap, and I sensed that intangible quality that I'd struggled to pin down when I set out to find a new friend. It's impossible to describe, because it's all intuition and feeling, and I could sense all that and more from this rabbit.

"He's the one," I announced. "Plus, he's a cuddler. Eight pounds of cuddle."

But that's when something happened from out of nowhere. Our every move was being carefully monitored from across the pen by two other beautiful rabbits, both of them white. Both of them female. And both of them, it turned out, were purebred American White rabbits.

"I can't believe you have two albino American too!" I blurted out. "They're gorgeous!"

I introduced myself to the two fuzzy does, which were just as inquisitive as their blue buck friend. One of the does was slightly larger than the other, with an extra air of confidence, while the smaller of the two had a face that was more petite and refined. Both looked at me with warm, vibrant eyes and expressive eyelashes. It was uncanny to be observed as closely as I was observing them. Somehow both seemed to be communicating with me in a language that spoke loud and clear.

My parents picked up on it too. They motioned me over to the side for a private little chat.

"I know what you're thinking," my mom said.

"Can we get all three?" I asked. "Thanks to Snickers, we already have everything we need."

Hearing those words come out of my mouth made me realize that my beloved perfect best friend was responsible for setting things in motion that led me to these rabbits. I suppose it was the first time I truly understood that hearts need to be open for love to flow through them. I definitely felt the love flowing through mine. If it weren't for Snickers, I wouldn't have been looking for a new forever pet. Neither would I have ridden home that afternoon in the back of our Prius with not one but three rabbits beside me, with the blue buck in Snickers's old carrier. It was a grand slam.

Paxton Peacebunny

In addition to being the same weight when we were brought home to join the Smith family in the blue house in Bloomington, the big blue bunny and I shared another similarity: the people who loved us spent a lot of time trying to pick a name that fit. Snickers came with his, as did the cats, and Mr. Mike had named Frosty, so it wasn't until I started to name the rabbits that

I thought about how people, places, and things get their names. Consider how randomly some names are chosen yet how important they are to shaping identity and expectations. Think about how, despite their randomness, names end up fitting the person or the pet perfectly.

Much to the chagrin of my grandmas, who wanted to buy clothes and gifts in advance, my parents agreed not to find out my gender until I was born, explaining that they wanted to wait like it was Christmas morning to find out what was in the gift.

My mom was in the hospital for less than forty-eight hours, and when it was time for the three of us to leave, I still had "SMITH BABY BOY" on my ankle tag. The staff gave my parents the appropriate form to register my birth, and as time passed, everyone from family and friends to hospital employees expressed their eagerness to learn my name.

My parents had spent months thinking about possibilities. They had only one rule: no names of anyone they already knew, which, after years of working with male hockey players from around the world, took out more than a hundred options.

Because the name would be paired with Smith, my mom and dad hoped to come up with something quasi-original. The world already had enough John Smiths, Michael Smiths, and Bob Smiths. Tens of thousands of them, in fact—including some in my own family.

Blessed with a pretty good sense of humor, my dad tried out a few random names that clearly didn't go together just to see people's reactions, especially his mom's, who was determined to be supportive no matter how ridiculous the ideas were. I don't know if he ever thought about naming me after one of Minnesota's sports heroes, like Harmon Killebrew Smith or Fran Tarkenton Smith or Kirby Puckett Smith, but I wouldn't put it past him, just to get a reaction from his mother.

Finally, they decided on the name Caleb, which means "devoted to God." Relatives on both sides of the family approved. At my dedication service at church, they committed to teach me Scripture, to do their best to follow the example of Jesus, and to model a life filled with prayer and service, guiding me until I was old enough to make decisions on my own. Their hope was that I would choose to devote my life to following God too. So I suppose you could say the name was both aspirational and providential.

I went through a similarly long exercise to name my rabbits. After we brought them home, I spent a lot of time getting to know them. The trait all three seemed to share was a sense of calm and peace, so I started referring to them as the peacebunnies. They seemed at peace themselves, and they had a way of bringing peace with them wherever they went.

The Peacebunnies.

To me, it was as clear and simple as describing the sky as blue or the grass as green or cheesecake as perfect.

The hard part was the first name. I needed one for the little blue buck that went with the last name Peacebunny, and one day, flipping through baby-name books at the library, I stumbled on the name *Paxton* and discovered that in Old English it has roots that mean "peace." Paxton Peacebunny. As soon as I heard myself say it, I knew it was right. Like music. Noah was the first of my friends to come over to see the new additions to our family. He tried it out and agreed with me.

"Did you think of that yourself?" he asked.

"Yes."

"Paxton?"

"Yep, and Peacebunny will be the last name for the whole family."

"I like it," he said.

So did I.

And just as important, I sensed Pax did too.

I thought about the which-came-first process of choosing a name. Do you give a name because of what the pet looks or acts like? Or do you give a name based on what you hope they will become?

The name Paxton Peacebunny was both.

So Long, Lemonade Stand

The rabbits lived inside the house, but I took them to the backyard every day so they could roam around and enjoy the grass and fresh air. Before the week was done, I had named the two female American White rabbits Star and Creampuff.

All the neighborhood kids and several parents came over to see what was creating such a buzz. Some of the older kids, who were in middle school now and no longer as available to play with us younger kids the way they once were, still enjoyed welcoming the new rabbits.

Of the trio, Paxton was the calmest and most peaceful, yet still quite outgoing. Star had a stronger personality, letting us know she was there and whether she was interested in being social. She paid attention to everything going on around her, especially at dinnertime—ours, not hers. She seemed to be begging to try my food and was annoyed that I didn't oblige. Creampuff's personality was like her name, soft and gentle. It explained why she and Paxton got along best much later, when we gave them a hoppy minute to mix and mingle and start a family of their own.

As their use of the litter box became consistent, Pax and the girls were allowed throughout the house—but no coed parties without a chaperone. All of them delighted in exploring and resting under my bunk bed. Like Snickers, Paxton tagged along with me. He wanted to make sure he wouldn't miss out on any of the action. Some people are like that. Some rabbits are too.

That summer, as always, lemonade stands popped up along our street. Almost everyone took turns opening their own stand. I liked working with all the neighbor kids; it was a fun way to spend the afternoon . . . until two friends decided to open stands on the same day. Then it was war. I went back and forth to be a good friend to both, but I got fired from both stands within the first five or ten minutes for talking to the competition.

There was much drama, and everyone went home mad. Things spilled out that never should have been said. A lot of tears flowed along our street that day. The worst part was that the block remained quiet the rest of the afternoon, and no one came back outside after dinner. Everyone stayed home and the hurt festered. I wasn't angry at anyone, but I was angry at the situation. This was not how things worked!

The following morning, I chose to open my own lemonade stand to try to coax everyone back together. As agreed in advance, I paid my parents for the ingredients, like taking out a small business loan, and they allowed me to rent the use of tables and chairs for the small fee of helping wash the car. I set up my stand in a prime location under the tree in the front yard that now replaced the one we'd lost. One by one the doors opened, and kids came back to play with Pax. We all congregated at the lemonade stand I'd set up beneath the celebration tree.

At first I thought it was awesome because after hugs, we were ready to join forces in a unified goal. In fact, the business was great for everyone except me, because not only did I not make any money, I *lost* money. Everything would have been fine if we'd had customers, but we were lucky if one or two cars drove by all day. And those that did were driven by someone's mom or dad, who generally slowed down, waved, and asked, "How's business?" They didn't buy anything.

Worse, my employees drank all the lemonade and then still wanted to get paid for their time. A quarter isn't much unless a quarter is all you have. When I closed the stand, I was broke. I couldn't even have a final going-out-of-business glass of lemonade because my workers had finished off the last drop. On the bright side, everyone was friends again, so I felt rich in a whole other way. With only eleven more weeks of summer, we needed to make the most of every day.

The following week was the start of vacation Bible school at a local church that always had it on the same week each year, so we blocked out the calendar way in advance. The five-day VBS culminated in an outdoor festival with arts and crafts, live music, and barbecues for the whole family. It was a big community party that drew a large crowd well beyond those affiliated with the church—including my family, because this wasn't our home church either. But I thought their VBS was the best, as they decorated the whole building and transformed it according to that year's theme.

During the first day of VBS, I spoke to the director and offered to bring my rabbits to the festival to share some joy. My parents gave me permission and helped me get the necessary approval, and I was so excited. The bunnies sat atop smaller tables provided by the church, allowing people to come by and say hello. They seemed to genuinely enjoy the gentle affection—the bunnies and everyone else.

I spent an hour answering the same five or six questions about rabbits from an endless line of parents and kids. I made a mental note that we should print out little fact sheets if we ever did this again. Every new family wanted to know if the rabbits had names, if they were friendly, what kind they were, how old they were, how much they weighed, and what they ate. Some of the kids asked if they had a favorite TV character, like Bugs Bunny, and their parents cracked classic bunny jokes, like: "How do rabbits travel? By hareplane." Or: "What is their favorite type of music? Hip-hop, obviously." Groaner dad-type jokes, but I saw how they made everyone smile and laugh.

Toward the end of the day, a man approached my parents and asked if we'd ever considered bringing rabbits to kids' birthday parties. His daughter was a couple of years younger than I was, and her party was in a week. It was a question we hadn't been asked before, so my mom took down his phone number, expressed our thanks for the invitation, and said we would call him back after we'd had a chance to talk about it. During the car ride home, we tried to figure out if there was a reason not to move forward. We had the carriers, the pen, some blankets, and of course the bunnies. The party would be in the family's fenced backyard and they didn't have a dog.

"We should try," I said. "What's the worst that could happen?"

"Never say that," my mom said.

"Okay, let me try the pitch again." I smiled. "Mom, I think we should try this. It'll be an adventure."

"Adventure," she said. "Now you're speaking my language."

Before the day of the party, I researched the rates for special events and learned that many companies in our area that hosted parties with ponies and petting zoos charged between $275 and $350. I was flabbergasted. Even if I asked for donations and everyone paid only what they could, I saw the opportunity for a new and viable income stream that could help pay for the cost of feeding and maintaining the bunnies.

"If we do more birthday parties and school trips and stuff, maybe they will help us afford even more rare rabbits," I said to my mom. "Maybe someday I could even make enough money that I could pay myself a salary too."

She rubbed her thumb and finger together. "After you pay off your lemonade stand loan," she said with a smile.

Because our families hadn't discussed any payment, I put it out of my mind and focused on the most important thing: having a blast and sharing what I'd been learning about bunnies while they created their magic. It took about fifteen minutes to pack everything in the car, five minutes to travel, and ten minutes to set up, during which time there were eight very excited party guests who were jumping up and down and squealing.

With more experience, I would have directed all the guests to wash their hands while we set up. In any case, the birthday party was a hit. The girls loved sitting in the pen with blankets on their laps and interacting with the bunnies and with each other. The parents' eyes were gleaming as they watched and kept edging closer until they finally played with the rabbits too. The guests had simple questions about their names, ages, favorite foods, and if they did anything silly. Everyone was gentle, but it was clear they hadn't interacted with rabbits before or seen a rabbit poop on a blanket, so if there were to be a next time, I realized I needed a formal opening, some simple rules, and a way to change expectations from a petting zoo to an educational playdate, where the bunnies learned as much about us as we did about them.

As we folded up the small white table, the girl's father took me aside and thanked me for making his daughter's party memorable and special. He leaned forward and began to put six twenty-dollar bills in my hand, a total of $120. I'd never held that much money before. But I politely declined and tried to give it back because we hadn't talked about payment and this was my very first party. Plus, they insisted that we stay and have dinner with them, including birthday cake covered with pink frosting and rabbit decorations.

"I want you to take the money," he insisted. "I worked out an agreement with the rabbits, and you can take it up with them if you have an issue."

Although I thought that was funny, I still politely declined. It seemed like too much money. But he persisted, and I finally gave in.

"I will consider it a donation for the bunnies," I said, thanking him on behalf of my business associates.

In the car on the way home, I did some quick calculations. His generous gift was enough to pay for rabbit pellets for one of the rabbits for an entire year. I knew right then that I was never going to set up my lemonade stand again.

3

Presents for Bunnies

"So many bunnies! My heart almost popped out of my ears!" exclaimed a little girl with amber hair in pigtails who couldn't have been happier we'd brought bunnies for a visit. This was at our second birthday party, and it confirmed my feeling that bunnies have a way of making great days even better. Her family also met us at the VBS family festival and asked us to come to their house for a backyard party.

But they added a twist that I hadn't thought about until we arrived at her house and set up. Instead of bringing the birthday girl presents, she'd requested that her guests bring presents for the bunnies. Parsley. Cilantro. Bananas. And yes, carrots. They added some homegrown yummies from their backyard garden too. One guest arrived with a six-pack of water bottles with a bow on top.

"For when the bunnies get thirsty." She beamed.

This second birthday party was equally celebratory, but the family approached it more like a fun science project. The girls wanted to see if the rabbits liked to eat cilantro or parsley more. Would they prefer carrots, celery leaves, or bananas? Would Paxton gravitate to different smells or tastes? How far would he go out of his way to get his choice? Did different rabbits have different preferences, or did they all like the same food?

I didn't know the answers either, and the girls' curiosity planted the seed of an idea that I would pick up on later. But this birthday party was most memorable for showing me the capacity people have for love and their eagerness to open their hearts if given the opportunity. One girl who had Creampuff on her lap caused every head to turn when she shouted to her mother to hurry and look at her.

"Did you see that?" she said. "The bunny just hopped onto my lap and said, 'I love you' to me. And just to me!"

See Rule #2

Many days that summer, my family headed to Wood Lake Nature Center for a short hike and one of their year-round naturalist programs. No matter what mood I was in, I found that being in nature helped. I knew all the staff by name and the trails by heart, including the nooks where the turtles hid and the ducks socialized. We marked the seasons there: pumpkin carving in the fall, moonlight hikes in winter, and the maple syrup ritual in spring. We hauled buckets back to the main visitors' center in black snow sleds and then sat for hours watching the liquid turn to syrup.

When we were there one day, we saw they were about to host a weeklong minicamp for preschoolers that showcased the wild rabbits often seen in the preserve. It was called "Bunnies, Bees, and Butterflies." Aware that I raised rabbits, the director asked if I would be willing to bring one or all three of my domestic rabbits for the little kids to meet, allowing them to touch a rabbit or two and helping them understand the difference between the ones kept as pets and the ones outside. It was an easy decision, and the giggles were priceless.

Less than a week later, the director invited me for a meeting to discuss the possibility of hosting a few birthday parties in the visitor center as a partnership. They would advertise the opportunity in their brochure and arrange all the logistics if I brought the bunnies and hosted a short educational program. I stuck out my hand and shook his hand vigorously before I even finished saying, "Deal."

That changed everything. One of those first Wood Lake birthday parties led to an invitation to the Richfield community egg hunt, which resulted in a stream of events. Because one of the preschool parents had an older daughter in Girl Scouts, the bunnies were invited to a scout meeting, which opened up the chance to host a booth at an elementary school's science fair, which led to two other birthday parties and the Eagan kids' expo. There, I met the head of scheduling for a childcare system that booked thirty visits over the next four years. Someone on staff at one of the preschools invited me to their son's birthday, which led to a Cub Scout meeting, which then led to my first senior-home visit, which brought me back to another party at Wood Lake, all without a dime spent on advertising except a website designed by . . . me. Phew! That just proved to me that things in motion stay in motion.

Somewhere along the way, I created a "key values" page in my journal that I could go back to whenever I struggled about what to do. It was a measuring stick, a mash-up of heuristics—or problem-solving techniques, as explained to me once by a guest speaker at a Rotary meeting—that helped guide my decisions then and still does.

1. Do your best to take care of God's bunnies.
2. Choose your attitude, and choose to be kind every time.
3. Bunnies are free to act like bunnies and are to be free from hunger, thirst, discomfort, pain, injury, disease, fear, and distress.
4. Every person gets VIP treatment, regardless of ability or willingness to donate. It's not about the pay.
5. Try to see each person the way God sees them. Maybe the bunnies were sent there just for them.
6. Be like Switzerland. Even though people have polarizing views about how rabbits should be cared for, choose to learn from everyone. If they are mean, refer to #2.
7. Choose to forgive and guard your heart. Refer to #2.

8. Don't be late or a no-show. Commitment means "no matter what," even if I'm tired or something fun and spontaneous comes up for the same time slot. What would be worse than a bunny party without bunnies?

9. Use your brain. Learn from mistakes and near-misses and things that worked well. Take time to debrief.

10. Did we come out with the win? Was the event a success in their eyes? Did we follow rules 1–9? Did we meet our outcome goals, such as teaching more people about rabbits? Did we somehow make the world a little better?

Summer flew by. We had more invitations than we had time for. I didn't know how to choose from all the emails and messages that came in and decided to accept invitations only for certain days and on a rolling, first-come basis, regardless of how much someone would pay. We didn't have a set fee anyway; we trusted that people would be as generous as they could be. I never wanted to send a bill or try to collect a fee afterward, and we didn't.

Every adult I talked to while I was figuring out how to start up the organization said I was making a horrible business decision, especially because I wanted to start an educational nonprofit, and they figured people would take advantage. To be sure, that has happened from time to time, but my goal at eight years old was to do just enough events to pay for the business expenses without focusing on the money or completely filling up my calendar. I wanted this to be fun for me, the other kids, and the bunnies. I wanted the spotlight to be on the rabbits, not on having to fulfill a contract or an obligation, and whether people realized it or not, it worked out gloriously because expectations shifted and it became about sharing time together.

In the end, it was all about attitude. See rule #2.

Wisdom Keepers

Although some people started pointing out how I was different from other kids my age, I think I assumed that just like me, everyone else in second grade spent their time working on projects like this and I'd learn about them during show-and-tell. Second grade was going to be awesome!

I was eager to participate in my first science fair and was giddy when I registered for another year in Cub Scouts. As a kid who liked to wiggle and run, I loved the weekly game time in the gym before the meetings as much as the formal activities involved in working toward Wolf rank. My favorite was the bicycle rodeo night, where we all learned proper hand signals, did a safety check, and finished by navigating a course of cones and obstacles through the entire church parking lot.

To meet the scout requirement of learning about hand tools, I built a pinewood derby car. Working under the supervision of my dad's father, Grandpa Smith, in his tool-filled shop, I sketched ideas, developed a design, and crafted the final product. My grandpa helped with some of the finishing touches, like weighing the car to add exactly the right number of pennies and washers to make it run smooth and fast. He was smart, patient, and willing to answer the endless stream of questions I threw at him about his own growing-up years.

I learned so much from listening to the stories he told about his life when he was my age. So many things were different, though I was surprised by how much was the same, and I was reassured by the way my grandpa said, "And they always will be."

I understood what he meant when my teacher assigned a genealogy project. My dad traced his heritage back to France and the Isle of Wight, while my mom's family story wove its way through records that included the Civil War, the Revolutionary War, and life in Europe in the 1500s. Long ago, my great-grandpa had made a cedar chest for storing treasures. When I opened it up, I found a large family Bible with records of baptisms, marriages, births, and everyone's favorite hymns and Scriptures. I carefully studied the items from the trunk as my parents handed them to me.

"What do you think?" my mom asked.

"It's like Paxton, Creampuff, and Star," I said, eager to share my insight. "All of them have papers that describe their family history too."

Others shared my interest in family history. They were friends from the Dakota and Ojibwa communities whom my parents had gotten to know at various local events. Over the years, we were fortunate to attend many of their gatherings, and I always sat with kids my age, watching and listening to the elders share their histories. They grew up in a culture that respected those who had come before and had seen more of life, and that resonated with the way I was raised. Like my grandparents, their elders were valued as wisdom keepers. Their culture was built on kinship—on being good to each other.

I was also influenced by their sense of time. Events started when they started and ended when they ended rather than revolving around the clock. Whether an event took thirty minutes or three hours, it didn't matter, as long as everything was from the heart. I had already modeled the end of our programs the same way, but my Native American friends gave me the words to explain it. When we scheduled a bunny event, we would agree on a start time but let things wind down naturally, rather than rushing out the door. Some of the best conversations happened after the events were formally concluded.

Over time, it helped to have my ideas validated by businesspeople who could share their wisdom. Every Friday morning, my mom took me with her to Rotary club meetings, where I listened to speakers from nonprofits, government agencies, and businesses. I went for the muffins but stayed for the inspiration and the opportunity to chat with people I really respected. I had been attending since I was just a baby, so they'd all seen me grow up. One day an insurance executive named Victor, who was close to my grandpa's age, struck up a conversation with me that centered on my business endeavors. He listened to me talk about wanting to breed endangered rabbits and end pet rabbit abandonment, and then he began to share ways to achieve these goals.

Our conversation would go on for years and touch on basics like how to structure a business plan, how to overcome obstacles, and how to shake hands. But in those early days, Victor also pushed me to think about prioritizing the topics I'd overheard at Rotary meetings, like service and values and applying the Four-Way Test: Is it the truth? Is it fair to all concerned? Will it build goodwill and better friendships? Will it be beneficial to all concerned? One week I introduced him to Paxton Peacebunny, who was on his way to visit my school for show-and-tell. I told him I wanted to enter Paxton in the next year's county fair.

"What's his specialty?" he asked.

"He and my other bunnies make people feel good," I said.

"How do they do that?" he asked.

"By being good rabbits," I said. "They bring out the best in people."

"It sounds like he has lots to show us all."

Sacred Ground

It wasn't quite the middle of December, but it was close enough to the holidays that we were counting down the days to Christmas. Brightly colored lights blinked and twinkled throughout the neighborhood at night. It was festive and pretty in the snow, which had been on the ground since late October—and super cold for anywhere except Minnesota.

This particular day was relatively warm for December, with the temperature expected to climb to thirty-eight degrees, but the morning had started slowly because I'd missed the bus. Then I found myself overdressed in layers. All day, everything was kind of off.

The next day I woke up early, and because it was the weekend, I hurried over to the Bachmans', where Noah and I worked on our snow fort. Each time I ran home to warm up, my mom was on the phone and too engrossed in conversations to ask me about the progress we were making, which wasn't like her. I sensed something was wrong—it didn't feel like a normal Saturday. Sunday was more of the same. When I asked what was going on, I caught a glimpse of tears in my mom's eyes.

I stepped closer and she pulled me close for a hug. "There are a lot of people who really need prayer," she said. "Be patient. Your dad and I will explain what we can, but it will be later."

I went to school on Monday as if everything were normal. But it wasn't. At the end of the day, my parents were waiting for me in the parking lot. I climbed in the car and saw my blue roller suitcase, which meant we were going to the airport. Before pulling out of the parking lot, they explained we were going to catch a flight to Newtown, Connecticut, a community that was grieving from a mass shooting at an elementary school named Sandy Hook.

"On Friday, some families had an empty seat at the dinner table because their kids got hurt at school," my mom said, being very selective with her words.

I moved closer to the front so I could see both of their faces.

"Was it anyone we know?" I asked.

"No, the kids live in Connecticut," my dad said. "We don't know anyone there."

I knew where that was from having worked on and memorized our United States map puzzle. Those states out East were so small that they were combined on the wooden puzzle pieces, and the purple part that represented Connecticut had a picture of a robin on it for their state bird. I also knew Connecticut had been home to the NHL Whalers hockey team before they were sold and became the Carolina Hurricanes. So, in some roundabout way, I felt connected.

But what had happened at Sandy Hook was beyond my comprehension. I had no context for understanding the magnitude of such tragedy—not yet, anyway.

This part is especially tricky for me to write about, because more than anything, I want to be respectful. In my mind, the community of Newtown became sacred ground even beyond where the children and staff lost their lives. Even though I will fumble the words, I need to try to share the experience from my point of view and the impact it had on me, because this visit in December was instrumental in my journey to creating Peacebunny Island.

Growing up, I knew my parents had volunteered in disaster relief before they got married. Because they stopped soon after I was born, I didn't see that part of their life, but those experiences greatly shaped their lives and worldview; I have no doubt the heart changes they underwent in those years trickled down to me, especially in the way they raised me to think about what is meaningful and important.

I was in first grade when I first heard a teacher bring up September 11 and guide a conversation about the plane crashes in New York, Shanksville, and the Pentagon. I'm pretty sure no one else in my class had ever heard about the event. Contrast that with my family, who had a tradition of eating sausage and peppers that day every year because that meal was served repeatedly to the volunteers at Ground Zero, where my parents were assigned.

I've learned that their experience in disaster relief is the reason they watch tornado weather reports so closely and lead us in prayer whenever one touches down or whenever a hurricane is heading up the coast. It's also why they know the names of so many little towns across the Midwest, all places where they've led teams filling sandbags and cleaning up. It's why they always pay attention to the bad mix of a late heavy snow and a fast melt, knowing it changes the water levels along our riverbanks. They remain acutely aware even though they stopped accepting disaster-relief invitations after they became parents. Eventually the phone calls stopped.

Then the shooting at Sandy Hook occurred, resulting in the death of six adults and twenty children between the ages of six and seven years old, and the phone in our house began to ring again. Friends had called to tell us that a group from Red Lake wanted to go to Newtown to be present for the funerals. They felt compelled to stand in solidarity with the community the way others had come to be with them almost eight years earlier when they had experienced a mass shooting at Red Lake High School in northern Minnesota. They knew firsthand the terrible shock and grief the residents of Newtown were going through, and they wanted to share their support and messages of hope in person.

They wanted to share something else too. In 1999, a school shooting took place at Columbine High School in Colorado. In the aftermath, Debra Gutowski, an elder in the Little River Band of the Ottawa tribe in Michigan, made a dream catcher, a net woven with feathers and other charms originated by the Ojibwa. Miss Debbie said it was a gift for kids at Columbine, intended to help them heal. After the shooting at Red Lake, Columbine students brought it to the reservation. Now several Red Lake students wanted to take it to Newtown.

One of the elders called my mom and asked her to make the appropriate contacts in Newtown, hoping she could help coordinate their travel logistics. Several of the children making the trip knew me, and there was a discussion about how (or if) it would help to have me there. She and my dad talked about whether it was right and respectful, as well as the psychological effect it would have on me.

It was one thing to hear something terrible on the news. It was another thing to go there and be immersed.

The Ministry of Presence

After the excitement of getting on the plane and reconnecting with the Little Thunderbirds, the kids close to my age, I slept a little on the second flight, and the rest of the trip went quickly. But time seemed to stop once we arrived in Newtown. The ground was still. The air was filled with sadness and unresolved questions. As I sat in the back of the car, I thought about something I'd overheard my mom say to my dad the night before: "How do you have a conversation with a second grader about something like this?"

The answer is in small bites. Over the course of the next ten days in Newtown, Mom let me absorb and process information on my own and ask questions as they came to me. One question I wondered but didn't ask: How do you have a conversation with *anyone* about a school shooting?

The reality is profoundly unimaginable, yet that was the reality the people from this town were facing. As we arrived, I imagined families sitting down at the dinner table with an empty seat. Empty beds and bedrooms. Parents walking past bedroom doors and darkened rooms in disbelief. Siblings numb. Pets waiting for them to come home.

Before we left the car, my mom asked if I knew why we'd come.

I nodded without saying anything.

"Because people here need comforting," she said. "And however we can, we are going to support the people from Red Lake who have come to bring them comfort."

I considered what that meant for me. I was there to support the Little Thunderbirds and to be their friend while the adult delegation from Red Lake did what they were uniquely positioned to do. And maybe I could find some ways behind the scenes to be directly helpful too. I figured if I just asked God to open my eyes, maybe I could see people more the way He does. Who knows—there might be something small that a kid like me could do.

Very soon our Rotary hosts began treating us like close friends. The rest of the delegation from Red Lake that drove almost thirty hours straight showed up the next day. Steeped in their own emotions from having gone through a similar tragedy, they understandably chose to stay in a hotel rather than in homes with others from Rotary.

Every step, every word, and every moment, even when nothing was said, was emotional, solemn, careful. Each of those who came felt compelled to be there, and, as I later heard one of the adults say, they could not *not* make the journey. The trip was important for the people they would meet and comfort in Newtown, but it was also another step in their own healing.

One person can't force another person to heal, of course. But as I started to learn, people rarely heal on their own, and we need to be there for one another. The right person at the right time can make all the difference in helping a community move forward. A man who epitomized this idea was Dr. Anthony Salvatore—or Dr. Tony, as everyone called him. My mom had contacted him early on Monday morning and informed him about the young adults from Red Lake who were driving to Sandy Hook with the dream catcher so they could attend the funerals. She had found his name listed on the Rotary website and simply called the school office, and the secretary gave him the message right away. Dr. Tony cried as he listened. But something else was behind his tears.

Only a few months before the shooting, Dr. Tony had been the assistant principal at Sandy Hook Elementary School. Due to budget shortfalls, the veteran educator's post was eliminated, and he transferred to a similar position at the nearby middle school. His mentor and close friend, Sandy Hook's principal, Dawn Hochsprung, was among the first of those killed.

That Tuesday morning was the first time we crossed paths in person with Dr. Tony. He met with us once we were screened and inside the middle school, where we were far behind police lines and away from the media. I will never forget seeing him welcome members of the Red Lake delegation. As they reached out to hug him, he stood with his arms wide open, welcoming them into his school, his life, and the community. The room was filled with love. It felt like God was directly reaching out and holding each of us tightly, reassuring us that He was going to keep everyone from drowning in sadness.

As we left to go to the first two of the children's funerals, Dr. Tony made introductions and helped open proverbial doors for the delegation. Some of those from Red Lake were ready to head to Honan Funeral Home. Others went to the community hall, which was becoming the main coordination area. Still others were there as pillars for anyone who needed to be held steady. It was just about being present.

In shock and disbelief himself, Dr. Tony said he was dealing as best he could with the trauma that had ripped through the calm and security that schools provided for kids and parents. I watched the way he consistently conveyed just enough strength and just enough compassion to the array of people he interacted with, including parents, police officers, federal agents, teachers, and students. He kept moving and serving others, trying to hold the remnants together, trying to hold himself together, trying to deal with the guilt and remorse stemming from the fateful question, *Why not me?*

One of his best friends had been killed. He also knew each of the victims beyond just a name, along with the fifty-one students who had been directly exposed to the horror in the classrooms, the parents, and the older siblings who were now at the middle school where he served. Though he was his district's safe school climate coordinator, which in theory helped prepare a person for a crisis, no manual or training would be able to scratch the surface of handling moments like this.

Dr. Tony said he was figuring out the next steps as he took them. He focused on the basics: inhale, exhale, repeat.

I watched as memorials sprang up around town, lining the fences and spilling onto sidewalks. Near where a fire truck displayed an American flag, a large white tent was set up to protect bystanders from the cold drizzle. Inside, people visited and left posters, flowers, candles, poems, stuffed animals, notes, and pictures. Floodlights allowed the tent to stay open late into the night, and we walked across the street to the Blue Colony Diner from time to time to warm up with something hot to drink.

Within the tent, each of the students and teachers who had died was represented by a little angel figure. I stood and looked at their pictures. Many of the people who visited the memorial had connections to one or more of the victims. They wanted to share a story or their reaction to what they were experiencing. But the sharing wasn't confined to the memorial. Whether we were at the Big Y grocery, the Newtown Meeting House, or the Booth Library, people wanted to talk, hug, cry, and most of all, connect.

I saw how vital it was to share the special, tiny, everyday, and sometimes very intimate memories of a lost loved one, even with complete strangers. Again, it was becoming obvious to me that people don't heal in isolation. They heal with their arms around each other. I was beginning to understand the power of presence.

"We can't replace the people who are gone," Mom said. "But we can show up and show that we care. We can do what we can to help if we're asked."

That explained a whole lot to me about my parents and those who had traveled all the way from Red Lake who said, "We went through the same thing. That's why we're here—to show that we care about them and that there's hope at the end of everything."

One of the men in the delegation put his arm around me and we shared a side hug. I trusted he was right about there being hope.

Comfort

The adults in the delegation had distinct and important roles, doing things only they could do. The Little Thunderbirds had their own special role too, and I tagged along when they visited with kids at the middle school, where classes were continuing as scheduled to help maintain the familiarity of routine. Of all the roles being filled in Newtown, though, none intrigued me as much as that of the specially trained therapy dogs.

I knew psychologists, counselors, ministers, teachers, and parents, among others, all offered help in times of personal crisis, but I'd never heard of therapy dogs before. Yet they were as visible and present as any of the other frontline volunteers. The Lutheran Church Charities K-9 Comfort Dog Ministry team had brought nine specially trained golden retrievers from Addison, Illinois. They were stationed inside the Newtown town hall, at the middle school, and outside the tented memorial. I noticed them one day as I walked out of the tent.

I stopped and studied the scene. Just beyond the exits, counselors were available for people who wanted help processing their thoughts and emotions. Beyond them were the therapy dogs for people of all ages, but particularly kids, who, as my mom later explained, weren't ready to talk about their feelings but found comfort spending time with the dogs.

I was at the middle school the next day during lunch and spotted the dogs again. I saw them when we went into town too. I was impressed with the way they did their work quietly and in the background, and I tried to do the same.

At lunch one day, an older kid sat at the table with me and several of the Little Thunderbirds and said, "It's nice that you kids came from Michigan, Montana, or Minnesota, or wherever you're from, to be with us."

One day I was in line at the middle school's all-you-can-eat ice cream bar for the second or third time when the kid behind me, who'd also been in line previously, said, "Man, you sure can put away your ice cream for a little guy."

We laughed, and the fact that we could—and did—was a surprise to me.

In town one evening, I saw a couple of kids my age in Cub Scout uniforms, and soon we were trading stories about making pinewood derby cars as if we were in the same troop.

The picture was becoming clear to me. Whether or not we knew each other was immaterial. We were all in this world together. That was the way it felt on Friday morning, exactly one week to the minute after the shooting, when the whole community in Newtown shared a moment of silence. We were in the middle school auditorium. Everything in the entire town stopped. Everyone stopped driving, walking, working, talking, doing anything. Then the middle school bell rang once for each person who had been killed. I'll never forget listening to the sound of the bell as it disappeared into the silence each time.

Afterward, there was just the silence. I felt the emptiness in my bones. And when I shut my eyes, I saw the faces on the wall at the memorial— pictures of people I'd come to know and yet would never know—and in the last vestiges of that silence, I saw everything that wasn't there and never would be there.

After the moment of silence was over, everyone remained motionless. Finally, life around us resumed. Later that afternoon, at the recommendation of someone we met from the *Newtown Bee* newspaper, we explored a park off Main Street called the Pleasance. The path there led to a special section known as the Bunny Garden, which included a cottage with a statue of a mama bunny outside. Inside was a tiny bed, a fireplace, tiny books open on the chair, and veggies in a basket. Down a nearby path was a statue of Peter

Rabbit and Mr. McGregor tending the garden. Although the park was covered in snow, I pictured it in spring. I pictured something else too.

"I could do something like this back home," I said. "But with real bunnies!"

"Real bunnies, huh?" my mom said. "Do you think the Peacebunnies would like to be in a garden like this one?"

"Yes, absolutely," I said excitedly, pulling her cell phone out of her coat pocket. "Let's take pictures so I can remember everything."

On our way back through town, I saw the therapy dogs again. I tugged on my mom's arm and signaled her to stop. Something about them clicked. From my experience with my rabbits, I realized that the dogs were making themselves available. Although they were trained, they seemed like they were just being themselves, eager to give and receive hugs and to get scratched or petted. Time after time, I watched kids sit down cross-legged and pet one of the dogs until that dog's head rested gently in their lap, and then, inevitably, it was as if the kids quit trying to be super strong and let themselves cry.

"It's almost like you don't need to be a grown-up to help or minister," I said to my mom. "And you don't even need to be a person. You can be a dog."

Or a rabbit.

I turned to my mom with a new idea.

"In my bunny garden, the bunnies will be like therapy dogs," I said. "They will be real and not just statues. The bunnies can help people who are lonely or hurting. And if the people aren't lonely or hurting, the bunnies will make their day even happier."

My mom rubbed the top of my head with her fingers and messed up my hair, which was something she did sometimes instead of hugging me. It was kind of a shortcut if she was busy. She happened to be talking to my dad on her cell phone at the time, and she told him what I'd just said. Then she smiled at me.

"It's the gift of presence," I said.

The next evening, I visited with one of the dog handlers, a man about my dad's age, who wore a red bandanna around his neck that matched the one his dog was wearing. I asked all the obvious questions about his dog, as well as what qualified dogs to be therapy animals. The biggest thing, the man said, was that they had to demonstrate that they were calm and could be quiet and listen.

I had the urge to tell him about my Peacebunnies—Paxton, Creampuff, and Star—and ask if they could qualify as therapy animals. He was polite and patient, but someone else approached him, and I stepped out of the way. However, the more I thought about my idea, the more sense it made. Even without training, my rabbits were already quiet and great listeners.

I knew from firsthand experience that I could talk to my rabbits about anything and they would listen. Other kids in the neighborhood knew this too. Creampuff's ear held plenty of secrets that she obviously wasn't going to tell. The same was true with Paxton and Star. They were perfect for the job.

I talked about this with my mom on the flight home. The rabbits would be sweet and gentle and would allow people who were hurting to share what was deep in their hearts. Bigger breeds like Paxton were easy to pet. They were also easy to move around in wagons.

"What if I could get kids to help me?" I said. "Kids want to help. Did you see all the cards and drawings and stuffed animals they left under the tent? And the Little Thunderbirds brought joy to everyone at the school's Christmas show. Besides, kids really like bunnies."

My mom handed me some snacks as we started brainstorming my idea.

"What about your other ideas for the bunnies?" she asked.

"I still want to do the educational programs and all the stuff we're doing," I said. "That's part of it. But listen. Listen to this. If I allow my rare-breed rabbits to have babies, I'll help save the rabbits from being extinct. Then kids can train them to sit in wagons. Eventually the ones who want to can become comfort rabbits. Then there will be a demand for the rare breeds, and at the same time we can help people who are sad or lonely. How does that sound?"

My mom looked out the window and silently patted my leg. That's when I saw more tears on her cheeks. She held me tight the rest of the flight home.

Hi, It's Me…Caleb

Returning to normal school life after winter break proved difficult. Emotionally, I was aware of a huge invisible chasm between me and my second-grade classmates. I didn't mention the trip to Sandy Hook to anyone outside of family while I attempted to process the experience. I felt the need to do something, though—something that would bless people in our community. Doing nothing and keeping it all inside left me with a sense of emptiness.

I wondered how the families in Newtown talked about the tragedy, if they did at all. I wondered how families across the country talked about it, if they did at all. It seemed to me that words were important. Hugs would help. It wasn't necessary to go across the country, as we did, in order to relate to the loss of the precious children parents had hugged in the morning and would never welcome home again. Or to recognize the gift of sitting down at night with those you love—a gift that shouldn't be taken for granted.

Sharing the holidays with family helped me process what I was thinking and feeling. The first half was spent with Grandpa Tractor and Grandma Deer at their cabin. I introduced them to my three rabbits and told them about my trip to Connecticut. Every night we sang around the piano, which was an effective antidote to the sadness that was so hard to comprehend. It's a long-running joke in my family that if you don't have a song to share, you don't get to eat. I knew to come prepared with a poem, a song, or a story; the holidays weren't the time to miss a meal!

Lest they worry, I told Pax and the girls that I would save the carrot peelings for them regardless but that they ought to plan ahead because they were part of the family now. I heard them nibbling on some apple chunks next to the hearth while Grandma Deer recited the Christmas story from Scripture by memory, just as my great-grandma had done and someday I will too, I suppose.

Christmas Eve service, held in the historic one-room wooden chapel where my great-great-grandparents met, was homey and warm. The chapel's history made every visit there feel like a step backward in time. After the pastor spoke, people stood up and shared how God had blessed them that year. Several expressed themselves with a song. It was all unscripted, yet super meaningful.

I was seated next to the woodstove at the end of our row, and it got a little too toasty, as I recall, but I forgot about any discomfort once my grandpa led the singing with his rich tenor voice while my grandma played the piano.

I shared the worn hymnal with my dad and tried to sing the bass part, only an octave higher. The gentle crackle and sizzle of the cedar logs in the fire carried the smell of cinnamon from the back pew to the front. From where I sat, I could see the treats someone had baked and set in the back of the church. How could I bottle that smell for later?

As the service came to a close, the elders turned off the antique hanging lights and distributed candles. They were lit one at a time as we all sang "Silent Night" a cappella. The acoustics and sentiment were perfect, even if not all the voices were. I imagined heaven would be like this, where you see the outlines of people and feel the closeness, seeing with your heart and not your eyes. I could actually feel my grandpa looking at me, smiling.

We spent the rest of Christmas break in Minnesota with my dad's family, which meant nineteen people camped in a duplex for nearly a week. Noise. Games. Every meal was a production. Prep and cleanup seemed to occupy most of the day. I played video games with my cousins, but there were never enough controllers. There wasn't enough sleep, either. Everyone stayed up way too late, trying to cram as much as possible into the time we had together, and that was the point. That's also what made thinking about Sandy Hook so painful.

We finished our holiday get-together with our traditional New Year's Eve parade, an ear- and side-splitting event that included banging pots and pans and stomping through the house. We filed up and down the staircase, where empty stockings still hung on the banister. We blew kazoos and noisemakers and left a trail of confetti in the parade's wake, offering goofy smiles to family paparazzi as we marched past. And at the end of the parade? Pax, Creampuff, and Star were waiting to join the pile of cousins who would be posing for a photo destined for my grandma's calendar.

Returning to school filled my head with complicated thoughts that some adults might have said were beyond my years, except for the fact that they were mine. How could someone celebrate holidays when their heart has been shredded? I suppose I was beginning to understand more fully what it means to put yourself in someone else's shoes.

In mid-January, we returned to Newtown for several days. While there, I heard the song "We Won't Be Shaken," which became the soundtrack in my mind whenever I thought of Newtown or visited there again in the future.

I was eager to contribute to the healing, if that was possible. During Christmas break, in the days when I wondered how families were talking about the tragedy and I struggled with the silence of those who didn't talk about it, I composed a prayer in my journal. Shortly after we returned to Newtown, I shared it with Pastor Jim Solomon of New Hope Community Church. I explained it was my way of breaking the silence and serving as a bridge between those who were suffering under the weight of unanswerable questions and God.

He asked me to read it at their Sunday service.

Dear God,

Hi, it's me, Caleb.

I want to start by just telling You that I love You.

Thank You for loving me even when I make mistakes.

Thank You that I can talk to You, just like I can talk to my dad.

I want to ask You this morning for Your help.

You are a God of miracles, and I ask You to do one for the United States.

We need You to remind us of what is important.

Help us to see people how You see them. Help us to love people how You love us.

Help us to serve people who need extra love right now, especially my new friends in Newtown.

Help us to take care of each other and to stop hurting each other.

Give us Your eyes for just one second.

Thanks for taking care of the children and adults who recently came to heaven.

Thank You that You have a special place for them and for my bunny Snickers. I miss him.

Please give Your special hugs from heaven to all the families that have an empty seat at the dinner table tonight. Help everyone who is sad or hurt or sick or alone. Thank You for the tears, which help.

Please help children show the big people that we are all neighbors and that we need to take care of each other. Help our leaders make wise and caring choices. Help them to get along and do good things that will make You proud.

Please show the adults how to make things better so they'll stop arguing about whose plan is best. Help them to stop blaming and start fixing. Help us kids to figure out what we can do to make our world better too. Help us not make the same mistakes over and over, and help us imagine a new, better way.

Remind us all the time that You are there.

Help us feel Your love when we feel alone. Help children everywhere to be safe and well.

Please bless Newtown. Bless the United States of America, and make it united again.

Thank You that You care about the little things and the big things, and hear us when we pray.

Amen.

4

Privacy, Please

The talk was going the way I might have expected. I was trying to explain to my friends that it was time for the Peacebunnies to have babies, and they kept interrupting me with laughter and silly comments. Reproduction is such a sensitive subject for many people, and anatomy terms can embarrass them or strike them as funny. At our house, my parents taught me with the proper biological terms, and it never seemed silly to me. When I had questions, they provided explanations. Sometimes they explained things before I knew I had a question.

By the time I was ready to breed the rabbits later that spring, I had also learned the anatomy parts of the rabbits, most of which are the same as ours. To address my curiosity about how their bodies worked, we downloaded coloring sheets that identified the names of different bones and systems, which made learning anatomy fun. I knew sharing this information with my friends and answering their bunny baby-making questions was guaranteed to end in laughter, and it did. I explained their curved back was known as the saddle, the furry wattle of skin under the female's mouth was a dewlap, and the area above their tails was the rump.

"What about the boy rabbits?" one of my friends asked. (I am purposely leaving out his name to avoid future embarrassment.) "What do you call his thing?"

"Just like us—a penis," I said.

My friend exploded in laughter. So did the two others with us.

"And the girl?" another asked. "Is it a va-va-va-va—"

"Vagina," I said.

More laughter. A thunderstorm of laughter. The three guys wobbled around and fell to the ground from laughing so hard. I'd heard jokes about rabbits and how they multiply like, well, like rabbits. And yes, the jokes are true. The names of their body parts alone never made me laugh, but I became accustomed to this uproarious reaction and knew it would be coming from then on, so it never fazed me.

The female rabbit is blessed with miraculously efficient and proficient baby-making anatomy. The gestation period of a rabbit is one month, which means the babies are inside the mom for a month. With six to eight baby bunnies growing per uterine horn, that's a lot of babies per litter—plus, she can get pregnant again the day after giving birth. She can have one or two litters a time, even staggered at different times, so she can have babies every two weeks. Get this: she can get pregnant while she is already pregnant. Her ability to procreate is staggering (and some might think exhausting).

For these reasons, I was careful to keep Paxton separate from Creampuff and Star until the time was right. I took Paxton aside and told him, "No dating, no kissing, no fluffing each other's fur."

Paxton and Creampuff were the most docile and therefore seemed to me the most compatible in personality, so I paired them together. Star would need to wait for a suitable mate, and we hoped to find an albino buck for her. Paxton and Creampuff seemed to hit it off right away, because within minutes, they danced together. (That's what I first called the baby-making act—the dance.) The whole engagement—from the time they were in the same pen until Paxton stopped and fell over onto his side, exhausted, signaling success—took only about fifteen seconds.

"Well, okay then," I said as I retrieved Paxton.

We only let them dance together once, because I didn't want Creampuff getting pregnant on both sides and having simultaneous litters of six to eight babies each. That would be too many babies at once. All of us were just getting started. It was wise to go slow.

As with all rabbits, there was only one month until her delivery date, and I was excited to observe the changes in her body and personality. The time flew by. As the due date approached, Creampuff rested more and squished herself into the tightest spots she could manage. On day twenty-five, I noticed she was busy rubbing herself against the side of the pen and picking up the hay with her mouth until she couldn't cram anything else in. Then she did the silliest thing: with the hay still in her mouth, she rubbed it all over the side of the cage and the nest box, stretching out her neck and rubbing her scent glands on everything too.

It was textbook behavior. She was building a nesting area for her babies.

Guided by instinct, she created a warm, safe, comfortable landing pad for her babies. As I watched, this first-time mom stopped and looked at me in a way that indicated she was a little annoyed by my intrusion. Her expression seemed to say, *Privacy, please.* My mom picked up on her message too.

"Are you giving Creampuff her space?" she asked.

"Argh, it's so hard!" I said. "I want to see how she's doing, and I don't want to miss when she delivers."

"She'll let you know when it's time to come say hello to the babies," she said.

My mom was right. I placed a fleece blanket over the side of the pen with the nest box for the final few days before Creampuff's due date and fought off the urge to peek. I still came with food and refilled her water bottle, but I was careful to be calm, quiet, and as unobtrusive as possible.

In the meantime, the entire neighborhood buzzed with anticipation. Noah and Markus stopped by every day. Jamaal and Qiandre checked in. The Troubles asked if there was news. Evangel and Bishop wanted to know when they could come over and see the babies. I was like the desk nurse in a maternity ward with no news to share with those pacing the waiting room. And I was one of the impatient ones too!

One day I noticed a lot of white fuzz floating around the cage. It appeared Creampuff had decorated the babies' room by adding a mound of her own fur. Like clockwork, her hormones had triggered the release of fur, and she began gently pulling off some fuzz with her mouth. She added the warm, soft fur to the nest—a signal that it was just about time.

Within minutes, I heard her hop back into the metal nest box. It became super quiet until I heard her hop out and get a drink of water. I figured she was resting and it must not be as close to delivery as I thought. This was my first time doing this too. I brought over a small snack and said hello to her. Then I noticed something moving in the poof of white fur in the nest box. She had delivered!

I welcomed them with a quick rendition of "Twinkle, Twinkle, Little Star," the same way I'd been welcomed upon my arrival.

Creampuff seemed to pay zero attention to my musical tribute. After devouring the snack, she hopped out of her area like it was any other day and made her way to play in the backyard. "Good job, Mama," I told her.

I knew from the book I'd read about breeding rabbits that human scent on a litter would not deter the mother from caring for them. I checked the nest box, counted the babies, and made sure they were all healthy. We pulled out the nest box and set it up on the table so I could see better.

Delicately, I unveiled eight little babies, each approximately two to three inches long. They were snuggled in tight because they wouldn't have any fur of their own yet for a few days. Their skin reflected the color their fur would be once it grew in. I saw blue-gray, black, and brown—a "rainbow litter." Their eyes were firmly shut tight and wouldn't open for about a week and a half.

I bounded outside to congratulate Paxton on the birth of his first babies with some banana slices. Then I returned to my parents with an expression that must have reflected the relief and amazement and pure joy I was feeling. Today was a red-plate day—a day to celebrate! So I took the special red china place settings out of the cabinet and set the table for dinner.

After that I went door-to-door in the neighborhood with the good news, and members of the pack joined the noisy entourage. The plan all along was that I would only show them pictures for a few days. My friends asked if they could see the babies anyway.

"What are they doing now?" Markus asked.

"They're sleeping," I said.

A couple of hours later, Noah came over.

"Can they come out and visit yet?" he asked.

"No, my mom says they're still resting," I said.

"What do they do all day?" he asked.

"They mostly sleep," I said.

"But when they're awake . . . what do they do?"

"The book says they drink milk for about five minutes a day and then they just lie around in bed with big fat tummies."

"Sounds good," he said.

Heavenfluff

The babies looked a little like baby mice at first. By the end of the first week, their fur began to fill in. After about twelve days, they opened their eyes but remained lumped together in a way that made it easy to picture what they'd looked like when they were still inside Creampuff.

I held them gently in my cupped hands and stroked their tiny, perfectly proportioned ears and counted every perfectly formed toenail. I delighted in seeing their itty-bitty tongues lick their lips. Two bunnies were blue like Paxton. Two were white like Creampuff. Two were brown and two were black. A perfectly balanced rainbow batch!

Every day they changed a little bit. Just two weeks after delivery, they were looking up at me with expressive eyes focusing on the world for the first time. They seemed to be asking, "Who are you?"

I decided that any babies from Paxton's line would have the last name Peacebunny, but I waited until their personalities started to shine before giving them names. I decided they should get names starting with the letters *A* through *H*, and I wrote the letters on their ears with a permanent marker to keep them straight. *G* became George because he was so curious. The bunny marked *H* was super gentle, with a wonderfully soft, fuzzy coat. As they developed, all of them were healthy except *H*, whom I eventually named Heavenfluff. She was smaller and thinner than the others, and one of her back legs was noticeably bowed, which was probably why she wasn't as active as her brothers and sisters and why she wasn't as strong in competing for Creampuff's milk.

After a month, Heavenfluff was the only one unable to jump out of the nest box. When I took the rabbits outside, I often carried her around in my shirt, letting her rest against my belly and handing her snacks while the others explored the backyard. I embraced her limitations as a personal responsibility and made sure she received her share of food, enjoyed playtime, and did all the things the other rabbits did but at her own pace.

The extra time and attention I gave Heavenfluff never seemed like a chore. Pretty soon, I forgot she was different from the other rabbits. It was like my friendship with Markus. I know people might wonder what it's like to be friends with someone whose health is extremely precarious, often to the point that he has to be taken to the hospital for treatment that keeps him alive. The answer is simple: I wouldn't know what it's like *not* to be friends with Markus.

Markus was the first of the kids in the neighborhood who engaged with the rabbits the way I did. He read a ton and became an encyclopedia of information on everything related to animals, especially rabbits. If *Jeopardy!* had a rabbit-themed show, he would have been the champion. Our shared interest in the rabbits drew our families closer together. We even had bunny time in our front yards.

Noah liked the more active and busy rabbits, while Markus preferred to hold a rabbit on his lap or gently help with grooming. It might seem like Markus and Heavenfluff would be best buddies, but they both preferred others. Perhaps it was because Markus and Heavenfluff already knew the lessons the other was sure to share.

In the spring, my second-grade teacher, Ms. Kellum, gave me permission to bring the Peacebunny family to school and try out the STEMbunnies program I'd mentioned to my parents in my original *Shark Tank* pitch. I figured rabbits could get kids excited about learning biology, environmental science, and the world around them, just as they had done for me.

I had another motive too. In order to save more rabbits, we didn't need another rescue organization. We needed an educational program that was good for kids *and* bunnies.

After setting up four pens, I explained the agenda. I would give a brief lesson about the care and maintenance of bunnies, hand out a worksheet, do bunny-related math problems, and lead a discussion on the difference between living and nonliving things.

"Is this going to be fun?" one kid asked.

"I brought rabbits," I said. "Why wouldn't it be fun?"

Considering it was the debut of my STEM education program, I deemed it a success. And at the end came everyone's favorite part: a chance to pet the bunnies. They were a hit. Several kids called it the best day ever.

I followed this event with my first public Easter egg hunt on the shores of Lake Minnetonka at the Excelsior Commons, about half an hour from our house. It was a combination egg hunt and bunny garden inspired by the one I saw in Newtown but with my real-life bunnies.

I measured the Easter event against my list of key values, and it was a grand success. My dad had barely pulled our Prius into the driveway and helped me unload the rabbits before the phone was ringing with several families wanting to book birthday parties. The timing was perfect, like having the exact number of buns you need for your hot dogs.

I was already thinking ahead to the next year, when I'd be in third grade. I wanted to expand my STEMbunnies program to all grades so I could teach kids about the rare heritage breeds and recruit kids whose families might want to join a crew of volunteers and together help me save more rabbits.

There was one catch. Just like me, my business associates likely wouldn't want an increased workload. It was obvious to me: the time had come to expand. I hoped my parents saw it just as clearly.

When I sat down with them, I shared some calculations that showed we could pay for more food if we said yes to more parties and events. "And by doing that," I added with gusto, "we could ultimately save more rabbits."

"But?" my dad asked. "Where's the *but*? There's always a *but*."

"I need more rabbits," I said. "It's time for baby bunnies!"

My parents had one of those conversations with just their eyes. They didn't say a word—not that I could hear, anyway. But they believed in me and my intention. My dad nodded, and my mom flashed a thumbs-up. I hugged both of them.

Despite my excitement, I had trouble falling asleep that night. While snuggled under my covers, I began making a checklist of things I needed to do, starting with Star. It was going to be her turn to dance. We needed to start looking for an albino American buck. Of course, we could have grown the Peacebunny family through rescuing more rabbits. But my plan was to raise the rabbits from birth and help them feel safe. Perhaps we could add some rescues later if they had the right personalities, but we were going to provide forever homes to the Peacebunnies. Not only was I committed now; my parents were too.

Do Rabbits Dream?

A few weeks later, my mom came home from a medical conference in St. Louis with a purebred albino buck that I named Casper. She saw a posting for him in a private online chat group for owners of rare rabbit breeds. It turned out a family who specialized in other rare species listed with the Livestock Conservancy had dabbled with rabbits but decided to change directions. As soon as Casper met the other rabbits in our backyard, he used his strong back legs to clearly announce that he was in charge.

Paxton didn't seem to mind the new alpha addition, and the girls were intrigued by this newcomer without getting crazy about him. Maybe that was because Casper was an over-the-top stereotype of a dominant male, which made his behavior downright comical. When I brought out the pellets at mealtime, he stomped around, grabbed the pen with his teeth, and vigorously demanded attention until I served him his food. Then, after scarfing down three bites and filling his cheeks with food, he dramatically plopped down and took a nap.

One day that summer, I stumbled into another source of income. A local gardener contacted me and asked if the garden center could purchase bags of rabbit manure. Without any idea what to charge, I asked for a donation—whatever they thought appropriate. Rabbit poop turned out to be a highly prized soil addition for gardens. Because it doesn't need to be composted long term, the manure is immediately safe to be placed on plants. Soon I had a small army of regular customers paying between five and fifteen dollars per bag. This unexpected revenue stream won me praise at my mom's Rotary club meetings.

"Caleb, you're turning into quite an entrepreneur," one of the members said.

"Actually," I quipped, "I'm an entre-manure."

Despite all I had going on, I still found time for normal kid things. Yes, I spent time updating my STEMbunnies program, making sure the materials and activities met state standards, which was the prerequisite teachers said they needed so they could incorporate it into the classroom. But I spent many afternoons playing baseball and organizing my hockey cards. I also made sure I enjoyed bunny time of my own. Watching Paxton dig around the tiny area near the fence in the backyard always amused me. He was looking for carrots, even though we never planted any for him to find. His optimism was impressive.

One day I watched Paxton lie down in a comfy spot, ready to take a nap, and I wondered if rabbits dreamed. I often saw my rabbits tremble, twitch, and move as they slept, and I assumed it was because they were dreaming. Star snored during her afternoon naps, which cracked me up. She snored even deeper now that she and Casper were expecting a litter soon. I was glad she didn't sleep in my room.

If rabbits did dream, I wondered if they could experience nightmares. I hoped not. What about good dreams? What kind of dreams would make them happy? Maybe seeing themselves hopping through a field speckled with daffodils, dandelions, and violets, with the bees buzzing and the birds chirping. Maybe Heavenfluff dreamed of hopping as fast as the other rabbits. Maybe Paxton saw himself flying over the neighborhood and waving down to Noah, Markus, the Troubles, and everyone else, as I sometimes did in my dreams.

I was lucky. Or more accurately, I was truly blessed. Many of my dreams were coming true when I opened my eyes.

I hoped my rabbits felt the same way. There was no question I was doing my best to ensure they did. But what about bunnies who were caught up in a real-life bad dream? I hadn't given much thought to what I would say or do if I was called on to help—that is, until the call came in.

Taffy and Oreo

Someone from the parks and recreation department found a rabbit hiding in the bushes at Taft Park in the nearby Twin Cities suburb of Richfield. Something about the rabbit indicated that it shouldn't be hiding in the bushes, and their staff called the Wood Lake Nature Center for a second opinion before alerting animal control. The director of the nature center called our number, most likely to talk to my mom or dad first, but I picked up the phone and took down some notes. Not surprisingly, the rabbit was scared and apparently had some fleas and ticks, but when approached, it didn't run away. It cowered, as if wanting help.

"They think it's an abandoned pet rabbit," I told my mom, who had come into the kitchen to see who I'd been talking to on the phone for so long.

"We aren't a rescue," she mouthed to me.

After I hung up, I filled her in on the details. She responded with a look that was the mom version of a high castle wall surrounded by a wide moat.

"You know we can't fix everything, right?" Her tone let me know she was stating a fact that happened to be packaged as a question.

I played dumb.

"The problem is too big for just us to tackle. Do you remember how many rabbits were on the spreadsheet you made?"

Yes, I remembered the spreadsheet. But I responded with really wide eyes and a puppy-dog look that was the kid version of a device that could hopefully catapult me over a high castle wall.

"Don't give me that look," my mom said.

"We can at least go see," I said.

Five minutes later, we grabbed a box and gloves and headed for the car.

"He said it's in desperation mode," I told my mom as we drove there.

Because the tiny doe was found at Taft Park, I started calling her Taffy. From everything I heard and saw, I could tell she'd been someone's pet rabbit. She had either been abandoned in the wild after they didn't want her anymore or she had somehow escaped out of their yard. Either way, she couldn't survive long term on her own, and she must have known it. Especially after the series of huge thunderstorms that had rolled through Minneapolis earlier that week.

I pictured her huddled under a tree, thoroughly soaked and relying on instinct to find cover, like me at our spring campout with my scout troop. I guessed she'd been on her own for a few days before she finally ventured from her safe spot in the desperate hope that some human would help her. That's what I assumed led to the park staff catching her so easily and taking her to the Wood Lake Nature Center so someone would have the chance to claim her.

Taffy looked up at me from her box. I knew my mom was watching us carefully, but I avoided looking at her and instead kept my eyes on Taffy. In a soft, soothing voice, I told her we were going to take her home and get her cleaned up.

"Then we'll figure out if we can help you more or if we need to take you to someone else who can do a better job," I said. "Will you let us?"

She nuzzled herself close to the side of the box with the saddest, most pathetic eyes. I needed to at least try to help. It was unlikely things would get worse.

Taffy allowed us to wrap her up in a blanket like a big burrito. I figured she was too weak or scared to disagree with our plan. We placed her gently in the cardboard box with breathing holes covered by some netting the park staff provided so the fleas wouldn't spread to our car.

Back at our house, we sat on the porch and took a closer look at Taffy. We weren't about to bring her inside or allow her to get close to any of the other rabbits for at least two weeks, especially with baby bunnies on-site and Star due to deliver soon. A veterinarian friend said that if Taffy was willing to eat and drink and her bowels and bladder were working normally, we should take a wait-and-see approach rather than bringing her into the animal hospital.

That's the course we took. As we went through the meticulous process of removing the ticks and fleas and picking out the prickly burrs stuck in her fur, Taffy seemed to understand that we were trying to help. Although it was likely uncomfortable and a little stressful for her, I think she knew that we were her best shot for the moment. She didn't put up any fight at all; perhaps she was too exhausted from the trauma of being alone and scared in the woods. It broke my heart to see her so frail, and I tried to picture her healthy and well and vibrant again.

While taking turns combing out the fleas, my mom and I chatted about the difference between being nice and being kind. I hadn't thought about the contrast before, but in the context of taking in Taffy, it made sense. If I was merely a nice person, I would calmly and pleasantly say things that made Taffy feel good, which would be, well, nice. But in her time of distress, she didn't need someone to talk nice and just make her comfortable, although we aimed to do that, too. Being kind to her meant being willing to pull off the bugs, get her cleaned up, and support her during this really hard time.

I chose to get close to Taffy and listen to what she was communicating with her eyes. I also wanted to let her look deep into my eyes in the hope that she could see my motivation. Working with her was a great lesson about how true kindness may not always feel pleasant at first, but it's the only way to really help. And from the way she surrendered to us, it was apparent that Taffy wanted us to help her. She didn't want us to just be nice.

At dinner that night, I marveled at Taffy's coloring and disposition. I couldn't believe someone wouldn't want a cute little Mini Rex like her.

"I know in my gut that she would have been euthanized if we hadn't taken her in," I said. "She's going to find a wonderful new home; I just know it."

"Well, today was her lucky day, because you answered the phone," my dad said.

For the next few days, Taffy was timid and guarded. When we finally introduced her to the other rabbits, she was slow to say hello. I'd never been the new kid in class, but I didn't blame her. I couldn't stop thinking about the trauma she must have experienced, going from the comfort of someone's home to a long-term camping trip she was unprepared for.

As she began to gain weight, I assumed my efforts were paying off. I felt better. Then one day I noticed much of her new weight was going to her midsection. Suddenly she looked a little too large there. My suspicions were confirmed when she started ripping her fur. On top of everything, she was also pregnant!

She and Star gave birth at the same time, but only one of Taffy's babies survived. Following the advice of experts, I put Taffy's light-brown baby, which I named Caramel, with Star's litter—the "Twinkle Twinkle babies," as

I dubbed them. Star didn't seem to notice another mouth to feed, and she nursed Caramel as if she were her own.

After Taffy delivered, she stopped showing any signs of fear and became more engaging and what I would call good company. When I sat in a chair, she hopped across the room and sat on my shoes. She wanted to be close to me. With regular meals, she filled out and grew stronger. Her dark-brown fur grew soft and velvety, a quality associated with Mini Rexes. She was like Cinderella, who was given a gorgeous gown yet remained unassuming and humble.

That was only part of it. In a sign that she was even more comfortable around us now, Taffy rolled onto her back in an obvious gesture to beg for a belly rub. What kind of weird bunny behavior was this? She was acting like Markus and Noah's dog, Champagne.

Once I was confident of her disposition, I invited her to go to a birthday party. She was immediately a star. When I trialed our foster program, she was one of the first and most frequently requested rabbits.

Before summer ended, we chose to formally adopt Taffy into our growing program. By this time, there was never any question about keeping her. Although she never had another litter, her new Peacebunny family made sure she was never alone. In fact, a week or so after my parents and I formally acknowledged that Taffy was staying with us, we met another Mini Rex that was about to be homeless once its family moved out of state. I thought she and Taffy could be roommates if they got along.

The new rabbit was named Oreo because she was white with black splotches, like the Holstein cow from the milk commercial. This was funny to me because I liked to dip cookies in milk. I never dreamed we would be collecting rabbits named after sweet treats.

We were the family's last call before they took her to a shelter. They were extremely worried that she might not find a forever home, an outcome that filled them with anguish. Coincidentally, we'd seen their ad on Craigslist less than an hour before they called.

With Taffy having opened our hearts to rescues, the timing was perfect for all involved. We brought Oreo home, and she turned out to be a birthday party superstar. Talk about fitting in and taking over!

Mini Rexes feel like velvet. In that way, they're unlike every other rabbit. This fact was confirmed at the second party I took Oreo to after she joined the team. She hopped into the lap of a little girl who buried her fingers deep in the folds behind Oreo's neck. As her dad took a video, the girl's face turned into one big smile and she said, "She's so soft! I never want to stop petting her."

I often felt the same way.

5

Paxton Liked the Ladies Too Much

At the end of summer, we went to the Minnesota State Fair. This was only my second time attending the annual extravaganza that celebrates agriculture and livestock but also includes dozens of rides, arts and crafts, big-name music performances, markets, and more food than any one person can imagine eating, though many try. Although I was impressed at finding more than sixty different foods on a stick, from alligator sausage to key lime pie, my goal was more narrowly focused. I wanted to check out the 4-H club rabbits.

They were housed in the sheep/poultry building, which was a cacophony of clucking chickens and guinea hens, plus human beings trying to talk over the noise as they checked out the animals. I peered around the corner, where the penned sheep appeared bored. Then I came to the rabbits. While I thought they deserved to have their own building and anything less was insulting, they seemed perfectly content. I anticipated seeing at least one representative of each of the world's forty-plus breeds of domestic rabbits, especially the rare breeds. Unfortunately, I counted only about sixteen kinds.

I plopped down on the metal bleachers by the fan and started observing kids and teenagers wearing matching 4-H club shirts and lining up for a competition showcasing their rabbits. Awards included ribbons, cool prizes, and bragging rights. Some of the teenagers led demonstrations from stages. When I learned they were paid to talk about their rabbits, I turned to my parents and said, "How cool is that?" I could talk for days about my rabbits.

They looked like they were having a lot of fun together, and I decided I wanted to compete the next year. However, as I read the rules, I saw that entrants needed to be finished with sixth grade and qualify through their county to earn a trip to the state fair. I let out a loud sigh. Sixth grade seemed like forever away—maybe further than forever. Someone overheard me groan about being too young and explained that there was also an open competition that didn't have an age requirement.

"I could do it next year?" I asked.

He nodded.

I punched my first into the air in celebration. "Yes!"

"What's got you all jazzed up?" my dad asked.

"Next year my rabbits can compete," I said. "I'm too young to compete with the Peacebunnies through 4-H, but I just found out that my rabbits can compete in the open rabbit show next summer."

"That's cool," he said.

"That means our rabbits would be competing against those brought to the fair by professional adult breeders." I was already picturing myself walking proudly up to the judges' table with them. "Wouldn't it be crazy if one of the Peacebunnies happened to bring home a ribbon?"

Two weeks later, I joined our county's 4-H club for rabbits, the Hennepin Hoppers. I wanted to learn as much as I could and meet other kids who owned rabbits. Markus also signed up, and I was super excited because our families could carpool to the meetings. In a year, Noah would be old enough to join, and I could picture the three of us staying in the club as long as they allowed, well into high school.

Meetings were the first Monday of every month, and I was happy to discover useful tips and tricks about proper cage cleaning, monitoring the rabbits' health and wellness, and good animal husbandry policies to prevent illnesses.

I was skeptical when I found out this club had members who focused on teaching their rabbits to conquer obstacle courses. I didn't know that was a thing, but it was, like dog agility courses. During training sessions and practice competitions, the rabbits wore harnesses attached to leashes and were prodded by their youth guardians to run up and down ramps, jump over hurdles, and sprint through tunnels. Paxton was in my lap the first time both of us saw this activity, and the two of us had the same reaction: *What is this craziness? Steeplechase competitions for rabbits?*

Everyone took turns with their rabbit. Paxton and I watched closely, though at some point his attention strayed. When we were up, I politely declined. Our club leader, Mr. Mark, was surprised and asked for an explanation.

"Is your buck an agility bunny?" he asked.

"Well, Pax does love to explore and to play," I said.

"Perfect! Let's get him out on the course and see how he does."

"Well, it appears that he's just too busy for that," I said.

"Too busy to go play?"

"As you can see—" I held him up—"my rabbit is extremely interested in all the ladies."

If it hadn't been obvious before, it was clear then that Paxton was drunk on the smells and attention that came from being in a room full of females. He was all gaga and in the mood for love. The last thing on his mind was an agility race. I put him down on the course, but he was literally dizzy and couldn't decide which direction to go first. Sniffing the carpet and turning around in a semicircle, he rubbed the scent glands under his neck on the side of the tunnel, but it was clear he had no intention of going all the way through it. He inched in and out, then rubbed his chin on the fabric and was just super goofy.

Mr. Mark suggested trying the course again next time, with Paxton going first. I shrugged and laughed, confident my Romeo rabbit was a lost cause.

"You should be sympathetic," he said. "Someday you might understand what Paxton is going through."

I didn't get it.

"But, Mr. Mark," I said, "why would I compete in an agility race?"

No Questions Asked

Halfway through Star's pregnancy, a man called and said his family wanted to adopt an albino American rabbit. English wasn't his first language, and we struggled to communicate, but he was adamant about his requirements. It couldn't be just *any* rabbit. It had to be a white American. And it had to be an albino. With red eyes. While speaking with him, my mom mentioned that we were expecting baby rabbits in a few weeks that would be purebred albino American rabbits, available after weaning.

"Will they have red eyes?" he repeated.

My mom reassured him.

Later, when she relayed this conversation to me, I cocked my head. "I would have thought he'd know that albino rabbits always have red eyes," I pondered.

Mom explained to him that we'd never considered permanent adoption before and that the rabbits were really the purview and passion of her son. When he asked to speak to me, she explained that I wasn't available.

"Is he at work?" the man asked.

"No, he's riding bikes with his friends."

The man came to one of my very first Bunny Bootcamps, the workshops that taught the basics of rabbit care with information gleaned from rabbit experts. This was still early in our foster program, but the basic format and messaging were already clear. I wanted families to enjoy learning and to leave knowing what the bunnies needed, setting everyone up for long-term success.

Throughout bootcamp, this man was the most attentive person there . . . and the only one attending without his children. He showed me pictures of his wife and daughters and bubbled about how happy a rabbit would make them. I shared my story about finding more than three hundred rabbits that were being sold or given away and then focusing our efforts on education to prevent abandonment and neglect.

The man praised me in front of class and said something along the lines of, "If only the whole world operated that way." He was adamant about providing a forever home for a rare rabbit, and it seemed like a great match.

The man called back every few days with much enthusiasm and

a persistence that was a little awkward, but it was fun to hear about his family's joy during the countdown to the birth. He gushed about being the best pet parent ever. As Star grew closer to giving birth, he organized a contest among friends, family, and coworkers to guess how many babies would be in the litter, along with their delivery date and time. I'd finally met someone who was even more excited about a bunny birth than I was!

As the leaves started to fall, Star and Casper's babies were nearly eight weeks old and were no longer drinking milk. Caramel was also weaned and eating pellets and hay, but because she wasn't a white albino American, she wasn't of interest to him. Whereas Paxton's babies' names started with letters, Casper's babies were numbered, and that led to their temporary names: Uno, Deuce, Tres, Katrina, and Fiver. We could tell the white babies apart only after writing on their ears with a marker.

The man had a bounce in his step the day he and his family visited our backyard and picked out which rabbit they wanted to adopt. They almost immediately chose Fiver, a little buck, and told us how their family had spent weeks thinking until they selected the *most perfect* name. Yep, they named him Fluffy.

I must admit I rolled my eyes and consequently felt a stern look from my mom. But really, of all the creative names one could possibly come up with, they couldn't be more imaginative than Fluffy? Oh, well. We were happy they were giving him a forever home, so Fluffy it was.

Before we said our goodbyes, we restated our agreements: because Fluffy was a rare-breed rabbit, they were not to sell him or breed him, and we would hold his pedigree papers. They were also welcome to give Fluffy back to us, no questions asked.

About a month later, I was scrolling through the local section of Craigslist, looking at the rabbits offered for sale or adoption. By now, this was a habit. I had permission to visit certain sites regularly, on the off chance that more rare breeds came up. In midscroll, I shouted for my parents to check out the picture on the computer screen.

"I can't believe it," my dad said.

My mom's mouth was gaping open.

"That's Fiver, the one that guy calls Fluffy, right?" I said. "I know it is."

I could still hear myself reminding the family before they left to call me if for any reason things didn't work out. It was my first adoption, so I wanted peace of mind. Now that was long gone.

One of our adult volunteers called the number in the ad and asked a few questions about the rabbit being listed, confirming that they were indeed trying to sell Fluffy. The next day my parents and I called the number and asked if we could have the rabbit back. The man wanted clarification: Were we interested in *purchasing* Fluffy? Did we want to buy back our own rabbit at a higher price?

This became a huge growing experience—for me and our fledgling organization. As uncomfortable as it was, it drove us to be more formal in our process, with an established classroom curriculum, a mandatory two-month foster-first period, written expectations and agreements, and required spaying or neutering for rescues.

A few days later, I welcomed Fluffy back into our family, redeemed with my birthday money. My mom made a cherry cheesecake, served on our special red plates, to celebrate the occasion. The bunny seemed well cared for, and if he had stories, we never heard them. We also never learned why it didn't work out for that family, but for our family, we knew we needed clear communication and boundaries.

The only issue with his return was what we should call him. To my mom, he was always Fiver. To Dad, he was Number 5, a nod to the movie *Short Circuit*. In the end, I stuck with Fluffy, although his pedigree remained unchanged. He was a Peacebunny, and he would always be part of the family, no matter what he was called.

Play like a Kid

Rather than get angry and blame the man or myself, I tried to use that episode to learn about who I was. What did it teach me about the person I wanted to become? How could it help me become a better version of myself, both now and in the future? Sometimes you see yourself in other people; other times you see the person you don't want to become. Being lied to or cheated is a way of being stretched and challenged to examine and develop your own character. There was only so much I could absorb and process at the time, but that incident stayed with me, as did Fluffy, and both of us moved on.

There was no time to stew. More bunnies were born, and now Paxton Peacebunny was a proud and happy grandpa at the age of barely two years old. During backyard playtime, he reminded the other bunnies that the yard was his first. He was loving to his kids and grandkids, licking their ears and snuggling close. I never saw him bite any of the babies, as alpha males are wont to do, but he did occasionally sit on them, probably to let them know he was the boss. Maybe like wrestling with Dad.

About that time, one of our foster families found three Lionhead babies and their mother on a hiking trail and brought them to us. Lionheads have massive hairdos and look either dramatic or silly. The jury was still out on these babies. When their mom died a few days later, the babies nursed with another mom and they grew with a fury. Leonardo had rich brown spots on white, Newtown's fur looked like chocolate-and-white camo, and Einstein was dark brown with a mane of fur that went beyond dramatic and silly. It was *crazy*. But he seemed to know how to work it.

Prior to the start of school, my mom and I met with teachers from Green Central School in the Minneapolis school district. I considered it my first big pitch meeting. There, teachers from all grade levels—kindergarten through high school—listened to me pitch my STEM program and suggest that the best way to teach about science and nature, endangered breeds of animals, and responsibility was with a bunny in the classroom. If you want to make your class fun and popular, put a bunny in there, I said.

The teachers smiled and nodded.

"It's good for the kids," I concluded, "and it's good for the bunnies."

Many of the teachers took me up on an invitation to bring their families to our house for a day with the bunnies. That closed the deal. Before Christmas break, we had twenty-three bunnies in classrooms across the district. In addition to hosting birthday parties and selling manure, it was another revenue stream. The money went to help pay for all the rabbit food and supplies.

But it also meant more work, because once a week we needed to deliver food to the different classrooms. Welcome to my Saturdays. Sundays included

Bunny Gardens and Bootcamps after church. No matter how jammed the schedule, though, I managed to find fun moments within the chaos.

One day we were driving back from a STEM class with Moe Moe Peacebunny sitting next to me in the backseat of the Prius and the other bunnies in their carriers. I spotted an endless sea of dandelions in a field, and we stopped to let the bunnies out for a snack. I kept a close eye on Moe, who always found a way to escape or hide. He was the smallest of his siblings and teeny-tiny compared to the others, so I fell in love with him right away. Kind of like Heavenfluff. We were on the letter M, and he was my little marshmallow—or "momo," as I called the confection as a toddler.

Between his size and proclivity to disappear, I was frequently asking, "Little Moe, Little Moe, where did you go?" One day he went missing after the young Peacebunnies were playing in our backyard. I simply couldn't find him anywhere, and it was even harder to find a black rabbit in the shadows.

Several neighbors came over to help look for him. Noah went one way, Alexander went another, Diego checked the corners of the yard, and the Troubles ran off in their own direction shouting Moe's name. I finally found him hiding under the leaves of a hosta plant next door. I looked under the canopy of huge broad leaves and there he was, peering up at me with a rabbit's version of a smile.

"*Okay, you caught me,*" he seemed to say.

I sat down and he jumped right into my lap, seeming to ask, "*Can we play that again?*"

Can I Borrow Your Farm?

Because our city code allowed only four adult rabbits six months and older per household, we would be over the limit if we needed to bring everyone home at the same time. We had plenty of foster homes, with friends from the neighborhood, school, church, baseball, and scouts, along with a few other random people, plus twenty-three rabbits living in classrooms—but it wouldn't be enough if the program continued growing. One of the older kids in the neighborhood said I worried too much about the regulations.

"It's not like there are bunny police who are going to arrest you," he said. "Who's going to know?"

"I'll know," I said.

That was the problem. I've always believed in following the rules and trying to change them if they don't make sense. But at that point I didn't have time to challenge the city ordinances. Neither did my parents, who had jobs and other responsibilities in addition to supporting me and the ever-expanding world of the Peacebunnies. I didn't have a solution.

At dinner one night, my frustration came out in an exasperated roar. "It's like we're running a couple dozen bunny farms . . . minus the farms," I practically shouted.

It didn't make sense. If this was something I was meant to do (and I felt it was), shouldn't we be able to meet the need? Or were we outgrowing the vision? Maybe we should scale back and place more rabbits with forever homes. But how could I help get these rare breeds off the endangered list if I cut back?

Then the light bulb turned on. "We need a farm," I blurted out.

"A farm, huh? I can picture that," Dad responded with a deadpan facial expression. "Yes, I can, indeed. Picture the Smiths as farmers: your ma is out driving the tractor, you in your overalls wranglin' up the rabbits from the range, while I'm . . ."

There was a long pause that stretched on and on. Finally my parents looked at each other, then at me, and then back at each other as a goofy grin burst across my dad's face. This was followed by an uproar of laughter that could have lifted the dinner table up a few feet.

"Why, sure," my mom chimed in with an exaggerated northern Minnesota accent with exceptionally long vowels. "I think dah you and your paw would look quite nahtural in duh overalls. Yeah. Don'tcha know? You know dat if Dad worked at your fahrm, he would become a fahrmer."

We were laughing so hard I wondered if the Bachmans could hear us from across the street. As my parents noted, we were anything but farmers. We respected farmers; we just doubted whether we were tough enough to do it. Also, where would we learn how to farm? Oh, and before we put the cart before the horse, we needed a farm. It's not like we could roll up to Sam's Club and put forty acres and a barn in our cart. How much did a farm even cost? I had no idea. We weren't rich—not in the dollars sense, anyway. My parents had never hidden the fact that we lived in a house that we could afford and there wasn't much left afterward.

These were all good questions. But they didn't seem to matter. After dinner, my mom showed me how to use Google Maps to search for farms within thirty miles of our house.

When I questioned whether we could afford a farm, she shrugged. "Who says we would need to *buy* a farm? Why can't we *borrow* a little piece of one?"

My research turned up a few options—not that many, because we lived in a metropolitan area. My parents agreed to let me explain the situation to the farmers I found and ask if we could use part of a barn.

Two weeks later, we pulled up the driveway of a beautiful livestock farm not far from the Mall of America. I didn't know such a farm existed in the city, and neither did my parents, who had lived in Minneapolis a lot longer than I had.

We'd come straight from school, and I changed into my old junky shoes in the back of the car. Because we were stopping by uninvited and unannounced, I wondered if anyone would even be there for me to meet.

The farmhouse was at the end of the long driveway, set on a slight rise, and the classic red barn sat back on the right. Craning my neck up high like a periscope out the back window, I saw white sheep munching pleasantly in the pasture. Huge, fluffy clouds floated overhead in an all-blue sky. It was like a picture of an idyllic farm from another era—"the olden days," as I sometimes thought of it—and I felt a shiver of recognition that told me I was exactly where I was meant to be. I just hoped the man I spotted up the dirt road felt the same way.

He paused to look at us, as did the two exceptionally large and hairy white dogs next to him. He was wearing big brown overalls, which made me chuckle. Dad wasn't so far off with his overalls comment.

With a small flock of butterflies in my stomach and without a preplanned speech, I walked up to him and said hello. I saw him look over my shoulder at what I assumed was my mom giving him a sign that he had her permission to speak with me. After introducing myself and finding out his name was Chris,

I explained that I was two years into breeding rabbits on the endangered list. I told him how I educated kids about rabbits through a STEM program and how I'd started fostering rabbits partly out of necessity and also as a way to curb the pet abandonment cycle.

"I have a lot of rabbits," I said.

"With what you've got going, it sounds like you need 'em," he said.

"Our program is like a library system," I explained. "It's a bad analogy, but schools and families can check out a rabbit for up to two months, and they can renew it if they want or bring it back in early."

"Hmmm," he said. "Sounds complicated."

"Sometimes," I said. "We're just starting out, but we've had a lot of families who really like the bunnies."

"And?"

"Well, I need some space to care for the rabbits, and they can't all be at my house," I said, finally getting to the point. "We can only have four over the age of six months. That's why I need a farm with some space in the barn where I can house them together, especially during summer break and over the winter."

"You don't need a whole farm?" he clarified.

"Someday?" I wondered out loud. "But right now, I think a corner of a larger barn would work. And I'm wondering if you might have space like that available."

"I might," he said, explaining that he only worked there but would share the information with the owner.

"Here's the other thing I need to tell you up front," I said. "I'm hoping I'll be able to keep the bunnies here for free. We're just starting out, and I only have enough income to cover food and supplies, unless we do a lot more events to cover rent."

"All right," he said. "I can relay that, too."

"But I can learn to help with chores," I added quickly. "I'm willing to do, you know, farm stuff."

"Oh, you are?" He gave a nod while sizing up my nine-year-old arm muscles. "It's not my decision, but give me your phone number and—"

"That's awesome! Thanks, Farmer Chris."

Later that week I was invited to return, and the owner came to show me a small barn just past the main one. There weren't any animals in it, but the side of the barn she offered me was packed with antique-looking things in storage. It was dirty and far from bunny-ready, but for what I needed, it was perfect. We made a deal.

A week later, a local sports team needing some community service hours helped us clean our part of the barn. Even with all that extra muscle, it still took most of the weekend before a space was cleared enough to move the bunnies and their cages into place.

Once we were situated, I had to remind myself I wasn't dreaming when we drove out to this gorgeous farm every day after school to care for the rabbits. Noah and Ms. Deb went several times, and when the fall weather was warm enough and he felt up to it, Markus came too. Everyone helped feed and water the rabbits, which took about twenty minutes in all and left plenty of time to play. I introduced everyone to Farmer Chris, pointing out his brown overalls, which he wore daily as if they were a uniform.

We said hello to some of the sheep across the fence, near where the donkey was grazing, and then headed over to greet the goats and peer across the Minnesota River Valley. One special day, I helped feed the chickens in the coop for the first time. From then on, each trip included another new chore. I was learning to farm. Somehow I was always dirty when I was about to get in the car. At first, I avoided the dirt and tiptoed through puddles. As the weeks wore on, though, I realized that trying to avoid getting dirty on a farm didn't just waste time; it missed the point of farming. It started and ended with dirt.

As a result, I was thrilled to put on a pair of overalls for the first time. Once I was outfitted in brown Carhartt bib overalls that went all the way down to my new work boots, my whole image changed from being a kid at the farm to being a farmer. One day our neighbor Mr. Mike saw me getting into the car in my overalls and yelled out, "Farm boy!"

I replied, "As you wish."

Later that week, just like that, the weather changed, and it was a normal Minnesota winter. Sometimes I forget that not everyone has winters where crawling into an igloo might be an improvement over the outdoors. During

Christmas break, my cousins visited from Texas, and for a fun outing, they agreed to brave the ten-degrees-below-zero temperature to come play with the bunnies while I did the chores. Two months later, it was even colder. And there was more snow. Lots of snow. A blizzard that lasted several days had dumped several feet, and the drifts were the size of small mountains.

"We're like the post office," I said. "Neither rain nor sleet nor snow—even lots of it—will keep us from feeding the bunnies."

"You're sounding very confident," my mom said, peering intently through the windshield while navigating the slippery road.

Somehow our tiny Prius had made the drive up to the farm the past few days. But that day we only drove close enough to see it before we became completely stuck. It was like being swallowed up by a huge mound of icy cotton candy. The wheels sank. We tried to dig ourselves out, but the fierce wind just blew the snow back in, erasing all our effort and then some. Thankfully, Farmer Chris came out on his tractor and pulled our car out—twice. It was blustery and my eyelashes froze, but the bunnies got fed, and I got hot chocolate at home.

Months later, as the weather warmed and trees sprouted green leaves and daffodils rose from the ground, the farm sprang to life in a magical way. Chickens clucked as I ran down the gravel road past their coop. The field was filled with lambs and their mamas. I watched enviously as baby goats pranced and bounded into the air like they had springs on their hooves. Surviving the winter at the farm gave me a sense of pride and accomplishment, as well as a deeper connection to the effort that went into maintaining life. It was pretty cool.

To show my gratitude for the space, I reminded Farmer Chris that I was available for chores. He gave me a job: cleaning out the goat barn. I arrived the next weekend in my brown overalls with the legs rolled up (because they didn't have my size) and heavy rubber work boots. I was excited to grab a pitchfork and a shovel, push the wheelbarrow into the barn, and deliver a good day of work. I'd never touched a pitchfork before, nor had I been in a goat barn, but I was geared up and ready to go.

I knew that spreading manure over a farm field is an important spring ritual that adds rich nitrates to the soil and readies it for planting crops. But no one warned me about the hazards of getting the manure to the field from where the animals are. The mix of dried manure and straw, only recently starting to thaw after an entire winter, was at least a foot and a half deep, and it covered the entire barn floor. Seeing that it was a huge task even for a grown-up, I resolved to do a good job to show my appreciation, even if it took me every day after school for a month.

Then I loosened the first layer from the floor and reconsidered everything from the job at hand to the rest of my life. Until then, the straw had acted as a waxlike seal over the manure, locking the moldering fumes below the surface. The moment I dug in with my pitchfork, the seal broke and released the foulest, most noxious odor I'd ever encountered. As soon as I turned the pile over, my stomach turned too. I didn't vomit, but only because I ran out of the barn gagging.

How will I ever do this? I asked myself.

I knew the answer before I finished asking the question. It was important for me to be helpful and to keep my word even if the work I'd agreed to do was different from what I thought. Every fiber of my being was telling me to run to the car and yell to my mom, "Let's get out of here." Instead, I dragged my pitchfork back into the barn and somehow gave it another good try. I made a little progress, but not much. At best, I made a small dent before my body gave out, only not from the smell this time. My arms had turned into wet noodles.

I thought Farmer Chris would be disappointed in me for not finishing the job, and I built up all sorts of worst-case scenarios in my mind. But when it came time to turn in my pitchfork, he inspected my work and thanked me for trying to help out. He was kind and gracious, and I made a mental note to treat others who do their best the same way. I respected him even more because he did this kind of work all the time.

As I made my way to my mom's car at the end of the day, he called out to me.

"Forgot to tell you something," he said.

"What?" I asked.

"Nice overalls."

Cinnamon and Captain Phil

That spring my Easter egg hunt in Excelsior was bigger than ever. I added Bunny Gardens at various churches in the days and weekends leading up to Easter. With practice, each stop became more polished and successful. My favorite part of the day was when I asked the bunnies who wanted to go. I truly believed those that stepped to the front of their cages wanted to spend the day hopping from lap to lap and snuggling with kids, and those that stayed in the back of their cages sent a clear message that they wanted their alone time to just be bunnies instead of party animals.

Business boomed. I'd updated the folders I gave out at events promoting bunny birthday parties. "For THE BEST PARTY EVER, we will bring at least six different breeds, a variety of ages, decorations, and a whole lot more!" the flyer said. "We are experts at throwing a Bunny Party." The new information highlighted our now-official foster program and Bunny Bootcamp. "Fostering is FUN and INFORMATIVE and a WONDERFUL alternative to jumping into rabbit ownership," it said. "And a lot less expensive. Think of our rabbits and supplies like a cuddly library book you can check out."

Our phone rang throughout the day and early evening. Calls came in from across the metropolitan area.

"Whose idea was it to include our home phone number?" my dad asked.

My mom looked at me.

I looked at Paxton, who was in my lap looking back at me.

Most calls were inquiries about fostering, but we had quite a few birthdays to schedule. Then there were the calls from random people, more frequent than I would have anticipated, who had other questions about their new pet bunny or about wild baby bunnies in their yard. We didn't advertise that we were running some sort of a hotline, but the questions came anyway. Believe it or not, we fielded several calls from people who were alarmed that their new bunny had lost a toe. This seemed particularly true in the hours after dinner, when people seemed to cuddle their rabbits or rub that lucky rabbit's foot, and suddenly panic that their precious bunny had lost one of its toes.

"I can't find it," a caller said, panic creeping in. "There are only four."

"Check the other foot."

"Oh no! They've lost one on *each* foot!"

"That's because rabbits only have four toes on their back feet," I said.

"But I count five on the front."

"That's correct," I said. "They have five toes on their front paws and four on their back."

"Are you sure?"

"Yes."

"Who am I talking to? How old are you anyway?"

"This is Caleb Smith, and I'm almost ten years old."

The foster program, intended to cut down on bunny abandonment, was so much more than that right from the start. The program began as an attempt to house our expanding bunny population, but in spirit I say it started the day Markus fell in love with Katrina. She was the fourth baby born to Casper and Star, the sister to Fluffy. Whenever Markus came over, he played with her. She was light enough for him to pick up and cuddle, and he took a special shine to her. After our moms spoke, "KitKat" went to the Bachmans' for a playdate with Markus in the Taj Mahal of hutches that Mr. Mike had constructed for the occasion. It turned into a sleepover that lasted a few weeks.

We still frequently checked the listings for rabbits online to stay on top of what was available and how the rehoming situation was shaping up. If we saw one of the rare breeds, we reached out. That's how I saw the ad for Cinnamon. It was different from the hundreds of other ads I'd seen. The attractive photograph of Cinnamon aside, the ad didn't seek someone to buy or adopt the rabbit. It was a plea for help. "She's not eating. Why? She's not acting normal. Why? Maybe she's sick."

With my parents' permission, I responded to the post and asked if they had ruled out the possibility of a pregnancy. "Not a chance," the owner wrote back.

A day later, I received an email from the same person and saw an update to the post that was even more frantic. The rabbit was nesting. The owner had seen the belly moving. The rabbit was pregnant, and they didn't want baby rabbits in their house. They wanted to get rid of Cinnamon and her impending litter immediately. The desperation in the post bothered me. I waited to see if there was another update, hoping the post would be taken down because they'd found a home. The next day, seeing no changes, I let them know that if the rabbit hadn't delivered her babies yet, we would come over for a visit.

The response was urgent: "Please come."

When we entered her house, I was shocked by what I saw. The owner wanted us to see the pregnant rabbit—and take her. She ushered us to her downstairs area, a room packed with rabbits, many that I'd seen on Craigslist in the days and weeks before. I was sure they were the same rabbits, because some had very distinct markings. I put two and two together and realized she was running a rescue, collecting animals for free and deceiving people that she was going to give them a home. My parents figured this out before I did, but it was the way I looked at her that caused her to unravel.

"I'm a flipper," she confessed, explaining that she bought and sold animals online for a profit. She took them in, fed them, and reposted them on multiple sites. Rather than deny it, the woman brazenly explained her system and bragged about her income. Then she tried to sell us the pregnant rabbit! Yet she'd never had a litter before and didn't know what to do, so she was pushing the expectant mom off on us, using all sorts of manipulative arguments.

I have a theory that the way we treat animals is a reflection of our hearts, and I could only wonder what had happened to make hers that way. Still, I was reminded not to judge during an emergency. Even if we only kept the soon-to-be mother until she delivered, this was an immediate rescue situation, and I was resolute in my determination to take her with us. Thankfully, so were my parents. We picked up Cinnamon and brought her home.

She was indeed a beautiful Cinnamon rabbit, a breed known for its rich brown fur, black ears, and patient disposition. For the first few days, she was uncharacteristically touchy, but I understood why when, less than a week after we brought her home, she gave birth. Only one baby survived, a tiny male I named Phil because he arrived at the end of January and I figured he would likely open his eyes around Groundhog Day, like Punxsutawney Phil. When the little bunny saw his shadow, he charged into it rather than running away. So as an acknowledgement of his courage, I changed his name to Captain Phil.

Markus adored him. Having a friend whose health was fragile and whose heart was enormous taught me many things about myself, including how special Markus made me feel by wanting to be friends with me. It made me happy that he was drawn to Captain Phil. Why he liked that rabbit compared to all the other bunnies we had was beyond me, but I'd been the same way with Snickers, and it seems to me that's also the way it goes with friends. Maybe it's like that when people fall in love too.

I once asked my mom how she came to like my dad, and she cracked, "Oh, he was just around." I could tell from the sparkle in her eyes that she was making a joke. I suppose I will find out for myself one day.

For the next ten weeks, as Captain Phil weaned himself from Cinnamon, Markus came over to observe and play with the little guy as often as possible. We set up a pen where he could sit on the ground with a blanket on his lap and enjoy Phil. Phil also seemed to look forward to Markus's visits. I noticed he wasn't as perky on the days Markus didn't come. The two of them understood each other. One day, as Markus sat with Phil in his lap, I heard him say, "I love you, little buddy."

There was no denying their special friendship. Our parents talked, and Markus happily agreed to take Captain Phil home as his own rabbit. We drew up official paperwork, and Markus paid me one dollar. In June, Markus and Captain Phil competed at the Hennepin County Fair and took home a blue ribbon for best senior buck among the 6-class breed, the category for rabbits weighing more than nine pounds. At home, their first-place victory was reason for much celebration. Their friendship was the reason for even more joy.

Did You Miss Me?

After overseeing dozens of Bunny Bootcamps and foster programs, I learned what was really going on. I introduced people to rabbits, and the rabbits connected me with people. Like Bonnie, a teacher with a PhD, who attended a bootcamp undercover, meaning she didn't introduce herself as an expert. She welcomed several pet bunnies into her science classroom. Taking an interest in my passion for learning, she helped me improve my STEM curriculum. Eventually, as our families grew close, she became Aunt Bonnie. Not incidentally, the first bunny she fostered, Andre the Giant, won "best giant" at the state fair.

Then there was Lucia, a shy girl my age who attended bootcamp with her entire family and fostered one of our rabbits. Two years later, she and her family had acquired their own rabbits because she wanted little Fuzzy Lops. Their two-car garage turned into housing for their bunnies, and she became president of the 4-H club, leading meetings and doing public presentations at the state fair.

While seeing other people open their homes to bunnies was gratifying, nothing moved me like seeing the way bunnies opened people's hearts. At the Bunny Gardens that Easter, I overheard several kids sharing their secrets with bunnies in ways that reminded me of the therapy dogs at Sandy Hook. The same thing happened when I heard about a group of local soldiers being deployed to Afghanistan from a nearby National Guard base. I wanted to take bunnies there to give the kids whose parents were shipping off overseas a little cuddle time after they said their goodbyes.

After the base commander gave permission, we went to the dollar store and bought red, white, and blue bunting and blankets and used them to decorate the pens for deployment day. I brought three white Americans—Uno, Deuce, and Katrina, the offspring of Casper and Star—and dubbed them Patriot Bunnies. They were perfect listeners as the families said goodbye.

"I'm going to miss my mom," one boy said in a quiet voice as his parents held hands nearby.

"I'm worried about my dad," another boy said.

I remember a little girl calling to her mom, "Come look. These are Americans just like us."

I saw that the bunnies had a power all their own.

One day a girl from a couple of streets over knocked on the door and asked if she could play with the bunnies. I recognized Tricia from school. She was in the grade below me and got on the school bus at the stop after ours. I welcomed her inside and watched as she took a liking to Caramel, who wasn't exactly like the rest of the group. I was always intrigued by the reasons people gravitated to certain rabbits and the way rabbits reacted to certain people. Sometimes it was obvious. Other times I didn't see it right away.

Since being adopted by Creampuff at birth, Caramel had grown into quite a beauty, with a white belly, a warm brown coat, and eyelashes with a soft

107

bluish-purple hue. Her coloring caused her to stand out, especially in contrast to her all-white adopted family and the dark chocolate of her mom, Taffy. People often remarked that she looked different from all the others.

I preferred the word *distinctive* and used her looks to make a point. During the STEM lessons, we explained that rabbits, generally thought to be color-blind, actually see the world in varied shades of dark and light and several hues of green and blue. They also see patterns and recognize the differences between people and between one another by look, smell, and personality. I have always found it curious that humans see all shades of color and all the beautiful differences in rabbits like Caramel, and yet we treat them all with affectionate cuddles and care. Why can't we do the same with each other?

Through my mom, I learned Tricia was being bullied at school and having trouble making friends. I had no idea. And I had no idea why, because I thought she was awesome. She started coming with us to events, and it was fun to see her insecurities disappear while she played and told other kids about the rabbits. She was a natural.

I don't remember how the conversation came about exactly, but it ended with her family taking Caramel home. Then, after a swap, she cared for Uno. Much later, she was exuberant when she came to the backyard to play and met the twins Pepper and Roni. Those two were fearless characters, I told her. At only two months old, they hopped over to the fence and told the neighbors' dog they weren't afraid of him.

Once Tricia began caring for those two rabbits, she adopted their same fearlessness and started to blossom. Mom summed it up well: Tricia was always a beautiful person inside and out, but she started to see herself that way too. She laughed and showed the softness of her heart. Her eyes sparkled. Other kids in her grade started coming to her house to see the rabbits and play with her, and the bullying faded into the background.

As the months passed, more birthday parties were booked, bootcamp sign-ups reached capacity, and more bunnies were fostered to people's homes. At school, my lunch-table friends nicknamed me Bunny Boy. I began to take it as a compliment. You can't own dozens of rabbits and spend weekends hosting bunny events around the city and not have people talk about you.

I was often tracked down by parents who wanted more than just a bunny experience. Like the mom whose son was eager to attend our next Bunny Bootcamp. She called my mom, and because we didn't have a bootcamp coming up, she booked a birthday party at their home. Her son was a grade younger than me but was homeschooled, and he invited all the other kids from his therapy group. He was extremely intelligent and one of the most eager and acute questioners I've encountered. He hovered nearby as we unpacked the bunnies, gave them a last-minute health check, and set up the pens. I saw the way he took in every detail and restrained himself from talking to us about the rabbits.

When the party started, he sat in the front, inches from the rabbits. During my overview about rabbit biology, his hand shot up as soon as I mentioned reproduction. How many days are in their gestation? How many nipples did the mom have for nursing? How did she make sure all the babies ate at the same time?

When it was time to get in the pen with two rabbits, he practically jumped in. But first he gave me a reassuring nod.

"I will let them come to me," he said. "I know that's how you do it."

Finally, as we were packing up, he let us know he wanted to foster a rabbit.

"I have a quiet room downstairs where I sometimes go," he said. "It has a swing. I think a rabbit would enjoy it."

He was right—they did enjoy it. They seemed to have insight that enabled them to understand people better than we understand ourselves, or perhaps the way some people want others to understand them. Once, after a scout meeting presentation, a mom flagged us down before we loaded our car. She had a son with autism who rarely spoke, and when he did, his voice was barely a whisper. She was searching for ways to get Tommy to talk more, and someone suggested she get in touch with us about fostering a bunny. I suggested they attend several bootcamps before taking that leap.

At the first bootcamp, Tommy met several bunnies before focusing on a shiny black American rabbit that had been born with a deformity on its back right foot. I'd bottle-fed Bandit and showed him extra affection when he was younger. Now, at almost four months old, he was strong and handsome but moved around with a noticeable hobble, which Tommy noticed within seconds of sitting down with the rabbit.

"Do you need help?" he asked the rabbit in a soft voice.

At the next camp, Tommy sought out Bandit again, and when they were alone in a pen, I heard him use a noticeably stronger voice. "Do you remember me?" he asked. "Did you miss me?" Then, in the loudest voice I'd ever heard from him, he exclaimed, "I missed you!" His mom hugged my mom, who then hugged me. It was a familiar story. We help the bunnies, and the bunnies help us.

"I think they need a bunny," I said with a smile.

Forgiveness

A family with three younger kids became foster parents to Heavenfluff. They all fell in love with her at Bunny Bootcamp and wanted to take this longtime sweetheart of mine to their home. Their youngest daughter wanted a calm rabbit, and we all agreed that Heavenfluff was an obvious first choice, a rabbit whose own early challenges taught her to put love first and greet everyone with a gentle smile.

We knew the family through friends of friends, so it wasn't like we were close, but I could tell they were the kind of people I would want to live on my street. They were attentive through bootcamp. Each of them asked great questions that showed they cared about doing what was good for Heavenfluff.

"Is she nice?" one of the girls asked.

"Do you know the song 'Don't Worry, Be Happy'?" I asked.

Her parents said yes, so she did too.

"Heavenfluff is the real-life rabbit version of that song," I said.

As with every family, we assured them they could bring her back the next day, the next week, or in three months and we would receive both the rabbit and them with open, understanding hearts and still be friends. Or we would see them in a few weeks for their check-in, when we would give them the next bag of food and hay.

"This is going to be so awesome!" I overheard the oldest boy tell Heavenfluff as he skipped to the van.

We watched them disappear down the long farm road, and then I announced to my mom, "Now *this* is how I pictured it." I started gushing about this batch of new foster families and how well their orientation class went. It felt like watching a home-run derby, seeing each of them soar out of the park.

They provided us with updates that always made us feel good about their experience with Heavenfluff. Then one day my mom answered the phone while we were in the car, and I heard the other mom sobbing and sounding distraught and apologetic. Heavenfluff was hurt badly on their watch. Their family was devastated, she said. Their tears wouldn't stop.

The news was difficult to swallow for everyone because Heavenfluff was so special, but through my sadness, I realized that this foster family was probably having a really hard time.

A few days later, we had our first and only funeral for a foster rabbit and invited the grieving family to be there with us. So were Heavenfluff's parents, Paxton and Creampuff, because we wanted to give them a chance to say goodbye too. I could tell from all the tears that our hearts were full of what mattered above all else: love.

The process of grieving Heavenfluff didn't happen overnight. Each time someone asked about her at one of our events, the wound reopened a little. Her sweet disposition had made an impression on a lot of people. They'd hung a tiny portrait of her in their hearts. As a result, our extended bunny family learned a lesson in forgiving others and forgiving ourselves.

We started sharing Heavenfluff's story at our Bunny Bootcamps. We emphasized the importance of following our safety rules and reminded people that sometimes saying "I'm sorry" doesn't fix things. Certain things can't be undone or wiped away.

But Heavenfluff's sweet influence didn't end there. Although nothing could bring her back, forgiveness could help bring the family back. When they were ready to open their home and hearts again, they got in touch with us, as we'd encouraged them to do, and visited the farm.

"It is okay for us to try again?" the mom asked.

Her three kids flanked her on both sides, and the daughter was looking down at the ground.

"I trust you would do a good job taking care of another bunny if you want to try again," I said.

My mom, standing off to the side, nodded in agreement.

"Do the bunnies know what happened to Heavenfluff?" the youngest girl asked.

"I think bunnies know more than we realize," I said.

"Well, do you think any bunny will ever want to go home with us?" the oldest sister asked.

"You know, I truly believe that the bunnies can sense if a person has a good heart," I said. "How's your heart feeling today?"

"Good."

"Then how about we ask the bunnies if they want to go with you?"

I ushered her to one of the grassy playpens and draped a colorful fleece blanket on her lap. A sliver of a smile appeared on her face as she watched us place several rabbits in the pen with her. Oreo came over immediately and rubbed her chin on the girl's legs before plopping down next to her in a calm, accepting way. The little girl's smile grew bigger, and she whispered something to Oreo. I think Oreo said something back along the lines of "Come on, we can do this."

They went home together, and eventually everyone felt restored.

There are some things only animals can do, and in this case, I believe God used a rescue bunny to love and rescue this family right back.

6

Don't Judge Me by My Haircut

My mom was at the Bachmans' one day, and I overheard her say to Ms. Deb, "If we ever think about raising a bunch of Angora rabbits, you have my permission to give me a hard smack on my head."

Earlier that week, Markus and I had been reading a 4-H book about rabbit breeds, and we were shocked to see how fuzzy Angoras were. I couldn't even begin to imagine how much work they would require. I had a hard time just taking care of *my* hair in the morning. Mom must have pictured the same thing, because she vowed with a capital *V* to avoid taking in Angoras. They just required so much care and upkeep.

Then we brought home Ginger and Nutmeg, two Angora rescues.

Ms. Deb came over to check out the newest additions. She took one look at these beautiful Angora rabbits that were finally recovering from my haircuts, sprouting soft, flowing fur like Chia Pets on steroids. Her expression said, *Should I be supportive? Or is this when the violence begins?*

No blows were thrown. It was too late, anyway.

Ms. Deb laughed, which caused my mom to laugh, and eventually that filtered down to me. The joke was on us, but really, we didn't care.

We were right about the upkeep. The Angoras' long, soft hair grew at least an inch every month, and they required thirty minutes to an hour each week of gentle brushing, grooming, and cleaning. Meanwhile, they did everything they could to wiggle their five-and-a-half-pound bodies free from their hair—as if they could take care of their dramatic shags themselves, which they couldn't.

We had enough going on as it was. In the fall, we placed so many rabbits in classrooms and with foster families that we said farewell to Farmer Chris at the picture-book farm. We had bunnies throughout Minneapolis schools, at preschools, at senior centers, and even in the lobby of the local Mathnasium, where they figured out that having bunnies made kids look forward to math tutoring after school.

"Every dentist office in the country needs a bunny," I said. "They would help people relax."

"Funny idea, but *no*," my mom said, with a weary shake of her head.

That wasn't all. An American Blue named Bluedini was wearing me out. Mischievous, playful, and inexhaustible, Bluedini had a knack for escaping from any place I put him. He was the Harry Houdini of our brood—hence the name. Barely a day passed without my asking, "Where'd Bluedini go today?" He was definitely Little Moe's kid!

Add not one but three Angora rabbits into the mix, each of them needing weekly appointments in the "hare" salon, in addition to the basics, and you understand why my parents, Grandma Deer, my great-grandma, my teachers, and nearly everyone else were skeptical about my ability to juggle everything and still have time for homework. But how could we have ignored a plea like the one we received?

It began with a phone call, which was nothing new in our house. Our phone rang two to three times every other day with someone calling to tell us about a rabbit that needed to be adopted or rescued. Somehow our reputation spread, and so did our phone number. This time, it was the woman who owned Ginger and Nutmeg. Sounding upset, she explained that her two Angora rabbits were covered with knots and filth. A twig had lodged deep inside one of Ginger's fur piles, and now she was in pain every time she moved. The woman didn't know what to do.

When Mom and I walked into the woman's backyard, she and her husband were embarrassed yet eager for the assistance. They seemed even more relieved when, after a quick inspection that didn't turn up any injuries, we offered to take the rabbits home. Just like with Taffy, I figured we could at least try to clean them up and help them start over. It wouldn't be easy because the tangles were all the way down to the rabbits' skin, which was troubling to both me and the rabbits.

Once we moved them into their new penned area, I used a soft voice and an even softer touch, explaining what I was going to do. They eventually relaxed and let my mom and me gently brush enough of the matting out of the way for us to use blunt scissors to remove the knots. Electric clippers would have made the job easier, but neither rabbit liked the sound. So we went slowly with the scissors, working in five-minute bursts. I wanted them to feel safe and secure, and that started with letting them choose how and when to engage. Both rabbits seemed to understand that we were willing to try our best. Their haircuts lasted days.

When I finally put down the scissors and declared the job done, we didn't see the chopped fur and uneven coat. We saw a fresh start. One of the Troubles was the first to see the Angoras, and his eyes were nearly as wide as the two rabbits' were.

"Buzz cut!" he roared.

"No, it's not," I argued.

"What is it, if it's not a buzz?" he asked.

"It's short," I said.

Ginger still had a little bit of a punk-rock stripe down the middle, but her skin was too tender to go any farther. This was something my dad remarked on later that evening too. I advised everyone who checked in with a critical review to simply wait for the hair to grow back, which it did rather quickly. The point was that the rabbits were clean and on their way to being healthy. None of us should be judged or defined by our haircuts.

I am, however, willing to concede that my scissor work left something to be desired. Poor girls. Too bad they didn't each have a hat.

The Starfish Story

Late one afternoon our voice mail filled up with messages from various sources asking if we'd heard about a barn fire in northern Minnesota. Some calls were more urgent than others, and some contained more details. But all of them painted a bleak and disturbing picture of a farm about four hours north of us where Angoras were bred, and although I didn't know how many rabbits died directly in the blaze, from what I pieced together, the few that survived suffered severe burns or distress from smoke inhalation.

I watched my parents as we listened to the messages, trying to gauge their reaction. I was crushed. I had tried to quit listening, without success. The imagery was too terrible.

"We need to do something," I said. "At least we could get the survivors through the winter."

It took my mom and dad a few minutes to respond. There was just too much tragedy to absorb. But I was ready to jump in the car and bring home every bunny that was still breathing. If I'd been older and able to drive, I probably would have already been out the door. My mom pulled me close and, in the softest voice, made it clear we weren't going to be able to help all the bunnies.

"This is just like the starfish story," I said.

We'd recently read the story about a person walking along the beach who came across hundreds of thousands of starfish washed ashore. They would surely die if they weren't returned to the ocean. The person began tossing the starfish back in the water even as there were still countless more left on the beach. Overwhelmed by a sense of futility because they couldn't possibly save all the starfish, the person stopped to question: *If they can't all be saved, is it worth the effort?*

At the end, the person concluded that even if they could save only one starfish, it mattered to that one.

I said the same thing. "Even if we can bring home only one bunny, it will matter to that one. And if we can bring home ten—"

I got cut off.

"We aren't bringing home ten," my mom said.

I didn't know how many we were bringing home, but I had a problem to solve before we went to pick up even one. We were already sheltering the maximum number of adult rabbits allowed at our house. I called our neighbors and explained the situation, and my dad and I moved Paxton, Creampuff, Star, and Casper to Evangel's house until we could find our next farm, which we now clearly needed. Other rabbits on the verge of the age limit were also hastily dispersed among my friends and their families throughout the neighborhood, which brought me back to my original plan: together the kids would save the rabbits.

Then my mom and dad and I made the long drive north to fetch the surviving Angoras, who were now being housed in another nearby barn owned by one of the family's friends. The farmer met us in front, and we walked around to the barn with our carriers. Outside the barn, the farmer asked how many rabbits we wanted to take.

"We brought four carriers," my mom said with an audible catch in her voice that revealed the emotion we all felt in the moment. "We can only take four."

The farmer said he understood and then lowered his head. Quietly and with an obviously pained solemnity, he said we could go inside and pick whichever rabbits we wanted. My mom shook her head and excused herself for a moment to dry her tears.

"We can't pick," she said. "It's just too hard. Will you please go in and bring out the four you want us to take home? Give us the ones you think have the best chance."

Whatchamacallit

Though the farmer was gone only a few minutes, it felt like hours. When he emerged, he was holding a female Angora with the saddest eyes I'd ever seen.

I greeted her with a tender smile.

Then the farmer brought out three others—another female and two of her grown sons. It made me wonder how and why they'd survived and the others hadn't. Did their mother protect them? Were they nestled under her and shielded from the smoke?

We took them home, and within days, the female with the sad eyes breathed her last. I named the surviving mama Willow, and her two babies became Westley and Wyatt, later dubbed Quiet Wyatt. Three weeks into their recuperation, Willow surprised us by giving birth to three girls and a boy. For the next month, Willow cared for her offspring like any new mom. As they grew and scampered around the hutch on their own, she seemed to nudge them into independence earlier than expected. Then one day Willow didn't eat anything. The next day she was gone.

It was as if she had willed herself to survive the fire and whatever health issues she incurred in its aftermath in order to have her babies, even if it meant leaving them too soon. I believe Willow knew that I would care for her offspring. Of the four babies, the little boy was my favorite. He developed slowly. While his siblings grew fur that turned them into cartoonlike fluffballs, his hair remained short and, well, it was odd. He had hair on the side of his nose, several tufts behind his ears, and a few patches on his back. He didn't look like the other Angoras.

"I don't know what he looks like," I said one day as he sat on my lap while his sisters played on the carpet by my feet.

I was trying to pick a name. The last two babies I'd named were Westley and Wyatt, and I was still in the Ws, as I tended to go through the alphabet, exhausting each letter before moving on to the next one. But this little guy defied all my ideas. Nothing I thought of fit. I was at my wit's end. He wasn't a Walter. He wasn't a Willie. He wasn't even a Wee Willie Wrinkled Wabbit. But I wanted a W.

"I don't know what to call him," I said.

My mom was nearby helping me print signs for the next event.

"What'd you say?" she asked.

I was about to repeat myself when the name hit me. I looked down at the little rabbit in my lap and smiled.

"I know his name," I said, getting up from the sofa and walking over to my mom with the rabbit in my outstretched arms.

"What is it?" she asked.

"Mom, meet Whatchamacallit."

He was Whatchi for short. One day I woke up, and it seemed that overnight he'd grown all this fur. Instead of being an odd patchwork of tufts and tangles, he awoke a silky-haired shih tzu with a little bit of Ewok thrown in. He also sported a distinct personality. It was like Whatchamacallit woke up and decided to be the sweetest-dispositioned dandy on the planet. He had gone through his own grieving process after his mom passed and come out of it with a huge heart and a zest for life. He was ready to live life to the fullest.

He loved going out. He took special pleasure going to birthday parties and social events, where he was always the center of attention—and he knew it. He arrived with a look-at-me attitude and seemed to bask in the fact that people flocked to see him. With all that hair of his, it was as if he were dressed and ready for a party.

I took to pulling him in a wagon while he sat on top of pillows, his long hair unfurling like a well-coiffed prince in black-and-gray designer frocks. No other rabbit I'd encountered made an entrance like he did. Kids and their parents said, "Look at that one!" and lined up to meet him.

Whatchi seemed to understand he'd been blessed with a Brad Pitt–like magnetism that attracted humans of all ages, and he responded with unforgettable charm. As soon as someone entered the pen with him, he wanted to touch them with his paws. More specifically, he pawed his way up someone's chest until his nose was right under their face, as if daring them to look down at him. And when they inevitably met his gaze, guess what happened? He planted a soft little kiss on their cheek.

He teased people with his looks and sweetness, daring them to drop their guard and act the same way: silly and sweet. At one birthday party, a little girl who had spent fifteen minutes straight making goo-goo eyes with Whatchamacallit suddenly let out a gleeful cry to her parents: "I want a puppy just like this one!"

Her parents approached me, wanting to clarify the type of animal their daughter had in her lap. Was it a rabbit or a dog?

"It's Whatchamacallit," I said.

"No, that's what we're asking you," the mom replied, thinking I'd made a joke.

I thought of all that had transpired to bring Whatchi and me to this moment where he was providing someone so much joy and basking in the affection himself, even if he was being mistaken for a puppy. And I saw that Whatchi was teaching us that life, though never easy to understand, could still be soft, fuzzy, and pretty wonderful.

Tator Tot with a Side of Fudge

Almost as soon as I posted pictures of the Angoras on my STEMbunnies website, I began to receive inquiries from people asking if I was selling their wool for yarn. I wasn't—not yet, at least. I had some idea there was a market for that, but I'd been too busy to give the option much thought. But these inquiries opened my eyes to the possibilities of a new revenue stream.

I did my research, as always, and found their silky-smooth fiber was valued among knitters and the fashion industry at large and sold for about $12 an ounce, or $192 a pound. My rabbits' fur was especially valuable because they were raised ethically and with genuine affection.

A local knitter was my first customer. The woman bought a small batch of fur from Ginger, Nutmeg, and Quiet Wyatt. She was excited. She called me "a find." A short time later, she met me at a local church where I was doing a Cub Scout event and gave me several samples of the yarn she had spun from their fur. Appreciative and impressed, I saw the potential for more and bigger sales—that is, if I had more Angoras. But with STEMbunnies, foster families, Easter egg hunts, and birthday parties filling our calendar, plus all the events of normal life, I did more planning than selling. In the back of my head, I could hear my grandmother say that just because you *can* do something doesn't mean you *should*. Our time was more valuable.

One day we were stuffed into the Prius en route to a rabbit event at an art center in Minneapolis, where kids would be able to draw the rabbits. We had a dozen rabbits in the back, along with the pens and blankets. My mom's cell phone rang and I answered, assuming it was the coordinator at the art center calling with details about where to park and unload. Instead, it was someone on staff with the Minneapolis housing authority. Apparently she'd heard about us and was reaching out to say they had two rabbits for us.

"Hold on, please," I said, before looking over at my mom.

She'd heard the conversation and was already shaking her head no. "Be firm," she said.

I gave it my best effort, explaining to the woman that our program didn't operate as a rescue. We were more of an educational program, I said. Undaunted, she insisted that we meet these two rabbits because they were so cute and adorable and engaging. I heard that all the time, but I tried not to be rude. Every phone call and email involved someone trying to convince us why the rabbit they were trying to give away was awesome and perfect for *us*. I asked the woman to please call back and leave a message with her info.

"I'm sorry—I don't have a pen or paper," I said. "But before we hang up, I'm just curious. How did you get our cell phone number?"

"Someone told someone—you know how it is," she said. "I just know that you're the right people and that these rabbits are special."

"Thank you," I said.

"I promise they're special," she reiterated. "I'll call back and leave a message."

As we set up for the event, something tugged at my heart and wouldn't stop the whole time we were at the studio. I didn't even make it through the event before I told my parents that we needed to call back and say we'd take in the rabbits. The woman hadn't given any real details, and she had no clue how to describe them except to say they were two abandoned rabbits, one really big and one pretty small.

Ordinarily I would have asked specific questions about basic details, including gender, health, whether they were spayed or neutered—and if one of the rabbits was female, whether she was pregnant. Then we would refer them to a rescue organization. I didn't know anything, and yet I had a feeling the woman was right—those rabbits were meant for us. My confidence convinced my parents to let me call her back and set a time to at least meet.

Later that day, we rearranged our schedule and took time to meet the rabbits. Resting side by side, they were definitely a pair. Somehow, without knowing anything more about them, I knew they were perfect together and, as she said, perfect for us. Our commitment to politely declining them melted like butter in a hot pan.

Once we brought them home, I named them Fudge and Tator Tot. While they were best pals, they couldn't have been more different in appearance and personality. Fudge, whose marbled coat reminded me of a swirl of chocolate and white fudge, was a Flemish Giant, but on the small side, weighing only about eighteen pounds. His ears were huge, and the rest of him was all heart. He loved saying hello to everyone and every bunny. His flaw was not understanding that others weren't always as eager to meet him. He had a small scar on his nose from sticking it too close to other rabbits.

I never worried about Fudge running away, and I never put him in a pen because he always wanted to be around us and the other rabbits. One day Noah and I were sorting through the superhero cards I'd made for my rabbits (similar to hockey cards, because why shouldn't animal superheroes have their own cards?), and I said, "I finally figured out Fudge's problem."

"What's that?" he asked.

"He's a golden retriever trapped in a huge bunny body," I said.

Noah put his face inches from Fudge, as if to see for himself. Fudge scooted forward and touched his nose to Noah's. It was super sweet—Fudge's specialty.

Tator Tot was a Dwarf Hotot—pronounced *oh-tote*, for the village in France where the breed originated. The full name of the large breed is Blanc de Hotot, which literally means "a white one from Hotot." I spent six months on a waiting list before a breeder took a chance and sold two does and a buck to me. They're gorgeous, with striking black eye bands that look like eyeliner. By contrast, "Tator Tot the Hot-Tot" was the less endangered dwarf version of this breed. Barely four pounds, and with the energy and agility of a gymnast, he could go to parties and events and give people an idea of the breed without putting the full-size rabbit at risk.

Watching Tator Tot and Fudge enter a room together was like seeing two best friends conspire to meet everyone. They met in the middle, whispered a plan, and then divided and conquered. Once, at a birthday party, I turned my back on them and suddenly all the does I'd put together in a single pen were out and running free around the room. I knew Fudge and Tator Tot were responsible. I fell in love with them. The family who raised them must have felt the same way. It made me sympathize with how horrible their life situation must have been to see no other option but to move and leave these two behind.

I hoped they found someone who helped them to a better life, the same way Fudge and Tator Tot landed with the woman who called us. I prayed for them, as I do for all people who are in tough spots, to address the problems that led them into that situation. I wish I had a way to let them know that Fudge and Tator Tot have been a blessing to me and to so many others. All things can work together for good.

Happy Bucks

The summer between fourth and fifth grade had all the signs of the start of a journey, even if I didn't know it. For the second straight year, I attended the Young Entrepreneurs Camp hosted by Junior Achievement with other business-minded kids eager to learn about developing their ideas, creating plans and pitches, and doing the research that will, as they say, "convince the sharks to invest in your idea."

The weeklong camp pushed me to work hard and dream big and then share what I was learning. Not that I needed the nudge for any of it. One of the camp's counselors suggested I consider attending the *Forbes* Under 30 Summit sometime in my business career. I received similar encouragement from Gina Blayney, Junior Achievement's dynamic CEO for the region, who told me about a new entrepreneur contest for kids through the MN Cup. When we looked up the events online and saw that the conference for young entrepreneurs would be hosted in Philadelphia that fall, I thought, *Why wait?* That might help me get started with plans for the contest too.

My parents agreed, and I emailed the organizers. I was transparent about being eleven years old, but I assured them my parents were on board. I attached a picture of me in business attire from a Junior Achievement event where I'd introduced Ecolab chairman and CEO Douglas Baker Jr. Then I waited to hear back.

"If dimples count, you're a sure thing," my mom kidded.

"Mom, please," I said, slightly annoyed.

I was picturing myself in my suit, the CEO of my own enterprise, and her talk of dimples cheapened the image.

"Caleb, if God gave it to you, don't be afraid to use it," my ninety-five-year-old grandmother added.

She was talking about brains. But whatever.

At the end of August, I showed the four original Peacebunnies at the state fair in the open rabbit show. Casper came home with the best-of-breed ribbon. Both Paxton and Star met the tough standards for fur color, body shape, and ear length, and Creampuff won the blue ribbon for best female, so we had quite a celebration.

Among the Angoras, Whatchi and Wyatt were in adjacent cages, and they drew attention from everyone who walked in the building. We placed a large fan by their cages, and with their five-inch-long fur blowing in the wind, people stopped to watch as if they were gazing at a *Vogue* fashion show. Whatchi won best English Angora and best fur, both of which were cause for more celebration.

The icing on the cake? No sooner were the blue ribbons on my bookshelf than word came from *Forbes*: my application was accepted, and I was invited to attend the conference in Philadelphia. Time to shine my dress shoes!

It seemed far-fetched—an eleven-year-old kid attending such a conference? But then again, why not? As hockey legend Wayne Gretzky once said, "You miss 100 percent of the shots you don't take."

At the next Rotary club meeting, I was eager to share the good news. I placed a dollar—called a "happy buck"—in the donations basket for the local food shelf and told everyone about the rabbits' success at the state fair. Then I added another dollar and beamed about the invitation to the *Forbes* Under 30 Summit. The congratulations and support I received made me feel like I was going to rise straight out of the building. Afterward, as we ate and visited, it hit me. I wasn't just someone's kid tagging along; the members treated me like I was part of the group.

Before we left, one of the younger men attending as a guest that day came over to shake my hand and asked what I needed to get to the conference. I didn't quite understand what he was saying. The conference was in three weeks, I explained. Everything had been slow to transpire, and then it all seemed to happen at once. We didn't have any travel plans yet, I told him, but I assumed we would be driving because we had an event in Chicago right before. My mom came over and introduced herself just as he offered to cover all of our trip expenses.

"When I was a young entrepreneur, there was no one to teach me what I needed to know," he said. "I didn't have a mentor or other adults to challenge me or hold me accountable, and I wasted so much time, money, and energy. Plus, I'm not proud to tell you this, but I lost some of my integrity. Now I'm in a position to help, if you'll let me."

I was stunned.

"You remind me of myself when I was your age," he continued. "Except I was more of a dog person."

A few more of the members approached as we talked about the trip, and each shared some tips. Bring plenty of business cards. Write cues on the back of any business cards you get so you can remember who you meet. Be yourself, because you want to attract the people who like you for you. Don't try to meet everyone; focus on meeting the right people. Each person has something to teach, so don't be afraid to share some of what you bring to the table.

Then Jeff Meacham, an executive coach I'd come to know as a person of integrity and deep personal faith, started a line of questions. I could tell he already knew the answers, but he wanted to see if I did.

"Caleb, what does your name mean?"

"Devoted to God," I replied.

He gave a knowing nod. "Then keep doing your best as you try to follow God. Find a way to serve others while you're there, and He will direct your path," he said. "For some reason your personal path is leading you to Philadelphia."

He put his hand on my shoulder the way he often did and bent down until we were eye to eye. "Caleb, somewhere along the way, maybe years from now, I'm sure you'll discover the reason you have the opportunities you have. Somehow I bet this trip will become an amazing chapter in your book and I'll get to read about it someday."

During school that day I tried to stay focused on what was in front of me, but my mind kept wandering as I pondered the good things that were coming together all at once and the amazing people who showed up at just the right time. The progression of events and the faces of caring guides raced before my eyes: Snickers, Paxton, STEMbunnies, the foster program, our Patriot Bunnies, Sandy Hook, Heavenfluff, comfort animals. Mr. Meacham's words resonated in my head. *"God will direct your path. . . . I'm sure you'll discover the reason you have the opportunities you have."*

I turned the page in our family journal and entered my thoughts. I wanted to remember some of the lessons I'd learned so far from my journey with the bunnies. I made a commitment to leave a journal behind for my future kids—and Noah's kids too—because they would never believe all the adventures we had.

- How can you fail if the goal is love?
- Everyone has the opportunity to be kind. Practice makes you better.
- Do good because you should do good. It may come back to bless you, but that's not why you do it.
- Do the right thing over and over, and it will become like breathing.
- Be courageous, but never be afraid to ask for help.
- Bloom where you're planted, but ask God to move the plant box.
- Look beyond labels and stereotypes. Open your eyes. Listen. Learn. And get ready to be amazed.
- Do what makes your heart sing. Figure out ways to share your song.
- Together, the kids will save the bunnies.

The Forbes Under 30 Summit

Setting out for Chicago, our first stop on the way to Philadelphia, my parents and I piled into our Prius, along with ten rabbits, including Paxton, Casper, Oreo, and Whatchamacallit. Once in the Windy City, we participated in a two-day pet expo. Although it was an overwhelming success, I encountered one person who was critical of our booth setup and suggested a different layout. She also pointed out that the young rabbits' paws could have been cleaner. My first instinct was to get defensive. But she did have a point—the rabbits had gotten messy on the long drive from Minneapolis. Despite a thorough wipe-down, they were still babies who got dirty. I figured that if I was able to accept praise, I should also choose to accept constructive criticism.

"GRANDPA TRACTOR"
teaching me (age three) how to drive

WATCHING THE COWS
& dreaming of farming

PLANTING
VEGGIE SEEDS
AT AGE 9.
Snickers, the rabbit puppet,
is supervising my work.

2007   2009   2011   2013   2015   2017

DAD, MOM & ME
on hockey team picture day
(2010)

**IN 2011,
I MET
PAXTON
PEACEBUNNY,**
*a purebred pedigreed
American Blue rabbit.*

Building a
**BACKYARD
RABBIT HUTCH**

2007   2008   2009   2010   2011   2012

STAR & CREAMPUFF

UNO, DEUCE, TRES & KATRINA IN MY ARMS
& Noah holding Caramel

2013　　2014　　2015　　2016　　2017　　2018

PATRIOT BUNNIES
*visiting a veteran at a
military sendoff for
National Guard members*

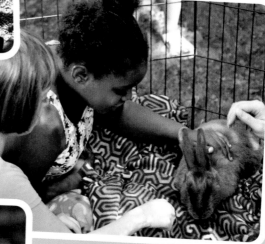

BLUE BARRY
at a birthday party

In love with
**HEAVENFLUFF
PEACEBUNNY**

2007   2009   2011   2013   2015   2017

SECOND GRADERS AT THE STEMBUNNIES PROGRAM, *weighing eight-week-old Moe Moe Peacebunny*

TINKERBELL
*roaming at the Excelsior
community egg hunt*

QUIET WYATT
*overseeing STEM
Days for Girls*

**EARL CELEBRATING
BEST OF SHOW**
in 4-H after the 2014 county fair

**JUNIOR
ACHIEVEMENT
STEM CAMP**

2007   2008   2009   2010   2011   2012

**FORBES
UNDER 30
SUMMIT**
in Philadelphia (2015)

**CHILDREN AT
STEM CAMP**
*learning that Willow just
got a four-inch haircut*

MARKUS & OREO

COMFORT
RABBITS RULE!
Lionardo da Vinci,
Willow, Morris, Tator Tot,
Thumbalina & Bandit

Spring litter of
BABY
ANGORA
BUNNIES

DAISY PLAYING
THE WHITE RABBIT
at an Alice in Wonderland corporate party

| 2009 | 2011 | 2013 | 2015 | 2017 | 2019 |

Holding baby
PERIWINKLE

WHATCHAMACALLIT, MY BUSINESS ASSOCIATE, *as the crowd voted us top one-minute pitch at the MN Cup (2017)*

LIONARDO AT A LIBRARY PROGRAM *where kids compare the textures of different kinds of fur at rotating stations*

PERS, A JERSEY WOOLY RESCUE, *in the hands of a woman in hospice. He knew his job was to warm her lap & simply listen. Often the best gift is just to be present.*

2007   2008   2009   2010   2011   2012

At long last . . .
PEACEBUNNY ISLAND
(2018)

SIGNING THE
SUMMER LEASE
for Peacebunny Island.
Paxton is preparing
to leave his stamp mark.

BOUGHT
AN ISLAND!
(October 2018)

2013   2014   2015   2016   2017   2018

WELCOME ABOARD!

Embarking on the 100-mile journey up the Mississippi River to the island.

OVERNIGHT AT WABASHA—

Huckleberry playing the night before we crossed Lake Pepin

JACOB DRIVING

from the flybridge area atop the houseboat as we approached a lock & dam

DELAY BECAUSE OF A POPPED BELT

on the port-side motor, assessed by Jacob & Kaden, who climbed in the bilge

ANGEL PEACEBUNNY
welcoming guests at Carrot Cake Bay

**EXPLORING THE
"FRONT PORCH" AREA—**
*crossing the logs from Kinderbunny
to the main island*

LIVING THE DREAM

**FUDGE,
ALSO LIVING
THE DREAM**
on Kinderbunny Island

AUTUMN REUNION CAMPOUT—
Jacob, Nic & Kaden joined me for the weekend

FULL MOON OVER THE MAIN 22-ACRE ISLAND,
with our houseboat parked at the sandbar (2018)

**CASPER & ME ON
PEACEBUNNY ISLAND,**
*enjoying the crackle of a warming fire
in the "Ring of Johnny Cashness"*

**HUCKLEBERRY AT SUNSET
ON THE MISSISSIPPI RIVER,**
relaxing on the upper deck of the SS Peacebunny

That spurred us to get additional quality carriers and to be more intentional about presentation details. I gathered new lessons.

- Listen to criticism; open up to hearing from people who have different viewpoints. Let this sharpen you and what you're doing.
- Don't make excuses; make better plans.

After the expo, my dad returned home with all the rabbits except Whatchi while Uncle Kris met us for the final leg of the trip to Philly. I sat in the back of his minivan with Whatchi, worked in my sticker book, and read a joke book. Uncle Kris not only tolerated but encouraged me to jam out to music in the backseat. "Eye of the Tiger" was on heavy repeat in preparation for doing the *Rocky* run up the museum steps when we arrived in Philadelphia. Whatchi bobbed his head like the long-haired rocker he resembled.

When we arrived at the conference, two name tags were waiting for us at the check-in desk. One said, "CALEB SMITH/STEMbunnies." The other said, "CALEB'S MOM." People crowded the lobby and the tables filled with schedules, pamphlets, and other literature. The air buzzed with conversation and energy. We'd planned to leave Whatchi at the host family's home with Uncle Kris, who wanted to rest after the long drive, but all that excitement gave me a crazy idea. I sought out the event manager and presented her with a question she hadn't anticipated: Could I bring my Angora rabbit named Whatchamacallit with me to the conference events?

I showed her how he rode in the wagon, and she was amazed that he was like a lap puppy who seemed more than content to have me pull him around. I explained that my furry business associate would model while I explained the Angora rabbit-to-yarn process. It was like taking people on a tour of my manufacturing plant. As she cooed and petted Whatchi, she enthusiastically granted me permission. No name tag necessary.

The three-day summit attracted more than two thousand young entrepreneurs from around the world. It included keynotes from Barbara Bush and Mike Tyson, numerous panels, a music festival, a food festival, and a final day devoted to community service. I attended panels in the fashion category, hoping to connect with people interested in Angora fur. Pulling Whatchi around in a wagon made introductions easy. One person said this showed a flair for marketing.

By the end of the second day, I'd handed out all three hundred business cards. In the end I have no doubt that more people knew the name of my rabbit than my name, let alone the name of our business, but they remembered how we made them feel. I told my dad on the phone that despite the demand for wool, I didn't think that scaling up to own more Angora rabbits would be the next logical step. But I wanted to tease the idea out more, and maybe the MN Cup process could help me decide what to do.

Before leaving Philadelphia, I was thrilled to be invited on a personal tour of a textile mill so the owner could show me how wool yarn is processed. As a bonus, this also counted as part of my very first Boy Scout merit badge. At the end of the night, I melted into the host family's chair, too tired to even get into bed. I don't know how long I spent staring at the wall, tapping at my face, which is something I did when I was lost in thought.

"What's going on in there?" Mom asked, kissing me on the top of my head and sitting down next to me. "You're tapping again."

"I was just thinking about how much space twenty thousand pounds of Angora wool would take up, how many farms we'd need to partner with, and how many years it would take to grow that much."

I was referring to the woman who had fallen in love with Whatchi and said she would buy that much wool from me if I was able to produce it. Although I'd told her my so-called operation consisted of half a dozen of Whatchi's friends—and I had other obligations, like school and scouts—the opportunity lodged itself in my brain like a jackknifed semitruck that blocked all traffic lanes. I couldn't get past it.

"Do you remember what your grandma always says?" my mom asked.

Although that wasn't what I wanted to hear, I nodded.

"Let's say it together." She smiled.

"Just because you can . . ." I stopped, but Mom coaxed the rest out of me. ". . . doesn't mean you should."

I crawled into bed and exhaled as I stretched out. My feet were sore from my dress shoes, and my brain was done. My mom gave me a good-night hug just as Uncle Kris popped his head in to ask if we needed anything before bed.

"Just the lights, monsieur," I said.

A few weeks later, I attended the Livestock Conservancy national meeting in California, where I spoke with a few Angora experts from across the United States and connected with several others from Ankara, Turkey, who were involved in a special academic program focused on Angora wool. A small breakout session I led on raising heritage breeds was a hit, and I realized my ideas could work far beyond Minnesota. I also realized that I didn't need to rush. The connections I was making wouldn't just disappear. I was only eleven years old—I could take my time to figure out a sensible plan and seek advice from business experts too.

Like everyone at the *Forbes* conference, I wanted to turn a profit. But money wasn't the way I wanted to define success. Whatever I did needed to first be good for the rabbits.

After the several-day drive home, we met up with the woman who had purchased the first wool clippings from my Whatchi, Westley, and Quiet Wyatt. She had spun more into yarn, which she knitted into booties for her new granddaughter. I was delighted to think these rabbits whose mom had been rescued from a barn fire were now helping to warm and protect a baby's feet. I relayed the story to Whatchi.

We thanked our lucky starfish.

Little did I suspect that as exciting as that adventure out East had been, a new, bigger, and crazier one was about to start.

PART TWO

Peacebunny Island

7

I Need an Island

I believe practically all truly great ideas are born one of two ways: either they come from an ecstatic burst of genius or from fatigue and frustration.

My long, challenging journey to Peacebunny Island stemmed mostly from the latter. On the day the island idea came to me, I was cranky and tired. I had just stepped out of a steaming-hot bunny costume, something I swore I would never wear.

Five years earlier, when I was seven years old, my parents had taken me to the Minnesota State Fair for the first time. In addition to absorbing the sights, crowds, and smells of the fair, I saw the rabbits competing for ribbons. I also helped out while my parents supervised the community service teams, whose members took turns dressing up as Smokey Bear in the Department of Natural Resources booth.

My role was to help escort the guy in the costume. He couldn't see clearly and needed a heads-up about curbs and small kids racing to hug his legs. I was fascinated by the different ways some of the adults treated him. Some traded high fives; others made naughty gestures as they took photos with him, and a few even tried to trip him.

The poor guy worked hard in the August heat, and when he took a break, he was dripping in sweat, like he'd been locked in an airless box in the Mojave Desert. Then and there I vowed I would never be a mascot in a costume.

Jump ahead to spring 2016. Now, at almost twelve years old, I was racing back and forth across a grassy field wearing a white bunny costume. Yep, I was a mascot.

We were hosting our annual Bunny Garden and Easter egg hunt at Wood Lake, and I was leading a group of preschool kids in a bunny hop race, a new feature we'd introduced to our events. The kids loved racing the mascot, and I admit it was fun skipping in front of them and then turning around to watch them hop, tumble, and land in fits of giggles while their parents and grandparents took videos.

Even the rabbits, watching from their pens, seemed amused. I got the sense that several of them wanted in on the action. Why wouldn't a bunny think they could beat everyone else in the bunny hop?

This hadn't been an easy day—or couple of weeks. For obvious reasons, Easter was our busiest time of year, and during this three-week Easter window, supported by teams of enthusiastic volunteers trained at Bunny Bootcamps, we said yes to more Easter egg hunts, Bunny Gardens, office parties, and birthdays than ever before. Business was booming. At home, we had a giant dry-erase board on our kitchen wall that had so many different colored notes and lines and arrows marking who went where and with which rabbits that it looked impossible to decipher, let alone execute.

I had stared at that board earlier while we finished breakfast and joked, "What does it all mean?"

My mom, already on overload, gave me that fed-up look.

"What *does* it all mean, Caleb?"

It meant we were operating on the brink of organized madness. Ahead of us were four back-to-back Bunny Gardens at Wood Lake and half a dozen egg hunts around the region that were being handled by our volunteers.

To start, I identified which bunnies would go to which events, knowing some would decline the invitation. We needed twenty rabbits for the Bunny

Gardens in order to allow adequate rest breaks for them throughout the sessions. Once there, the rabbits could opt out at any time. Mostly they just played and nibbled the grass. The other teams needed ten bunnies each for their events.

We sat down and figured out which rabbits were out with foster families and which were at the new farm we were renting in Hastings, a beautiful organic orchard about forty-five minutes from our house. Foster families were called and arrangements were made to pick up the bunnies and drop them off later, after the events. The days of keeping a few rabbits in the living room were long gone, my mom told one of the foster moms on the phone, adding (while giving me a playful wink), "Be careful what you promise your kids."

Things ran quite smoothly—until around noon. That's when several volunteer families called to say they were going to be late or had to cancel altogether because of sickness. Such last-minute glitches rarely occurred. Our volunteers were an A-team of friends, coworkers, neighbors, teachers, grandparents, families, and people of all ages with a passion for long-eared furballs.

Like a fifteen-year-old girl named Greta, who volunteered after her pet bunny died unexpectedly, and Deneen, a young woman whose job change required her to live on-site and surrender her beloved Basil, a six-month-old English Spot that she described as "a total jester." She was right—Basil was a hoot. And then there was Milton, a bank lender and dreamer who started by fostering and gradually did more and more until he was delivering used cages and an endless supply of free pallets and building supplies.

This particular Easter season, our volunteer teams included Noah and Markus's older sister, Heather, and her college roommate. But when five families dropped out that morning, our busiest day of the year, it created the perfect storm. My parents, who are oddly hardwired to handle such emergencies, went into hyperdrive. All the volunteer cars were loaded. Foster rabbits were fetched. And while I can't guarantee speed limits were always obeyed, every event started on time, including the four back-to-back events we hosted at Wood Lake Nature Center.

The day was a happy blur. Our early-morning logistical issues were quickly replaced by the joy of watching kids and families having fun during the events, especially all the tumbling and giggling in the bunny hop races. The only downside to the day was my empty stomach. With only fifteen minutes between the multi-hour events, I forgot to eat and probably didn't drink enough water to stay properly hydrated, considering all the running around I was doing in the bunny costume.

I kept telling myself, *Next break, ditch the costume and eat.* But then I'd get distracted, another group would arrive, and it was back to bunny business. Toward the end of the day, as I was dragging the metal pens across the field to fresh spots of grass so the bunnies could continue nibbling, I grumbled, "At least one of us gets to eat." I told myself to keep moving; there was just one more session to go.

I adjusted my grip on the heavy metal pen while nearly stumbling over my costume's huge white rabbit feet. Frustrated, tired, hungry, and thirsty, I propped my fuzzy white elbows on the edge of the pen and let my mascot face fall into my hands. My head was beginning to throb. I knelt down and looked at my mom, who was trying to corral our Flemish Giant, Tinkerbell.

Better her than me, I thought. Tinkerbell still wore the little bell around her neck that she came with after we rescued her, and it was ding-a-linging as she hopped away from my mom. The family we got her from didn't want her anymore because "she kept growing and growing." *Um, you knew she was a giant, right?*

My mom saw me on my knees.

"You all right?" she asked.

"I'm done," I blurted out. "We just need to get an island."

"What?"

"I can't keep doing things this way," I said. "We need an island for the rabbits so I can stop carrying everything."

I adjusted my massive mascot head so the eyeholes aligned and I could see my mom's reaction.

"Well, that's a new one." She smiled and got back to moving Tinkerbell.

"See, if we had our own place, people would come to us and we wouldn't need to drive around and haul everything everywhere. We would only need to set up once for the day!" I was making up the details as they came to me but thought they sounded pretty good. "It would just make things so much safer and easier."

"Well, that does sound nice right about now," she said, shifting Tinkerbell in her arms so she could speak directly to the giant rabbit. "Huh . . . an island for the bunnies? What do you think, girl?" She deposited our furry pal in the pen and sidled up to me. "Where do you expect to find this island?"

"Oh, I don't know," I said. "Just the thought of it gave me a little boost."

She gave me a side hug and peered inside my costume head to see my face. "Come on, kiddo. I'll finish this. Go help your dad and then take a minibreak."

The final Bunny Garden of the season was less than ten minutes away. I opened the gate, and my dad drove the car into the fenced area to bring in a few more carriers from the last egg hunt across town. He parked on the back side of a clump of trees. I lumbered behind the car, opened the back door, and collapsed into the very full vehicle, which barely had room for me. I couldn't remove my whole costume, but I pulled off the head and let out a sigh.

"Ahhhhhh."

"You doing okay?" my dad asked.

"Somehow we need to get an island," I said, staring up at the roof of the car.

In my head, I felt this idea progress from a lark to a question. *Hey, why not an island?* My mind worked that way. I got an idea and then immediately began to put the pieces together. It didn't necessarily mean I wanted to pursue it; I merely enjoyed thinking of the possibilities. In this case, however, the more I thought about it, the more I wanted an island. No fences. No pens to carry. It would be so much easier than all we had to go through for every event.

A private island for rabbits. It would be perfect.

My dad leaned his head against the headrest and shut his eyes.

"Someday, when I'm old," I continued, "when I'm like thirty-five, I can go there with Noah. And when we both have kids, we can all vacation there. Maybe it's on a lake or just off the coast. Or maybe it's out in the middle of the ocean. But I know it's out there. Somewhere."

"When you're thirty-five."

"Yep."

"What would you call it?"

I hadn't thought about it before, but I knew instantly. "That's so obvious." I smiled.

"Not to me," he said. "Tell me."

"Get this . . ."

"Come on, Caleb."

I leaned close so I was right up behind him.

"It'll be called Peacebunny Island."

Our eyes met in the rearview mirror. He nodded approvingly.

"That sounds so good," he said. "Very, very good."

Hastings

We made the round trip to the Hastings farm a minimum of once a day for the usual check-ins with the rabbits we kept there—now more than three dozen. They were delighted by their cozy accommodations, and so was I. The arrangement was almost too good to be true. Through a friend, we'd met a passionate produce entrepreneur named Rick, who was growing organic vegetables on the farm. He introduced us to the owner, and I pitched him the idea of housing my rabbits there.

The farmer had a vision for a wholly sustainable farm built around biodiversity. He was raising chickens and guinea hens, and tending fruit trees and prize-winning roses. A beekeeper used a section on the property for his honey-making business, and Rick was growing his organic vegetables. The rabbits were a perfect fit—their manure would be prized as a natural fertilizer. The farmer enthusiastically agreed to give us space.

As the seasons changed, we planted luscious orchard grass near where the bunnies stayed. The long, cool blades became their favorite snack, and it gave them a place to munch and rest as I moved them in the newly constructed "rabbit tractors," which were basically pens on wheels. It was also a comfortable place for me to stretch out and take a quick break from all the heavy lifting and physically demanding chores. If things got too busy, I snuck in quick naps on the drive to and from the farm. After one or two yawns, I was out and homework needed to wait.

Like Albert Einstein and Thomas Edison, I was a proponent of an afternoon nap. One day, as I sat in the back of the car and slipped into that dreamy place between awake and sleep, I saw Peacebunny Island. It rose from the water and summoned me with unavoidable clarity.

When I woke up, I told my dad about it. It was pretty simple: I needed an island for the bunnies. Sooner rather than later.

"I thought you were going to wait until you were thirty-five," he said.

I shrugged. "That depends on how quickly I can figure stuff out."

Like most big dreams, there was so much to think about, starting with how I could locate an island and convince someone to let me use it or sell it to me. And perhaps that was the easy part.

But the wheels were further set in motion when my dad began to think about retooling his skill set and changing careers. The hockey league had folded, and he started going to a weekly outreach dinner followed by a job transition group.

At these outreach dinners, my dad met Kaden and his mom and his two younger sisters. After about two months of hearing about this super-fun family, my mom and I started joining them for dinners. We all sat at the same large table together, and our families became good friends. Kaden and I were slow to connect, though both of us were amused by our parents. It was fun to hear stories I never would have heard otherwise. Kaden's sisters were intrigued by my stories about the rabbits, even though they hadn't met them yet. Each week they asked for updates about Paxton, Whatchi, Wyatt, and the others.

Kaden was a grade older than me, and he had an engineering-type mindset that gave him an original, creative approach to problem solving. He was in the school orchestra and took all advanced classes. During dinner, he usually wore headphones and did his homework. Then one night he passed me his phone and said, "Look at this video."

It was a clip from the movie *The Princess Bride*, one of the all-time greatest films I've ever seen—with some of the all-time best lines.

"Inconceivable," I said, quoting the movie.

"You keep using that word," Kaden said. "I do not think it means what you think it means."

"When I was your age, television was called—"

"Books!"

Both of us laughed. It was clear we shared the same sense of humor. And our friendship took off from there. *Thank you, Inigo Montoya.*

I considered telling Kaden about Peacebunny Island. Although he was less than excited about rabbits, he was smart and analytical, and I was interested in his reaction. But I decided the timing wasn't right. At that point the idea still wasn't solid enough in my own mind to mention to anyone outside of my family. I had only told my parents and grandparents and the Bachmans. All of them expressed support and encouragement, none more so than my ninety-five-year-old great-grandmother, who matter-of-factly said, "Why wouldn't you want an island?"

Bingo.

One day, on a lark, I sat down at the computer, looked up islands, and stumbled across Disney's Discovery Island, an old wildlife attraction that was shuttered in 1999, locked down, and left to the elements. Although it was 1,500 miles away in Florida, I wondered what they were doing with it (nothing at all, it turned out). I also found a list of celebrities who owned private islands with interesting names that ended in Islet or Peninsula or Cay.

In another search, I learned about Ōkunoshima, an island in Japan where the Japanese military had produced poisonous gas during World War II and tested it on rabbits. According to local legend, in the 1970s, visiting schoolchildren left eight rabbits there and they reproduced without the natural check of predators until the place was so overrun it was dubbed Rabbit Island. Now it was a tourist destination—and the antithesis of the way I envisioned Peacebunny Island.

As I saw it, Peacebunny Island would be a safe and gentle harbor away from the craziness and complications of modern life. It would be a place to unwind. A place to play in the woods and the water while we trained rescue rabbits and the young ones (which I called "kinderbunnies") to become comfort animals.

And Peacebunny Island would be more than an actual, physical island.

It would be a state of mind.

A shareable dream.

A place where anyone could travel in their imagination.

It might take a while. And I would need a bunch of dreamers with pure hearts to help make it happen. But that was okay. The journey would be fun.

And the destination would be *amazing*.

Why Not Name Him John?

It was the Fourth of July—my birthday and the reason Grandma Smith has always referred to me as her little firecracker, born on America's Independence Day.

We were at the hospital. But don't worry—nothing was wrong.

See, my family has some slightly odd but meaningful birthday traditions. We give the people closest to us presents on our own birthday as a thank-you for another year of care and support. We also host a huge picnic with build-your-own tacos for the same six families, including the Bachmans, my grandparents, and my cousins. And I have to admit, it's pretty cool getting fireworks at the end of every birthday.

But one of my favorite parts is starting the day with a visit to the hospital where I was born and thanking the doctors and nurses in the maternity ward for working on a holiday and missing their barbecues and fireworks. I suppose delivering babies is like fireworks, though: it always results in a *wow*! I also leave behind an envelope for the baby born closest to my birth time, 9:42 a.m., containing one dollar for every year I have been alive—in that year's case, twelve dollars—and a handwritten letter welcoming them to the world.

My handwriting has gotten better since we began this practice, but the sentiment has stayed the same. We wish the baby a life full of wonder and adventure, surrounded by all the love and closeness they felt on the special day they arrived.

It's like I get to be the first stranger to wave hello.

Each year the nurses allow me to push the button that plays "Twinkle, Twinkle, Little Star" over the hospital PA system, as is their routine every time a new baby arrives. That year they also surprised me with a small cake that we all shared.

A few days after my birthday, I was caring for a new furry arrival of my own. He was another "You've got to meet this one" rabbit. A woman called us, upset and apologetic that she had to rehome such a cutie, but she'd developed a severe allergy, and she pleaded with us to take her little loppy.

"I'm dying," she blubbered over the phone. "I'm itching. I'm sneezing.

And all this little guy wants to do is cuddle. He's literally killing me with his affection."

He was an older blue-gray rabbit, rounded like a loaf of bread. He had long, droopy ears, which meant he belonged to a breed known as lop-eared rabbits—hence her reference to him as a loppy. They have the same anatomy as other rabbits, except the muscles behind their heads aren't as strong, making their ears droop.

We didn't have any lop-eared rabbits in the program yet, and we were adding more bunnies for the growing biodiversity program, so we took a chance. My dad suggested a name.

"Why not John?" he said.

I had many reasons why not, among them the idea of introducing him with the other rabbits at events. "Here is Paxton, Quiet Wyatt, Whatchamacallit, Tator Tot, Fudge, and . . . *John*."

My objections didn't work.

Over the next few weeks, my dad offered numerous variations of John. He tried Yohannes, Little Juan, and Ivan. None of them stuck. When I filled out his official paperwork at his naming ceremony (with Whatchi, Pax, Tator Tot, and Quiet Wyatt as witnesses), I wrote the name *Little John*, and somehow it fit him perfectly.

Little John was an older bunny, yet he was determined to keep up with me and everything that was happening around him. He also adopted my dad, waiting for him at the door when he came home, snuggling next to his feet while he watched TV, and following him down the hallway until Dad gave him treats.

Like all new rabbits, Little John stayed at our house for the first two weeks, meaning no trips to the farm, no events, and no contact with the other rabbits. This quarantine policy was designed to help keep the Peacebunny colony safe in case the new rabbit carried germs our bunnies didn't have immunity for. We especially needed to protect the rare breeds. This period also gave us time to get to know each new furry pal and for them to get to know us.

Little John kept an eye out for when I got ready for bed, knowing it was time for fun. As part of my nighttime routine, I played the song "We Built This City" by Starship, partly because it was five minutes long, like my bedtime routine. Besides, it was a good song. When I began brushing my teeth, Little John hopped in figure eights around my legs, then hopped down the hallway and came back as if he were on a long stage. Sometimes my toothbrush turned into a mic while we jammed, and he seemed to hop in sync to the catchy tune.

As time went on, he zipped in and out between my legs as I walked through the house. He did it for fun, like he was born to run agility courses. This gave me an idea. With some birthday money, I bought supplies from the hardware store and built him a little course. Little John was thrilled. Without any prompting from me, he jumped over obstacles, ran through tunnels, and got Michael Jordan–like air leaping from one platform to another. In midair, he gave me a look that said, "Nothing's gonna stop us now!"

Unfortunately, he didn't get along with my other natural ham and agility ace, Tator Tot. Even though they got along with the other bunnies, they wrestled and nipped at each other. It was too bad, because I pictured them soaring through the air in tandem like a pair of Olympic skaters. Alas, there was too much ego involved.

On the bright side, I now had two rabbits who could spice up any event.

Housewarming

Once his two-week quarantine was complete, I was eager to take Little John to the next party and watch his outgoing personality in action. We didn't have to wait long.

A family of four invited us to a combination housewarming/birthday party. They had recently moved into a rental house, and it coincided with one of their kids' birthdays. They asked if we could bring bunnies as part of the celebration. All their guests would be excited, they said, and I knew they would too, especially with this little guy.

Because they'd known my family since I was very young, they skipped filling out the party form on my website and called us directly. We accepted the invitation and arrived with Little John, Moe Moe Peacebunny, and Tinkerbell, our plus-size princess.

All three rabbits were litterbox trained—important at an indoor party—and they didn't need to be reminded to bring their personalities. As we unloaded the rabbit carriers, it dawned on me that until now we had never been invited to visit this family's house. Neither had they come to ours. Our families' paths crossed a few times a year at community events, but I hoped this visit to their home would elevate our friendship into more frequent get-togethers. I knew the rabbits would also enjoy exploring during the party.

After opening the door wide, the family showed us around the house. Within minutes, we ditched our parents and went chasing down the short hallway to the kids' bedrooms followed by a deliriously happy Little John and the other two rabbits, which were hustling to keep up. Tinkerbell's tiny bell ding-a-linged behind us. Later, after dinner, our playtime was interrupted by the always-joyous announcement, "Time for cake!" In the kitchen, someone was proudly cutting up a store-bought sheet cake decorated with big globs of frosting.

They didn't have any birthday candles to blow out, but no big deal. He still asked his son what he would wish for if there were candles.

"*This* is the best present!" He smiled, turning his head from side to side as if scanning the house and making sure each of us, and especially his dad, saw his happy expression. "We have a new house. And my own bedroom. And my own metal fork. And a glass full of milk!"

"Cheers, everybody!" his sister said, holding up her glass of milk.

Applause filled the small kitchen. Only later did it dawn on me that during the tour of their house I didn't see any furniture other than a sofa in the living room. There weren't any beds in the bedrooms. No bookshelves. No toys in the closet. I guess I figured they hadn't moved in all the way from their last house. I hadn't thought twice about sitting on the floor, and the bunnies loved being so close to everyone. And Little John clearly found this to be the party of his dreams, because after cake, he was able to scoot between everyone, climbing into laps and leaping off, to the delight of his audience.

As we visited and ate more cake, we learned more about the recent journey this family had weathered, culminating in this special night. Yes, this was a birthday party. But they were also celebrating having a more permanent residence after many months of moving from house to house, sofa to sofa, and eventually parking lot to parking lot.

I thought back to the elderly couple with the cats who had been homeless for several weeks. Then I looked around the room: here was a whole family who had lived in their car too. And for even longer stints. Four people, two of them kids, living in a car.

The kids were playing peekaboo with the bunnies, and their laughter warmed the room. The kids had no idea, but two of the three bunnies were rescues and had their own hard-luck stories. And now, just like the kids, they had a forever home.

I was beginning to see that all of us have stories. Most people focus only on our differences. But the rabbits helped me see how the stories that really shape us are very much the same. If you ask me, that should make us all more understanding of each other.

"Caleb, try this," the boy said, turning a somersault across the living room floor.

I did one of my own. Then his sister followed. Little John hopped back and forth and did some crazy flops.

"I think Little John is trying to figure out how to do one too," he said.

Everyone laughed, and it was obvious that this party wasn't about what this family didn't have. It was about what they *did* have—an abundance of love and gratitude and contentedness—things so many people with far more money never find.

Wonderfluff

"What's going on with your island?" Grandpa Tractor asked over the phone.

"I'm still thinking about it," I said with a timid laugh. "Lots to think about."

"There always is," he said.

As we talked, I stared at the note taped on our refrigerator door. *What would you attempt if you knew you couldn't fail?* I must have read that sign a zillion times. It was a good question, with potentially life-changing consequences for those who took it seriously. I already had a huge list of things, and of course the island was on there. But as I saw it, the question wasn't only about projects and careers or even dreams. It could also be about taking a chance on love, friendship, an apology, or trusting again.

"Hey, Grandpa," I said. "What would you do if you knew you couldn't fail?"

He responded after a long pause.

"More," he said.

At the time, I happened to be struggling with the idea of "more." This was right after someone who had signed up to foster taught me some painful lessons. She was a recent college graduate who burst into our world with an enthusiasm that was impossible to resist. "I loved watching your bunnies this weekend," Wendy emailed, following a bunny event. "I would love to support your organization and a little bunny! I finally convinced my parents to be open to fostering a bunny, but I don't think they're going to remain that way for long. Is there a way we can speed up your process? Thanks in advance."

Our online information and foster forms clearly advised people not to rush into taking rabbits home. But Wendy had raised a rabbit in the past, so she knew what was involved. So did we. We had already placed bunnies with more than one hundred foster families and had worked with an equal number in the past. We knew there was a normal tipping point around week six when people are either in it for the long haul or ready to move on. We also knew that best intentions and massive bunny love didn't guarantee a perfect fit.

I recalled the wonderfully sweet family who wanted to take a rabbit home but said they didn't think they could convince their two pit bulls to open their hearts. I might be Captain Obvious, but I was shocked that I needed to tell them no. The dad looked at the kids and shrugged. "Well, at least we tried."

We tried with Wendy, too. She agreed to attend our next Bunny Bootcamp. In the process of communicating with her, we learned she was living with her parents after graduating from college with a STEM-related degree. On paper, she looked like a fantastic candidate. She requested a lop-eared rabbit, but Little John was our only lop and he wasn't available for fostering. Then, the night before the Bunny Bootcamp, a family donated another little lop to the program specifically because she was so gentle with their children.

It's amazing how things sometimes aligned like that. They knew we were about to start a comfort unit to visit senior homes, hospitals, and hospices, and they said, "We love the idea of our bunny brightening the day of everyone she meets."

We picked her up on a Wednesday night after church activities, and after one look at this tiny white Holland lop whose bold blue eyes reeled me in, I was in love. I named her Wonderfluff.

"She *is* a wonder," my mom said.

"We're definitely going to have to caution everyone that they can't fall in love with her," I said. "Just like with Oreo and Taffy, she can only go out on short-term fostering, and she isn't available for adoption. I promised the family she would be invited to be part of our comfort rabbit unit."

"You're probably right to give a warning," my mom said with a wink.

"I have no doubt," I said. "This little girl is so eager to be around people she's going to break some hearts."

Wendy was thrilled when we told her about the new lop. She also understood that Wonderfluff would only be a short-term foster and that the arrangement was contingent upon Wendy coming to class. She repeatedly expressed her excitement to see us and to meet Wonderfluff. So when Wendy didn't show up to the required class on Thursday afternoon, we were surprised and disappointed. Then, as we were packing up, she drove up hurriedly, parked right behind us, and apologized profusely for missing class. Because we'd brought supplies and a cage for her, we sent her home with Wonderfluff in exchange for her promise to attend next week's fostering class. After all, she was an adult and she'd cared for a pet rabbit before, so I bent our policy to make an exception. I trusted her.

"She seems like a great first foster home for this sweet bunny," I said.

"Maybe she'll choose to volunteer with us at Easter events," my dad replied.

"I like that she has a science degree," I said. "That's cool. I bet she's a great role model."

Only she wasn't. Wendy missed the next Bunny Bootcamp and didn't respond to our emails. More than a month passed before we heard from her. "Hi! Wonderfluff is amazing," she emailed. "She's happy and healthy and really social. She runs around and 'binkies' all the time. Also, she has worked *wonders* for me and my mom. Both of us are in a difficult part of our lives right now, and she has made a positive impact on our mental health. I know you said adoption wasn't possible, but I would like to provide a permanent home for Wonderfluff. Let me know if this will work out. Attached are some pictures of this sweetie angel bun."

Although Wendy's note and accompanying photos confirmed my hopes for the rabbits in our foster program, we had committed that Wonderfluff would live with the Peacebunnies. Wendy had agreed to the arrangement. We gave her and her family space rather than pushing for an immediate return, but we made it clear in another email that she'd given us her word and we expected her to keep it.

She had other ideas.

"I want to thank you so much for bringing Wonderfluff into my life," she responded. "It has been nearly six months since I got her, and she is the perfect pet for me. I love her more than anything. That said, I will not be returning her to you. I am positive the original owners would have no problem with her being in a loving, caring forever home where she has stability, fresh greens, space to play, and a loving companion (me). However, I do want to make this right. I am willing to pay any adoption fee you have in place."

My parents and those who advised us were stunned. So was I. This woman had completely lost my trust. She had also damaged my ability to trust adults in general. Completely ignoring our agreement, Wendy had taken something that didn't belong to her, and she was now offering to pay for it, as if this rabbit were a commodity and she was in charge of the transaction. I didn't know what to do. Nothing like this had happened before.

We didn't have a policy for a person who chose to keep a foster rabbit. *Who steals a rabbit?* I wondered. *Will I ever get Wonderfluff back? How far should I push to try to fix this?*

The other thing that really bothered me was that Wendy's actions made me a liar. They reflected poorly on my character. My word to the original owners had been broken, and if I didn't have my good word or my integrity, what did I have? Why would people believe me in the future?

At the next event, I confided in several of my adult volunteers, and they shared memories of times they first felt betrayed or taken advantage of by someone. One dad put his hand on my shoulder and said, "Caleb, as you get older, you'll see that big things become smaller over time."

While his advice was probably true in many cases, I found reasons to disagree. I imagined certain big things that would never become small, like losing Snickers or my joy at finding Paxton. I also didn't think I needed to compromise my values in this situation that might work out for Wendy but failed the ethics sniff test. This was a big deal.

"Is accepting bad stuff part of adulthood?" I asked my dad.

"Yes and no," he said.

"Then I'll take the no," I stated emphatically.

How do you find forgiveness when you fall short of something you've committed to? I knew how to ask God, and that part was resolved in my heart. But I couldn't reach the previous owners. I couldn't clear things with them. How could I move the business forward without beating myself up? How did I forgive myself? How could I trust my gut again? How could I trust again? Or should I just "grow up" and accept this as the way the world works?

I needed resolution, and I couldn't have it without a conversation with Wendy, who had ended her last email by attacking my motives and accusing me of wanting Wonderfluff returned only as a tactic to get her to pay for the bunny. The fact was, she hadn't paid anything. Our agreement was based on trust. How could I clear the air with her?

She sent two more emails, the second one coming about a month after the first. "I'm sorry things didn't work out the way you wanted," she wrote. "I have no doubt this rabbit will be well taken care of for the rest of her life. I am definitely going to pay for the bunny and her supplies."

In her follow-up message, she apologized for not having sent a donation yet, explaining that her father had died after a brief illness and the little rabbit that we had brought into her life had provided much calm and love to her whole family. Reading that note gave me the resolution I sought, and I felt the weight begin to lift as my family added Wendy and her family to our nightly prayers. I couldn't imagine losing a parent, and I was so thankful she had a furry friend to help her. We truly hoped she would find peace. I trusted that the bunny would have a forever home and would receive plenty of love.

Grandma Deer reminded me that like all the Peacebunnies, Wonderfluff was God's rabbit—she didn't belong to me or Wendy or the people who had her before us. No matter how badly anyone wanted to claim that adorable lop bunny as their own, she was on a mission to be a blessing. Wonderfluff taught me that regardless of how negative and convoluted things can get, all things work together for good in the end.

All trust is built on faith, and though my faith in people was shaken, God was big enough to rebuild the foundation. I wanted to live my life assuming the best and trusting people—trusting that they would do the right thing. Hopefully I'll be proven right. When you have an open heart, nothing is impossible.

A View from Above

It was cold and drizzly when we finally got back in the car after several hours in the memory-care unit of a senior center. The rabbits were in the back, the car engine was idling, and the heat was starting to flow through the vents. Taking bunnies to visit seniors dealing with issues ranging from mild dementia to severe Alzheimer's disease never failed to produce a range of reactions, whether it was a meek smile or a chatty string of childhood stories. Invariably someone said, "Hello, Peter," while petting a rabbit and then looked up at me and said, "This one's name is Peter Rabbit."

In the car, I recounted the way an older man who had been quiet and seemingly uninterested in our visit suddenly turned to me and said, "You know, I used to eat rabbits."

"What did you tell him?" my mom asked.

"I nodded calmly and said, 'Yeah, some people do that.'"

"What did he say to that?"

"Nothing. I think he wanted to get a reaction from me. But my calm defused everything."

When we got home, I went straight to the pantry and grabbed a box of crackers. I sat down at the kitchen table to work on our upcoming schedule. Compared to the rest of the year, winter was our slower period. It provided more time to manage the requests for parties and events that people wanted to schedule for spring and summer.

It was often a ho-hum exercise, but not this time. We had a request from a city recreation department for an event they wanted to hold at a park on a large lake. Because I wasn't familiar with the area, I looked up the address, and in the process, I spotted a good-sized island on the lake. That got my motor running. I quickly opened Google Maps and zoomed in and in until I found Minnesota, the Twin Cities and—*boom*—a lake island that wasn't located in the park.

Using the online measuring tool, I estimated that the island was roughly five acres in size. I clicked over to the county property identification records and found the owner's name. My heart beat faster. Amazing. Unbelievable. A private island! And relatively close to us. I began to yell excitedly for my mom and dad and Paxton and whoever else was home at that moment.

My parents rushed upstairs. I think they expected to see flames or blood. Instead, they found me pointing at the computer screen.

"I can't believe it!" I exclaimed.

"Can't believe what?" my mom asked.

"It's not owned by the city!" I babbled. "The island is privately owned."

By this time, almost a year had passed since I started looking online for a private island that might become Peacebunny Island. Because Minnesota was the land of ten thousand lakes, I assumed I could find at least *one* island. But every island I found that seemed viable was owned by the city or state and I figured the bureaucracy involved in trying to lease the land and start a business was way more than I could undertake, even with my parents' assistance.

This privately owned lake island seemed different. The almost serendipitous way it came to my attention made me feel like it was meant to happen. Excited and hopeful, I jotted down the contact information and wrote to the family foundation that was listed on the county's website. Surprisingly, a response came within the week. Essentially, it said, "We're curious to learn more about your bunny proposal. Let's talk."

We did, and that opened the door to several months of negotiations and preparatory work. The more I looked into the island, the better it seemed. It was close to a public boat launch, and there was plenty of room. But there was also so much to figure out—like which permits would enable us to have more than four adult rabbits there. Could we build on the property? And if so, what were the specifications? Where would we park a boat that would ferry rabbits and visitors back and forth? What about bathrooms? Garbage? Security? Insurance?

The questions were endless, confusing, exhausting, frustrating, and exciting. Every day I had the same thought: *What do I have to do to make this work?*

Topic du Jour

During one of our regular Thursday dinners with Kaden's family, his mom suggested getting together on Saturday. I couldn't believe the game-changing brilliance of this idea. I poked my mom to get her attention. She turned and saw me looking at her with a classic expression of surprise—wide eyes and mouth hanging open.

"We can do that?" I said. "We can have dinner with them on Thursday *and* see them again on Saturday?"

She nodded.

"Sweet."

This was just about the best news I could imagine. But it did dawn on me that I should learn the names of Kaden's two younger sisters before we got together again. That may sound rude, but they didn't know mine for the longest time either. We were friends beyond names. We were all simply each other's people.

Saturday came, and Kaden's family met us outside the building where we were taking some bunnies to a corporate party. Our normal volunteers could have handled the flow of people ourselves, but it was way more fun to have "Our Peoples," as we called them, see our bunnies and the way we ran events.

This was our first outdoor, middle-of-winter event of the season, and we were all bundled up. The party hosts provided straw bales for guests to sit on, and people on their way to see Santa filed past and took pictures next to the bunnies, which were enjoying digging their noses in the snow. Little John was full of antics, and the kids streaming by oohed and ahhed. All of us took turns warming up in the indoor break room and sampling the sugar cookies and hot cocoa.

Afterward, as we packed up the bunnies, we agreed that we couldn't wait to get together again on another non-Thursday. I took my dad aside for a quick chat. The island's owners, confident we were going to reach an agreement, had recently given us permission to visit the island and look around. I suggested inviting Our Peoples. My dad gave me the green light.

Kaden's reaction was something I never want to forget. He went totally bug-eyed when I told him about the island and asked if they wanted to go there with us.

"So, what you're saying is that you want to buy an island," he said, clearly trying to make sense of something that was utterly loony but at the same time the coolest, most awesome thing he'd ever heard.

"Right," I said.

He scratched his head. "And you have no money to buy an island, but you're actively searching for an island to rent to find out if you want to buy an island?"

"Correct."

"And this island is going to provide space for rabbits to play and be trained to sit in wagons and on tables so they can serve as comfort rabbits if they want to?"

"Yes."

"Could a person *fish* from said island?"

"I suppose," I said, momentarily confused by the unexpected question. "It's surrounded by water. In a lake. With fish. Yeah, why not!"

His face broke into a giant smile. "That. Is. Awesome."

From then on, the island was our topic du jour at Thursday night dinners. We planned and dreamed of things to build and add. My favorite group exercise was creating plans for a twelve-by-sixteen-foot wooden lighthouse that the rabbits could climb up using a ramp. At the top would be a lookout for the kids. We constructed a miniature model out of cardboard. We also talked about creating a garden maze, building tree houses, and camping in hammocks. Our moms suggested planting various wildflowers. For "bursts of color," they said.

I nodded politely. Adding bursts of color was way down the agenda compared to picturing a lookout plank atop a lighthouse.

One mild February day—it was about five degrees above zero—we met Our Peoples in the parking lot near the public boat launch. In our heavy winter gear, we didn't look like a bunch of island hoppers. No tropical shirts were in the vicinity. Ordinarily we would have traveled to the island in canoes, but since it was winter in the great North, the lake was frozen solid. So we made our way down to the lakeshore and then stepped onto the ice.

I'm walking on water, I said to myself, thinking it was kind of a funny observation. As I looked around, though, I noticed that dozens of people were doing the same thing. They were also riding snowmobiles, sitting in chairs while fishing through small holes cut into the ice, or hanging out in ice houses that had carpeting, TVs, and beds. In other words, walking on water was no big deal—as long as it was frozen solid. Still, I was nervous and used a heavy walking stick to test the ice before I stepped onto it.

Kaden's younger sisters took turns riding in the sled we were pulling and calling out "Mush!" to us like we were sled dogs. Wind gusted in my face. Despite all the layers of protective clothing I had on, I was still cold. I always wondered how those dogs did it without stopping for hot chocolate. But nothing was going to stop our expedition.

The island was about a mile from where we parked, but with all the slipping and stopping for silliness, the walk took about forty minutes. I shared the little background I knew about the island: the family that owned it lived too far away to visit often; other people apparently went there to hike or ride ATVs.

"I wonder how they get those out to the island," Kaden said. "Guess you need to bring everything heavy in the winter, before the ice melts."

I could see his brain at work. He was already making plans.

"We could do ice-fishing contests in the winter," he said. "And regular fishing contests in the summer."

He was still spinning up ideas when we finally reached the island.

"And campfires," he continued. "With s'mores, of course."

"Maybe we could have a kite-flying festival," one of his sisters added.

Even though there was little difference in height between the ice and the edge of the snow-covered ground, it felt like a big moment. I made my way up the slippery ledge until I stepped firmly onto the flat plateau of island. After a few steps, I stopped and looked over my shoulder. Kaden was right behind me, and behind him were our parents and his sisters.

"I wish I'd brought a flag to plant in the ground," I said. "To make it official."

"Don't get ahead of yourself," my dad said.

"But I know in my heart it's going to be Peacebunny Island."

I was already imagining coming back in the spring. My mind flooded with ideas. I pulled a small journal out of my pocket and began to write everything down, but I couldn't keep up with all my thoughts. I couldn't believe I was standing on this island. It wasn't on a computer screen or a map. It was real. I put my journal away and told myself to remember everything.

Everyone seemed to share my excitement. Kaden imagined doing science experiments and building things. His mom talked about the opportunity to teach kids about the environment. I surveyed the topography, looking from one end of the island to the other. The five-acre island seemed to be roughly equivalent to a Major League Baseball field. I trudged through the snow from tree to tree, trying to identify each kind. Ahead of us was a small peak.

"Perfect for a lighthouse," I said.

My dad nodded.

"It's big enough," Kaden said.

"What are you thinking, kiddo?" Kaden's mom asked me.

"I really like how the elevation changes in places," I said. "It's amazing. I can picture it in the spring even though I've never seen it. It's just so clear in my head."

As we continued to walk around the island, I was also able to visualize the summer ahead: building small forts, exploring, bringing volunteers for Bunny Bootcamps, and holding events through the fall.

"With so many people out on the lakes in the winter, maybe we could host a Christmas event with Santa—and bunnies in place of elves," I said.

The next day I shared my impressions of the island with several of the adults helping us navigate the paperwork and city laws. Then I emailed the owners. I told them it was perfect and I wanted to move forward with our deal. I tried hard to contain my excitement. Considering all the paperwork and daunting fundraising still ahead of us, it wasn't yet time to ask my mom to make a celebratory cheesecake, but I could already taste it.

Celebration of Life

It goes without saying that Noah and Markus knew all about the excitement brewing around the island. Unfortunately, they weren't able to see it themselves. Markus was having an especially difficult winter, and his parents were seriously considering relocating to Texas to be near a hospital that specialized in combination heart and lung transplants. They even began preparing their house to move if necessary.

Not being able to share the adventure in person with Noah and Markus made me double down on keeping them in the loop. Good news is never as good without best friends to share it with. Besides, providing them with descriptions of the way I imagined developing the island forced me to think through my ideas in even more detail.

As I sat in their bedroom, their dog, Champagne, seemed to listen attentively to every word we said. I imagined Captain Phil eavesdropping too.

Being good listeners made bunnies naturals at events where people were dealing with grief and sadness. This part of the program was new but had always been part of the larger vision. I'd wanted to use the rabbits to provide comfort ever since going to Sandy Hook. Although it wasn't a service we promoted, requests came by word of mouth following visits we made to senior centers and memory-care centers. It was as if people instinctively recognized bunnies' ability to listen, calm, console, and comfort.

One day we got a call from a local high school administrator who was hosting a tribute for two students who had died that week in a car accident. He wanted to provide bunnies along with grief counselors, and he asked if we could bring some rabbits. He didn't have any specific requests beyond that. As he explained, he'd heard about us and had a feeling the rabbits might help by being there.

A few days later we showed up at the high school. We positioned three bunnies on a table by the door to the auditorium, where people entered. A few people acknowledged the bunnies on their way in, giving back scratches and saying hello. But it was clear they were preparing themselves for an emotional day. When the doors opened again a couple of hours later, though, the reaction was different. Nearly everybody stopped to talk to the rabbits. They needed bunny time as they processed their grief.

A short time later, the bunnies were invited to another celebration of life, this time for a nine-year-old boy named Daniel. In a scene that was all too familiar, we watched parents, teachers, classmates, and friends file into the elementary school gym to honor this fourth grader who had drowned at a classmate's birthday party days before. The air was thick with grief at first, but soon there was a hint of peace and hope as the kids went between craft stations and visited with the bunnies. I remember thinking it was one of those moments when time stops and changes everything going forward.

Throughout the day, nearly all the kids came over to Tinkerbell, Andre the Giant, and Creampuff to share hugs and whispers and their sweet memories of Daniel. Their parents also lined up for bunny time of their own. After a long, thoughtful snuggle with Tinkerbell, one woman looked up with tears in her eyes. Suddenly, Andre hopped into her lap, delivering more bunny time.

"I've never held a rabbit in my life," she said. "It's like he knew I needed him and picked me."

"He probably did know," my mom said.

"And those precious white bunnies sleeping in the teacup just filled me up," she said, referring to some baby rabbits we'd brought. "I can't explain it."

She stroked Andre and gently blew the hair on his back.

"I guess Andre knew you needed a cuddle as much as the kids did," my mom said.

"He was right," she sniffled.

Once again, I was discovering that the things people need to hear most sometimes came from those with the softest voices. This was particularly evident during our visits to people in hospice. Spending time with hospice patients was a suggestion from one of the staff directors at a senior center. I talked it over with my parents, and we agreed it was something we had to do.

I was a little nervous when we made our first trip to a hospice center. I made sure to select our most patient and gentle rabbits. On the way to the center, I was quiet, wondering what the visit would be like. I'd never been around people who knew they were nearing the end of their lives. As my mom explained to me, some had a month or two or maybe longer. For others, it was a matter of days.

"Do they know?" I asked.

My mom nodded.

"Do they have many visitors?" I asked.

"Some do. Some don't."

"I can see why they'd want time with a comfort animal."

Inside, we were escorted to a floor that reminded me of a hospital. Most of the people were lying in bed. Some had private rooms; others shared a room separated by a curtain. A few were in wheelchairs. It was very quiet—maybe too quiet. About half acknowledged us either with a gentle wave or with their eyes. Some showed curiosity when they saw me pulling a wagon with bunnies in it. A few smiled.

I had eight bunnies with me—Oreo, a Jersey Wooly named Pers, and Whatchi among them. I left it up to the caregivers to decide if the timing was right for a visit. If they motioned to me, I wheeled a bunny next to the person's bed and stood nearby.

At first, I didn't know if the point of the visit was to make the patients more comfortable as they were dying or to remind them that they were still alive. I don't know that I ever figured out the answer or if it was even mine to know. What I did conclude, though, was that this time with the rabbits gave most people a time-out from pain, anxiety, and worry. For however long they had the bunny next to them, whether it was sixty seconds or ten minutes, they were able to run their fingers through its fur and receive tiny whisker kisses. Instead of lying in bed alone, they enjoyed pure affection. When time is limited, what more could anyone ask for than love?

Sometimes the visit seemed to be as much for their family members as for the ones in hospice care. I got to give a few hugs too.

After the visit, we went downstairs and gathered our cages and blankets by the nursing station. Before we left, I noticed several of the staffers saying hi to the rabbits, talking in baby voices as they came around the wagon to take turns petting the soft bunny fur. The rabbits seemed to know the staff needed a boost too. Our volunteer took Whatchi out of his carrier and put him on the head nurse's lap, where she'd draped one of our fleece blankets.

"Oh, my, how I needed a visit with a bunny today," she said.

"Somehow bunnies make every day better," I said.

Word spread. Without advertising or fanfare, people found us when they needed bunnies. The Peacebunnies enjoyed all the extra love and attention they received. One afternoon my parents were with a small team of volunteers at a local university where we brought bunnies set up to help students destress during finals week. As they wrapped up, a woman approached and asked if she could have a private word with someone in charge. She and my mom stepped to the side.

"I know this is going to sound kind of crazy," she said.

My mom put up her hand like a traffic cop.

"Stop right there," she said with a smile. "We've heard all types of crazy. No one is judging here."

"Got it." She laughed. "One of my closest friends is hosting a celebration of life for her baby next weekend. I talked to her on the phone just now, and we think it would be amazing to have your rabbits there."

Normally we are booked several months in advance, but that Saturday we had an opening. It was the end of the school year, and our only plan was to hang out as a family.

"Saturday would have been her first birthday," the woman added.

My mom didn't need to hear anything more. She reached out and gave the woman a long hug. "Of course we'll be there," she said.

That next weekend we met the host couple and learned they had held a family-only funeral when their daughter died. They kept it small, preferring to process their grief privately. My mom's eyes teared up as she listened. I don't know how she kept herself together. Now, about seven months later, they wanted to celebrate their daughter's life in a way that was memorable, special, and fun for their friends and family.

"We want it to be about laughter and love," they said. "It will help us all heal."

They transformed their yard into a carnival-like setting, with food, face painting, crafts, and games for the kids. We set up in the front yard so that the bunnies were the first and last thing everyone saw. The party activities were designed primarily with the kids in mind, but experience had taught us that the adults were likely the ones most in need of healing. And the bunnies seemed to meet everyone right where they were.

One moment captured the essence of what I believe the parents had hoped for. Near the end of the party, two little girls and a younger boy were in the pen with Fudge. The girls looked to be about five, and he was probably three. He leaned in and whispered something in Fudge's ear and then tilted his ear next to Fudge's mouth, awaiting an answer.

The sister asked what he said, and in a deep, overly serious voice, he replied, "The bunny said to give the boy another hot dog."

As the laughter spilled over the whole yard, everyone was reminded that the same God who gave us tears to express our grief also designed our bodies to laugh until our cheeks hurt.

Mission accomplished.

Rabbit Spit

By the beginning of spring, we were finally in a position to move forward. After months of talking about legalities and logistics, I had the green light to start using the lake island in the summer. I'd visited the island several more times since that first trip with Our Peoples, getting there most recently by canoe and slogging through glorious mud. Now the snow and ice were giving way to willows rising gracefully along the banks and trees that couldn't wait to burst to life. The ground was blanketed in soft, brown leaves left over from fall. I admired all of it and told myself that God's creation was indeed glorious.

That wasn't all that was making me feel good. Markus was spending more time at home than in the hospital, and that was reason enough to rejoice.

In March 2017, I redirected energy onto our Angoras and the opportunities for developing a business around them. To learn more, my family took Amelia Earhart and Quiet Wyatt to the national Angora competition in Amana, Iowa. We got there late Friday night, and I rolled out of bed the next morning with the speed of molasses on a cold day. I had to inhale breakfast in order to get to the competition on time.

We went to observe and gather information from other breeders. We also entered Amelia and Wyatt in the junior division competition. As long as we were there, why not?

Amelia and Wyatt had their nails trimmed before we left home, and they spent the morning licking each other's fur through the walls of the pen—their way of primping—while I slept. I thought they had done a pretty good job touching each other up. They looked stunning as we wheeled them into the nearby event center.

That's when I got a crash course in a whole other level of perfection. As we passed through the doors, we entered a parallel universe of extreme rabbit beauty and grooming. It was like we'd worn polos and slacks to the Academy Awards. People had their Angoras on pedestals that reminded us of lazy Susan spinners or pottery wheels, slowly turning while the owners brushed and blew out the rabbits' fur with large commercial hair dryers until they resembled giant cotton puffs.

"Wow," I said, my eyes bulging in disbelief as I looked around the convention. I was not trained as an elite judge, but I could easily spot some rabbits that stood out from the rest, like a brown French rabbit that looked like a book photo come to life.

"Is there any hair out of place?" my mom said, laughing at her play on words.

I could only stare and admire the extreme grooming on display. "These rabbits are amazing," I said.

After placing Amelia and Wyatt in their spots, we walked past all the cages. It was like a gathering of supermodels. Most of the owners were still busy beautifying their bunnies. Everyone seemed to know each other and shared an earned respect. We were disappointed to learn that Betty Chu, the unrivaled queen of Angora breeders, wasn't there. A former professor from northern California, she had raised Angoras for three decades, won more than fifty top prizes, and raised the Guinness World Record holder for the longest rabbit's hair—more than fourteen inches. I would have liked to meet her.

For all the attention to detail going on around us, people were still surprisingly welcoming and open. They wanted to show off their hard work and all the love they'd poured into their rabbits. At one point my parents and I traded looks that clearly asked whether we belonged there, whether our rabbits belonged there.

We had only one encounter with major snarkiness. It occurred after Wyatt scored a surprise win for best wool. My rabbit was not the best looking at this competition, but apparently the judges fell in love with his fur. And in the world of Angora rabbits, being awarded best hair is something to envy. And at the end of the day, this would drive up the price of my Angora fiber considerably.

One of the participant's moms eagerly approached me and asked what hair products I used on Wyatt's fur. She looked at Amelia and said, "Her, too. Tell me, what do you use?"

"Rabbit spit," I said, thinking back to the way Amelia and Wyatt had licked each other all morning.

I was still utterly shocked by Wyatt's blue ribbon, so I might have sounded too glib or casual. But I was being honest.

Still, the woman appeared to be offended by my response. She glared at my mother.

"Fine if you don't want to tell me," she said. "But you don't have to be snotty about it."

"I don't use any products. They just live in colonies and clean each other," I tried to clarify.

She had no idea we were new at this game, and she had no more patience for our Cinderella story.

"Rabbit spit, I'm sure," she said, and walked away.

The Unbirthday Party

Once back home, I spent the next couple of weeks finalizing my application for the MN Cup entrepreneur competition.

I'd learned about the competition several years earlier when I attended STEM camp through Junior Achievement. I entered it for the first time with my STEMbunnies project, but I didn't make it past the first round. That was fine with me. For my first time, it really was more about learning than trying to win (although the significant cash prize awarded to the winner and two semifinalists in each division would have been incredible).

The competition was run through the University of Minnesota's Carlson School of Management and provided winning entrepreneurs from across the state with exposure to funding, coaching, mentorship, connections, encouragement, and seed capital. There were several divisions and categories, including the one I entered for entrepreneurs under eighteen years old.

For this second effort at winning the MN Cup prize money, I pitched my Angora business under the banner Peacebunny Island, Inc. My application included a write-up of my idea, the business plan, the market, and the way I saw the business progressing. It also included a picture of my trusted business associate, Whatchamacallit.

The semifinalists wouldn't be announced until late summer. Depending on how I fared then, the finals—an in-depth pitch in front of a panel of judges—would be held in the fall. In the meantime, we moved into our increasingly busy Easter season. It seemed like only the other day we'd been battling months of cold winter storms and frigid temperatures. Now I wore shorts any day the temperature got above fifty, and the rabbits—Pax, Little John, Bluedini, Wyatt, and company—were out and about in the new spring grasses, nibbling on plantains, basking in the sun, and chasing after the sweet scents of violets and petunias.

As we got closer to Easter, I wanted to tell our volunteers about the island. But we were so busy with events that there just wasn't time. Even as negotiations narrowed and we began discussing a signing date, the island remained a relative secret. I was bursting to share the good news with the people who regularly donated their time at our events. I didn't want any of them hearing about it secondhand or reading about it on the Peacebunny blog without first hearing the news directly from me.

"I don't know when to tell everyone," I said. "Or how. Do I call everyone? Do I send a mass email?"

"How about making an announcement at our Unbirthday Party?" my mom suggested.

"Genius," I said.

Our Unbirthday Party was an annual celebration we threw after Easter to say thank you to all our volunteers. This year's party was at Wood Lake, a big step up from our backyard. We started throwing this Unbirthday Party in the earliest days of our bunny events. As the number of events grew, so did the number of volunteers, and so did the party.

To get things going, I flung open the metal gate and shouted, "Welcome, everybunny! Let the hoppiness begin!" Little John helped me greet people. Dressed in a tiny silk hat and bow tie that I'd taken off a stuffed animal, he hopped along a big table covered with a multicolored blanket and lapped up all the hugs he could get. Spying familiar faces, people traded hugs with each other, caught up, and introduced their families. They ate, laughed, and told stories. I took a moment to soak it in.

This was what Peacebunnies was all about. Friendships, joy, the opportunity to serve, and the sweetness of the bunnies. Oh, and lots and lots of food to share. Finally, just before cake, I decided it was time to get everyone's attention and make my announcement. I tried to paint a picture of what I saw in my head.

"I see this as a sanctuary for training kinderbunnies and rescues to become comfort rabbits, a place where kids make a difference, and an island known far and wide for manufacturing kindness," I said.

"What do you need from us?" one of the volunteer dads asked. "Our family would love to help out."

"I want to go to the island!" a little girl nicknamed Bubbles chimed in.

We finished the party with everyone blowing out candles to celebrate our Unbirthdays. It was truly a day to celebrate where we'd been and where we were going.

Nothing Personal?

A few days after I posted about the island on the website, I learned we had a serious problem. Up until that point, we'd had a warm and open business relationship with the island's owners and their lawyer. They said they admired me for being unafraid to pursue a big dream. Our most recent face-to-face meeting had culminated with a formal handshake photo. As a final step, my team was drafting a lease with an option-to-buy purchase agreement.

All was proceeding according to plan until the owner's representative called to inform us that the family had decided to go a different direction. Over speakerphone, I heard the sentence start with "I'm sorry" and end with "No offense, it's just business." I could barely process what I was hearing. My heart broke.

I had never heard anything as deafening as the click of the phone as that call ended. I turned toward my parents and shook my head.

"What just happened?" I said. "Is that the only explanation they gave? They changed their mind? Is our deal really over?"

My parents were equally stunned and confused.

Upset at myself and everything about the situation, I went from one disappointing thought to another. My brain played a loop of discouraging chatter. *You're just a kid. As if this dream was ever going to work out! Why did you ever think you could pull off something like this? No one ever thought it was a good idea; they just didn't want to hurt your feelings. What a cosmic waste of time. Just give up. It's too much. It will never work.*

Much later, we learned the owners decided to build a house with a lakefront-access point. I recognized that it made financial sense for them to make a quick profit rather than lease their island to a kid heading up a fledgling educational nonprofit and that it was their property to sell or not sell until the paper was signed.

However, that didn't mean it wasn't crushing to have my happily-ever-after snatched away. Having come so close, I couldn't begin to imagine getting another opportunity like this. Did I even want to try? How do you grieve the death of a dream?

The bunnies helped. But I had to figure out some things on my own. Like how to tell everyone.

Grandpa and Grandma Smith asked what I was going to say to the other kids. "I have no idea," I told them.

When Thursday night rolled around, I dreaded going to eat dinner with Our Peoples. I felt like I was letting them down. I also knew it was going to hurt to say it out loud.

And it did. "It's not going to be our island." I looked up and down the table and then looked down at my spaghetti dinner. It was a mound of mush, just like my dream.

"What happened?" Kaden asked.

"I thought we were close," I said. "Then they called and said they were going another direction."

Kaden's mom was quick with a hug for me and for her girls—one of whom had slid off her chair and crawled under the table.

Kaden tried to understand. "So all the island plans were for nothing? Is the dream on hold? Or is it all done?"

"Good questions," I replied.

At least school was almost over. Stuck in the quicksand of disappointment, I found it hard to think about anything else. Summer would create a fresh start. Time to regroup, play with rabbits, spend more time with Noah and Markus, and do what I did best: be a kid. Several of the members from the Rotary club helped give me some perspective.

"Caleb, this is only your first major setback," one said. "And sadly, I can guarantee it's not your last, because the only way you won't have another disappointment is to quit."

"It's a gift," another member said. "The gift is that now you get to find out if you were in love with the idea or committed to making it a reality."

"But they liked me," I said.

"I'm sure they did," he said. "But you have to learn to separate your ideas and outcomes from your identity. It is personal. But it's not *personal*."

Later that weekend my great-grandmother reinforced what all four of my grandparents and my parents had shared in some fashion, yet somehow this time the words finally hit home. "Some closed doors are a blessing," she said.

It didn't feel like it. For my own sake, I took one last trip to the island. I needed to say goodbye to the dream in person. Somehow as I walked along the lakefront, I got a sense of peace. Maybe we were being protected from something that wasn't right for us, or maybe there was something better in the future. I received what I'd prayed for, even though it wasn't the answer I was expecting. I was still sad, but I chose to believe that God wouldn't close a door without opening another one.

Later that night, I went into my bedroom and sat on the floor next to my bed, thinking in the dark. After a few minutes, I noticed two little eyes looking up at me. It was Paxton. He had hopped in from the living room and sat down beside me. He wasn't there to offer comfort and understanding as my rabbits had done so many times before. Nope, I knew those looks. This one was asking, "Okay, what now?"

Replanting Hope

This setback led me to add a new catchphrase to my business dealings: fail quickly. It seemed counterintuitive at first, but if things were going to fall apart, I didn't want to waste any more time, energy, and resources than I needed to. I wanted to learn what I could from the experience and then be ready for whatever came next.

I was thinking about closed doors as my mom chauffeured me and several rabbits to a residential therapy facility for boys about forty-five minutes north of her office. From what I'd heard, it was a specialized juvenile detention center. We arrived after dark and had trouble finding the entrance. Once inside, we immediately became disoriented because the campus was so large and the buildings were unlabeled and separated by long roads. On top of that, all the doors we tried were locked. Our frustration was growing.

The directions said we should go to the yellow building. Because everything was so dark, we couldn't figure out which one was yellow.

We didn't want to be late or miss appointments, and the stress was squeezing all the joy out of the trip. We finally found someone—a therapist who explained he was just "going off the clock" confirmed we were in the right place and told us to wait in the lobby. I tried reading a magazine.

After thirty minutes, he passed through again and said everything was delayed because of an incident. A few minutes later, we were shown to another building and told to expect five participants. *All this effort for five kids?* That began an inner conversation about how many people were enough to justify hosting a program.

I was tired, it was a school night, we had a long drive, I was going to get home super late, my mom needed to go to work in the morning . . . was this really worth it?

Then I heard a crowd of teen voices, the rising sounds of excitement. I looked out the window and saw not five but fifteen guys and their staff walking toward the building. My heart raced. Suddenly I felt nervous. *What will they be like? Why were they sent here?* Yet it was now too late for such concerns. As they filed into the room, I was swept up in their energy and anticipation. They didn't know what to expect, just like I didn't, but now the vibe was completely upbeat, and we were all expecting good things. After we moved some chairs and cleared space, they helped set up the pens. Then it was time to introduce them to the bucks I'd brought: Little John, Sherwood, and Fudge.

It was friendship at first sight. They asked tons of questions and were respectful to all the guests, regardless of how many legs each of us had.

"This one is so huge! Is that one the dad?"

"Nope. That's just his breed, like some people are taller or bigger than others," I replied. "And Fudge is actually pretty muscular. Feel him right here. He's buff, right?"

"So they aren't related?" another asked.

"Technically, no. But they all live together and act like brothers. I guess it depends on how you look at it."

Two of the guys were clearly afraid of the animals; neither of them knew what it was like to have a pet in their home. Another guy had never even *touched* an animal with fur. That completely shocked me. Even before our rabbits, I'd had plenty of animal interactions: we regularly visited the nature center and attended plenty of animal programs at the zoo. It stretched me to think about how I'd ended up where I was. Was it Providence, privilege, or simple luck? I had no idea. I started to explain about what I did know.

"Domestic pet rabbits live about ten years," I said and began with the questions I usually asked during our programs. "How old will you guys be in ten years?"

"I'm sixteen now," one guy said as his arm shot up. "So I'll be twenty-six." I tried not to stare at the long bandages along his wrists and forearms.

"I'll be twenty-four," another guy said as he poked the guy next to him.

"Think about the next ten years," I continued. "At twenty-two, maybe you could be graduating from college or already working full-time. At twenty-four, maybe you'll be getting an apartment or starting a family."

There were some nervous snickers. But I clearly had their attention.

I addressed the first guy. "That means if you started caring for a pet rabbit tonight, picture when you're twenty-six and you have roommates in your apartment or you're buying your first home. Chances are you'd still have a rabbit. That's why when people get a rabbit, I tell them to think about the next ten years. You need a plan—a plan for taking care of the rabbit and a plan for taking care of yourself and your family, if you have one."

Normally people are challenged when I ask them to think about a ten-year plan, but this time the conversation had more weight to it. I encouraged the guys to think big, dream big. What was next for them? What would they like to do? What would they do if they knew they couldn't fail? One guy asked me the same thing, and I told them about the island.

"The deal just fell apart, and I was—and still am—disappointed," I said.

Another hand shot up. "So how old do you need to be to volunteer for Peacebunny Island?"

"Yeah, I want to go there," another guy piped in.

Soon there was a buzz of animated chatter. I had no idea how their program worked, how long they had to spend in there, or what happened to them next. It was immaterial, I suppose. In some form, they were envisioning Peacebunny Island, even if each person's vision didn't look the same as another guy's, or mine. Those guys reinforced that even if they never got to go, the world would be better just because a place like the island existed. Together they shared a moment of hope, and they recharged mine.

My mom and I briefly explained how our volunteer program worked and challenged them to think about what their personal mission was. The bunnies had found their calling, and I was really starting to find mine. Then a staff member indicated that the guys needed to head back to their rooms.

"Hope to see you again, Fudge."

"Later, Little John. Be cool. You're all right, bro."

"Don't give up on that castaway bunny island idea," one guy said, flicking his head to move his long hair away from his dark, sunken eyes. "Maybe I'll apply someday when I get out."

After they filtered out, I noticed how quiet the room was. My mom and I folded down the pens and began taking the rabbits to the car. I looked at the time on the car dashboard, and it was late. It had been a weird night, a different kind of night. Nothing like I'd expected. But the bunnies weren't surprised. For an hour, they brought everyone together, slowed time, provided comfort, and sparked joy. Later, as I drifted off to sleep on the way home, I thought about the wide range of emotions I had seen in the boys' eyes. Exhaustion. Loneliness. Frustration. Defeat. And . . . hope.

And some of that hope had rubbed off on me.

9

Wait a Minute!

Summer flew by, and before I knew it, it was time to start middle school. In order to help my parents with their new work schedules, and also to prevent me from coming home to an empty house in the afternoons, I changed school districts and spent several weeknights with my dad's parents so I could take the bus from their house. Like with any change, it took a while for all of us to adapt, but it came with a big perk: it meant lots more grandparent time. Mom and Dad picked me up before dinner, and we spent evenings together even if we didn't sleep at the same house every night.

Our other routines stayed pretty much the same. One Thursday night after visiting late with Our Peoples, I slept at home rather than at my grandparents' house. When I woke up, I just couldn't get my body to move. It was as if my eyes were taped shut and forty-pound feed bags were attached to my legs. My mom tried to hustle me along so she could drop me off at the bus stop and cut some time off the commute to her office.

"Come on, Caleb," she prodded. "Every five-minute delay adds fifteen minutes to my drive."

"Got it," I said, wiping sleep from my eyes. "I just need to figure out how to put on my socks and find my shoes."

By the time I made it to the car, my mom was waiting for me with the engine running. She knew all the side roads that would get us to school quicker than the standard route. I stared out the window at the passing scenery, letting my morning eyes and brain sync.

The homes we passed were all familiar to me, including the five-acre farm behind the white picket fence along the roundabout. It was the last remnant of a dairy farm that had once stretched for acres in all directions. Every time we passed it, I looked at the three-story white barn and fantasized about how much easier our life would be if we kept our rabbits there instead of the farm in Hastings, which was forty-five minutes in the opposite direction.

If I had ever seen a vehicle parked in front of this old dairy farm, or any other sign of life, I would have asked my mom to stop so I could inquire about the possibility of using the farm for the rabbits. Unfortunately, not once in the months of driving past did we ever see a car, truck, or person on the property. We never even saw a light on inside the house.

Several times, acting on a whim, we stopped to leave notes in the screen door, but no one ever responded. I even found the name of the owners online and wrote them a letter, but I never heard anything in return. Still, the front yard somehow remained well tended even if the pasture needed some help.

Then on that Friday morning, as we reached the roundabout, I glanced at the farm and spotted a car in the driveway.

"Wait a minute!" I exclaimed. "There's a car."

My mom skipped the right-hand turn she normally made and circled back around, driving back past the property and down the gravel road. Curiously, we eyed the massive white barn with the silver weather vanes on top, abutted by two silos, and pulled up the driveway, where, sure enough, there was a car. We parked behind it. An older gentleman greeted us with a kind smile. We walked up, waving and smiling, eager to make friends.

I had already leased two farms and had plenty of business meetings under my belt. I was always ready to give my quick pitch about the bunnies, and I made it, crisply and concisely. I was sure I'd nailed it, and judging from the man's expression, I thought I'd connected with him.

"You're looking for a place for your rabbits to live between events?" he asked.

"Yep," I said.

"Well, that sounds great." He took off his hat and ran his fingers through his hair. "I'm just sorry to let you know I sold the farm yesterday."

I felt the air rush out of my lungs.

"To my brother," he added quickly. "His daughter is an animal lover. You should call her. Here, let me give you her number."

Farm Lady Yeah!

I spent much of the day at school thinking about playing in that giant pasture with Noah, Markus, and Our Peoples, and my head was swirling with thoughts about the potential new farm when my dad picked me up from the bus stop and drove me home. I tossed my backpack by the door and headed into the kitchen to see what Mom was cooking for dinner. Pax was waiting for me in the hallway, and I couldn't wait to tell him about the farm.

But first, something to drink. I opened the refrigerator and looked over at my mom, who was stirring a pot of cheesy tortellini while talking to someone on the phone. She switched to speakerphone. At first, I assumed the woman on the other end was someone who had a bunny their family wished to donate. In our house, that was a safe bet anytime the phone rang. But I quickly realized the call was about me and the farm, and my mom introduced me to the person on the other end.

"Caleb, this is the woman whose family owns the farm we stopped at this morning."

I looked at my mom with wide eyes. *Really?*

She nodded toward the phone with big eyes that made me focus in right away.

"Hi, nice to talk to you," I said. "I just got home from school. But I really want to speak to you about your farm. I have an idea."

For the next couple of minutes, I gave one of the most important pitches of my burgeoning business career. At the end, I suggested we meet in person, explaining that face-to-face was always better. She agreed and said, "I can meet you tomorrow at the farm at 5:00 p.m. Will that work?"

I looked at my parents.

"Will it work?" I asked politely with my folded hands under my chin, mouthing, *Please, please, please.*

I got the nod from them, and my mom leaned toward the phone. "We'll see you then," she said.

Amazing! After two years of dreaming, it seemed like it might actually happen. The bunnies might move to that farm. I told Paxton that his children and grandchildren and great-grandchildren, as well as their cousins, friends, and furry neighbors might have a brand-new home. That is, if I could get my own act together. When I stopped to enter the woman's name in the contact list of our family cell phone, I forgot what it was. It had all happened so suddenly that I hadn't written it down. So I entered her name as Farm Lady Yeah! (complete with the exclamation point).

I woke up the next morning feeling blessed and in awe of this turn of events. A few weeks earlier, I had been devastated after losing the island. Now my spirits were soaring. Still, I reserved some of my enthusiasm to cushion potential disappointment. I knew that people sometimes offered more than they intended to give. They also changed their minds. I stroked Paxton's ears and thought of my prayers the previous evening when I had asked God to close the doors quickly if this wasn't where the Peacebunnies should be housed.

But . . . how cool would it be?

I spent the day watching the clock and thinking about the progression of our farms. At the first one, the small barn served as a perfect home for my newly expanding crew of bunnies. The goats, sheep, and pastureland helped me discover if I was cut out for farming, and Farmer Chris was a patient instructor. And I would treasure the memories I made there with Noah and Markus for the rest of my life.

Our current farm in Hastings was a working lesson in biodiversity. We saw how chickens, bees, and pick-your-own berries complemented each other. With its organic orchard, lush grasses, and leftover veggies, it was a gorgeous and welcoming home for the rabbits. We test-hosted some events there too. In this fertile paradise, the Peacebunnies had grown and multiplied, and we had a safe, comfortable shelter for our new rescues. If only it weren't so far away.

On the relatively short drive to the farm in Savage, I considered the potential for this new place with the white picket fence. The farmhouse, which I'd already started calling the cottage, had a warm, welcoming feel, and with its proximity to the Twin Cities, the site had the potential for attracting more volunteers. The pasture was gorgeous; I pictured hosting events there. I realized I was grinning as I imagined Paxton exploring the farm, sitting in the sunshine and retiring to the barn as if he were king of the castle.

I heard gravel under the car tires and realized we'd turned into the road that went to the back entrance to the farm. When I looked out the window, I saw the long row of trees, the barn with its weather vane glistening in the late-afternoon sun, and the two silos.

"I can't believe we're already here," I said. "It's so close."

Then we waited. Our five o'clock meeting time came and went. I compared the clock on the car dashboard to our cell phone a thousand times. Each minute ticked by slowly. I'd waited all day for five o'clock to arrive so I could meet Farm Lady Yeah! in person, and she wasn't anywhere to be seen. Still, I decided to be optimistic, no matter what.

I wondered if we should call or just wait. Five thirty. Five forty.

Forty minutes late.

My heart began to sink. Had we misunderstood?

Snickers Would Have Loved It Here

Ten more minutes passed before I heard the distinctive sound of tires rolling over gravel. A car pulled up and a woman got out, waved, and hurried over to us.

"I'm so sorry," she said. "I ran very late at work and got here as fast as possible. I'm so glad you're still here."

She led us inside the two-story white farmhouse, and we sat down in the living room. My heart was pounding. I had spent all day thinking about the story I wanted to tell her and rehearsing it in my head, starting with Snickers and including my recent MN Cup entry. I would conclude with my dream of someday acquiring an island where hope and kindness would flourish while I raised and trained bunnies as comfort animals.

I planned to explain how this farm would be the rabbits' home—really, the home base between trips to Peacebunny Island, wherever that might be. This would be Peacebunny Cottage.

But I never got that far. After only a few minutes of getting to know each other, a cursory mention of our STEMbunnies program, and some of the ways Whatchi, Oreo, Taffy, and the others had touched people's lives, she smiled and put both her hands in front of her as if to stop me from saying anything more.

"I know enough to make a decision," she said, pulling an envelope from her purse. "I want to give you the keys."

The keys to the farm?

It sounded too good to be true. Only it *was* true. She was an animal lover who told us about the four-legged friends she'd cared for on her family's farm while growing up and her fond memories of visiting her aunt and uncle at this farm. She now ran a demanding business and lived on the far northwest side of Minneapolis, which was going to make it difficult for her family to maintain the property while her dad figured out their long-term plans.

"I'm thrilled you'll be able to watch over the farm, take care of it, and prevent squatters or vandalism," she said. "I'd also like to learn more about your educational and comfort programs, but right now I need to go home to my family. I'm so sorry to cut our first meeting short. My whole schedule is off."

She handed the envelope with the keys to me. All of us stood up.

"I'd like to begin moving in tomorrow, after church," I said.

"Everything about this makes me so happy." She smiled. "This is such an absolutely perfect match for both of us."

After she left, we stayed behind to look around. No part of me wanted to leave. I was in the middle of an out-of-body, out-of-mind experience, as if my spirit were floating above the lush grass. I needed a little walkabout to convince myself that I wasn't dreaming up this whole thing. Just outside the front door, I spotted a large lilac bush that was trying to decide whether it should flower or wait for the air to warm up. I pointed it out to my parents.

"Snickers would have loved it here," I declared.

The long row of pine trees formed a windbreak in front of me. I could see myself running around with Noah and my other friends. Stickball games would be mandatory. There was so much room to play and set up tents and let the bunnies out to munch and dig. There was also so much work to be done.

I ran from building to building, shuffling the large clump of keys and matching them to locks. I flipped on light switches and slid open doors and drawers, each new room and structure more exciting than the next. My mom took pictures of the exterior and insides, and my dad looked around carefully, surveying spaces and offering his thoughts on the place, while I mentally sketched a basic plan for where to put the rabbits.

I still couldn't believe how quickly everything had come together. The former owners were snowbirds living in Florida, which was why we never saw their car. They had only returned for the week to sign the paperwork necessary for the sale to his brother. How was it that we happened by at the exact time the owner was there? Or that Farm Lady Yeah! insisted that she wouldn't accept rent or utility payments? And did I mention all the friends who said they'd help with the move?

God is good.

The Crew

The transition was smooth, and the bunnies breathed new life into the long-dormant dairy farm. Peacebunny Cottage was up and running.

I was grateful for all the help and proud of what we'd accomplished. There were families carrying rabbit pens, cleaning cages, and running around the pasture with the bunnies. My uncle Kris drove up from Missouri and spent two weeks helping us with electrical work and constructing model pens that others could make using his design instructions. As time went on, volunteers created tables and play areas for the rabbits, built shelves for the barn, planted a vegetable garden, donated vehicles, and cleaned and cared for the animals. Vet techs like Barb did nail trims and well checks, and Farmer Todd helped ensure we got quality bales of straw each season.

To prepare for increasing chores, we had amassed an assortment of power tools and heavy machinery, including a tractor and a front loader purchased by Dr. Bonnie and her husband. How had everything come together? How had it grown from three rabbits into all of this?

I began to formulate a theory—the open-heart theory. Our programs helped people celebrate special occasions. They helped people connect a passion for animals with a very basic human need to care for others. Our programs served people who were hurting and lonely, sick and grieving. I saw that people of all ages and backgrounds, including our volunteers, were standing in some level of dirt and mud, and somehow the bunnies helped them rise to a better place rather than sinking deeper.

But for the rabbits to do their job, they needed humans to help provide food and water, clean their cages, provide wellness checks, drive them to events, unload shipments of hay and forty-pound bags of rabbit pellets, help spread the word, and so on. In other words, people needed to open their hearts to the bunnies. In the process, the bunnies worked their magic. They got people to open their hearts to each other—to friends, family, and even strangers. With open hearts, all of us turned into Peacebunnies. It was just my theory. But it seemed to work.

I hosted a weekend campout for my scout patrol at the farm and connected with Jacob, who was becoming one of my closest friends. We had been in the same troop for a few years, but our friendship deepened when he started to understand what I did away from scouts. He took an interest in the rabbits and the farm itself, particularly the tools. After the campout, he and his family attended a Bunny Bootcamp and volunteered at several events, though I joked that he did all that in order to use the power tools and the power washer outside the barn.

Late that spring, the two of us finished off our welding and metal-working merit badges together, skills that would come in handy at the farm. We also gained Nic, our scout troop's senior patrol leader, who began volunteering at events and sometimes brought his sister, Maggie. And we added *seven* new Flemish Giants, courtesy of Aunt Bonnie, the teacher with a PhD who fostered Andre the Giant and was excited about having large bunnies in more classrooms. She rescued them from someone who was ready to put them in the meat locker if they didn't get rehomed that weekend.

"I'm sorry to do this to you," she said, laughing. "But I needed to get them out of there. So I just scooped them up and brought them here."

"Welcome to Peacebunny Cottage," I announced in a way that my dad said sounded a bit like Mr. Roarke on the old TV series *Fantasy Island*.

Dr. Bonnie cautioned that all the rabbits seemed friendly except one, a regal blue doe. I greeted her, and sure enough, she tried to bite me. As Dr. Bonnie set her down, the doe gave an emphatic, annoyed thump with her back legs. She turned slightly sideways to see me better. I got the message. To say she needed a little more time to warm up to me was the understatement of the year. She raised one eye, looking down her nose at me in a taunting way that said, "You want a piece of me?"

I tried again to pick her up, and she promptly chomped down hard on my arm and almost took a piece out of it. "That's it, you win," I said, putting her down. "You're just too feisty. I'll check back in tomorrow."

Her bite left a welt that lasted nearly two weeks, which was how long it took to convince her that it was safe when I came with her food. Despite my open heart, I had to give her the space she needed until she could trust me and open her own heart. It was a profound lesson in safety and in life.

Do Not Touch!

I couldn't have scripted the end of summer better. In early August, I was notified that I was one of ten youth companies chosen as semifinalists for the MN Cup entrepreneur competition. After volunteers filmed drone footage of the bunnies, I submitted a one-minute video and a fifteen-slide presentation. At the end of the month, we celebrated our selection as one of three finalists. The next step was to put the finishing touches on my business plan and prepare a twelve-minute pitch I would give in front of a panel of judges in mid-September.

But first things first. It was Minnesota State Fair time!

I had a bunch of rabbits on display in the sheep/poultry building. Several of my rabbits, most notably my Angoras, were defending champions. Jacob and Kaden both came to help for a few shifts, and we all enjoyed the chocolate milk booth a little too much.

On one of the last days of the fair, I was taking a breather with Jacob. It was late afternoon, and we were regrouping after a long day when I caught sight of a crew of six guys heading into our area.

They looked to be in their late teens or early twenties. They stood out, since by that point the crowd had begun to dwindle and go in search of anything fried and on a stick.

"Check these guys out," I said.

They were clearly having fun, in a loud and obnoxious way. They stooped for closer looks at the different rabbits, mispronouncing the breeds and making fun of their names. A couple of them posed for selfies with the Angoras. When they started looking at the row of Flemish Giants, I had a feeling something was about to happen.

"Wait for it." I gave Jacob a nudge.

"Look at that massive rabbit," one of them enthused. "Man, that's bigger than your dog!" He read the card I'd made for the front of the cage. "The name is Feisty." He chuckled. "Guys, come here. Check out this *huge* rabbit."

"What's it say on the card?" another guy said.

"'Do not touch. My name is Feisty. I have earned my name. Please be kind and leave me alone, and I will leave you alone too. When I bite, I don't let go. I also scratch. You are warned. Wash your wound well. Help yourself to bandages in the box next to my cage."

They inched closer.

"Feisty! What an awesome name. Come here, Feisty."

"It says not to stick your fingers in the cage."

"Oooh, I'm scared," he said in a mocking tone. "Come on. It's just a rabbit."

"Maybe like the Monty Python rabbit."

"Okay, what'll you give me to stick my fingers in the cage?"

"I'll buy you a bucket of cookies."

Then came a chorus of cheers and encouragement. "Do it! Do it!"

He stuck his fingers in the cage.

"Come here, bunny bunny . . . Hey, girl . . . You don't look so tough . . ."

Chomp!

[Expletive deleted.]

[More expletives deleted.]

"Toss me that Band-Aid box!"

I couldn't believe those guys ignored all the warnings. I guess sometimes people just don't pay attention to the signs.

As soon as the fair ended, I worked hard to prepare for the MN Cup finals later in September. Except for school and chores, I did practically nothing for two weeks except rehearse my presentation and prepare for the eighteen minutes of questions that would follow. On the day of the finals, I felt confident and ready.

The two other youth finalists—an organic baker and a headphone designer—both had multiple people on their teams. But even though mine was a solo project, I wasn't exactly going onstage alone. I had Whatchi and Wyatt next to me in a wagon, so I'm not sure who had the advantage. I was also wearing a pretty sharp suit, with a perfectly tied tie—a new skill I'd perfected the night before.

"How are you feeling?" my parents asked before it was my turn.

"Ready," I said. "Nervous."

"Butterflies?" my mom asked.

"Yeah," I said. "But they're a reminder that great ideas are coming out of their cocoon."

The Rare Hare-Brained Idea

I didn't win the grand prize. I'd be lying if I said I wasn't disappointed—after all, I didn't enter the contest to lose.

But I counted plenty of consolations that still made me feel like a winner. The event allowed me to continue honing my networking skills. I became adept at carrying on conversations while balancing a plate of food *and* a drink. I got feedback from business professionals. I gained confidence. And as runner-up, I received a good-sized check and another cash prize for winning the People's Choice Award for best pitch.

Whatchi and Wyatt were outstanding in their roles as rabbits, helping investors understand the demand for Angora wool—and that this was the rare hare-brained idea that worked.

"What a journey!" I wrote in my journal. "Special thanks to Dad for pitching in more at the farm and to Mom for helping me with the business side this summer. We did it!"

Later that fall, readers of the *Minnesota Business* magazine voted STEMbunnies/Peacebunny Island "most likely to succeed" in the educational category of their annual poll on local businesses. I won other business pitch contests too. The reception that followed gave me an excuse to quip, "Knowing how to tie a tie is a horrible skill to waste."

I spent the next few months focused on school, planning our calendar of events, and dealing with fosters and parties—what Grandma Smith called "going with the flow." The checks I'd won sat on my bookshelf in the exact place I'd put them when I brought them home. I hadn't even opened a separate bank account for Peacebunny Island yet. Occasionally, a relative or a friend asked what I was going to do with the money. I didn't know for sure yet.

I had ideas but not a specific plan. I could try to ramp up the Angora business or focus on the STEM program and therapy rabbits. I could try to build the Peacebunny Island brand and sell branded merchandise. I could become more active on social media and try to attract sponsors. Or I could save for college, invest in the stock market, or put it aside for a car, which I might want in a few years when I was old enough to drive.

I chose none of the above.

The money sat on the shelf while I put my time and energy into finding a real-life island—the future Peacebunny Island. I thought an island would be the best investment and the best opportunity to make the bunny programs sustainable. My advisers all agreed.

Talk about hare-brained ideas.

If I Had a Houseboat

One of the realities of Minnesota winters is that large amounts of snow falls, and on some very rare but special days, there is so much snow that everything stops, including school.

I can't imagine a kid anywhere in the Twin Cities who doesn't pray for the occasional snow day. Adults probably do too. For me, a snow day meant sleeping late, hanging out in my pajamas, and playing with the rabbits instead of sitting in a classroom. Unfortunately, the heavy snowfalls that particular winter all happened over weekends. So no snow days.

I mention this as a way of lodging a weather complaint. I hate to get snowed in on Saturdays and Sundays and need to cancel or reschedule bunny events and do farm chores without any helpers. But if it weren't for a really serious snowstorm in January 2018, things might have worked out very differently.

It was a Saturday, and one of the first days in a long while when I had nothing to do, thanks to the paralyzing effects of the storm. So I decided to reengage with my search for an island. I got my notebook and some hot chocolate, and I sat down in front of the computer.

All the island-related websites I'd found before the Great Disappointment of 2017 were still bookmarked. I'd just been ignoring them. Launching another search felt like emotionally risky territory. But Grandma Deer had reminded me that risk is the building block for any success.

I searched for hours and saw a handful of islands but nothing close enough to pursue. I went to Google Earth and zoomed in on lakes in and around the Twin Cities. I had a sense of déjà vu but with a bunch more insight. There were twenty-two lakes in Minneapolis alone. Many of them were home to islands, though I knew from experience that figuring out whether they were government owned or private was a longer, more involved process than window-shopping on the internet.

Still, over the next few weeks, I created a spreadsheet of all the islands that seemed like they might have even a sliver of potential. At this point, the bar was not that high. All I was looking for was land surrounded by water. If that criteria was met, I looked up the owners and sent them a handwritten letter introducing myself and what I was hoping to do.

Hi, I'm Caleb and I'm thirteen years old. I have permission from my parents to reach out to you and ask about renting your island for the summer. I'd like to set up a time to tell you more about how we would use it for training comfort rabbits. Feel free to contact me or my parents at the number or email below.

Kind regards,
Caleb Smith, bunny guardian

I figured everyone likes the personal touch of a real, handwritten letter. I wasn't worried about the cost of these islands—not yet. Having been through this before, I knew there were so many other factors beyond financing that would determine an island's viability. Was there electricity on the island? Water? Did it have any existing structures, or would one or more have to be built? What were the environmental regulations governing the property?

Oh, there was one other huge issue. The owner needed to respond to my inquiries. None of them did. Not for the next two months, anyway.

In the meantime, I made a flow-chart decision tree with goal dates, deadlines, and issues that needed to be considered. Two logistical questions kept tripping me up: How would we safely transport rabbits to and from an island? And how would the rabbits take shelter during an emergency like a sudden thunderstorm?

They lived safely at the farm, but we needed emergency plans for an island.

And a restroom. That was also very important.

"Perhaps a houseboat is the solution," I mused later that day while in the general vicinity of my mom.

Translation: I was in the kitchen getting a snack, wondering why it didn't snow on weekdays, and looking to debate my latest brainstorm.

"Solution to what?" she asked.

I looked at her as if that should be obvious.

"We need a boat with a cabin," I continued. "It could be parked at the island. Guests would still come by canoe or pontoon or something."

"Wait, are you shopping for a boat now?" my mom asked. "On a snowy day?"

"No, not *a* boat," I clarified.

"Oh, good. For a second, I thought you were talking about buying a boat."

"Multiple boats," I said, waiting for her reaction. "Specifically, I'm researching houseboats."

She laughed to herself and then looked up at me.

"Sounds like you're searching for an adventure. Be careful, or you might find it."

Blue Moon

On Wednesday, January 31, 2018, astronomy buffs like me headed outside to watch the first of two highly anticipated blue moons of the winter. The phrase "once in a blue moon" refers to the rare occurrence of two full moons within a calendar month, and people generally employ it to mean "very rarely." A blue moon happens approximately every thirty-two months, about every three years. After these two, the next one wouldn't be until October 31, 2020.

I paused to think about how far off that was. I would be a sophomore in high school and old enough to have a driver's license—that is, if I finished the requirements for Eagle Scout. My friends thought I was crazy, but when I was all of seven years old, I voluntarily committed to not get my driver's license until I achieved the rank of Eagle Scout or turned eighteen, whichever came first—just like my uncles had done. Nic was close. Jacob and I were both chugging ahead, and Noah was right behind, but all that felt light-years away.

In addition to being a blue moon, this moon was closer to Earth than normal, making it a so-called "supermoon." It also had a reddish tint as a result of passing through Earth's shadow, making it a blue moon, a supermoon, and a blood moon all in one. For moon gazers like me, that meant this was a super freak-out exciting night.

Grandma Deer was the one in the family who originally drew us into watching the night sky. Looking up at the cosmos from my grandparents' cabin in the Midwest outback, the night sky was spectacular, an immense canvas of stars in an ocean of unfathomable depth and darkness. In August 2017, we drove there for a three-generation memory-maker when we watched the total solar eclipse that crossed the United States.

I couldn't stare up into the nighttime sky without feeling slightly hypnotized into dreaming big dreams and asking questions, most of them without answers. It was as if God put the finishing touches on His creation with one of His greatest mysteries, the stars. Within that mystery was a message: You're not alone; the heavens are here to remind you to stay humble and grateful. Appreciate the gift of every breath; find your purpose and pursue it. Feel small, humble, grateful, and blessed; share this gift of life by being kind. The heavens are infinite, you are not; don't waste time.

As I was about to crawl out of bed, my eyes were drawn to a colorful sign I'd painted years before that was hanging on the bunk bed slats above me:

IYADWYAD YAGWYAG.

It means, "If you always do what you always did, you'll always get what you always got."

And it's true.

The message came through loud and clear. Needing to try something new, I started surfing online boat sales. I needed to find a boat that a teenager without a license could learn to drive and that was also big and sturdy enough to transport the rabbits to and from an island. Kayaks, canoes, and fishing boats were all out. A pontoon? Maybe. I needed a boat with a cabin for shade on a sunny day and a roof on a rainy day. And a bathroom.

That's when I came upon a section for houseboats. There at the top was a houseboat that had been listed within the last two hours—and it looked perfect.

Not only that, it fit my budget.

According to the ad, the *Channel Surfer* was stored for the winter out of the water on blocks. I looked at the picture and easily visualized playing cribbage with my friends while we grilled out on the upper deck. The boat had a fridge and a bathroom with running water and a shower if we hooked up to shoreline power. We could have even more options, like a flat-screen TV and air-conditioning if we added solar panels or a generator.

I read my parents the description in the ad and showed them the accompanying photograph.

"It's like a floating tent with benefits," my dad said.

"We can keep mint chocolate-chip ice cream in the freezer!" I said.

"Sounds like a once-in-a-blue-moon opportunity," my dad added. "How much is it?"

"With my prize money, I basically have enough," I said. "I'm a little short. But I have a plan for that, too."

With my parents' permission, I emailed the owner and left a voice mail for good measure. Within two hours, my mom was talking with one of the two men who co-owned the boat. I stood nearby, kicking myself for not having answered the phone. My mom took a bunch of notes and relayed my questions as I read over her shoulder and tried to eavesdrop. I attempted to keep my enthusiasm in check, for obvious reasons—and I failed miserably, for even more obvious reasons.

"The boat is about two and a half hours away, in Winona," my mom said after the call.

"Amazing," I said.

"What's amazing about *that*?" my dad said.

"Everything."

We arranged to meet one of the owners on Saturday. In the interim, he followed up with a series of emails that answered our questions and listed details about the boat and its motors, along with improvements that he and his co-owner had made over the past few years. They impressed me as thorough and meticulous. Both were college professors who treated the boat as a pet project and gave it plenty of TLC.

I spent the next two days figuring out how we could get the boat back to the Twin Cities. The marina where it was dry-docked was on the right ascending bank of the Mississippi River, near mile 726, which was technically in Wisconsin, a state that claims even more lakes than Minnesota, depending on your definition of *lake*. We could get a trailer and drive it back, or we could travel by river. According to my calculations, the river trip would total about one hundred miles and amount to the most incredible journey of my life.

"Hey, Mom," I called to her. "With two tanks that hold 110 gallons each, we could fill up once in Winona and make it all the way to the Twin Cities without refueling."

"How long would that take?" she asked.

"It doesn't matter," I said. "We have all summer."

"You haven't even seen the boat," she said. "You don't own it yet."

"Doesn't matter," I said. "The trip will be amazing."

The Answer to the Riddle

My dad had to work, so my mom drove me to Winona. The sky was silvery, with the clouds just starting to open. According to the forecast, it was going to warm up to nearly 20 degrees by midday, with the winds picking up as the day progressed. And snow—more glorious snow—was starting to accumulate. But we now had an SUV, thanks to someone who had donated it to us for safe winter transportation, so the weather would need to be a lot worse to deter a couple of hardy Minnesotans like us from making the drive.

Even with the SUV, the weather did slow us down some. Thanks to heavy fog and blowing snow along some of the curvier stretches, the drive to the marina took well over three hours. Mom and I used the time to talk through a plan for negotiating the price with the professors. Should we go into the discussion with a default yes? What would be a deal breaker? What would be our signal to call a time-out and go outside to talk privately?

By the time we got there, we had a pretty solid plan. No matter how much we liked the boat, we would still process things before making a final decision. Besides, I didn't have an island yet—or even a lead on one. Why did I need a boat now, in February? But my parents made it clear that the decision was ultimately mine to make.

Then I saw the boat up close with my own eyes. I don't know if I believed in love at first sight before that moment, but that's what it was. I fell in love instantly and dreamed of our future together.

The houseboat was forty-three feet long. I felt so small standing next to the hull.

"It's even more impressive looking in person," I said.

"Climb up the back ladder," the owner said. "Look around inside and sit behind the wheel."

About five minutes later, he found me resting on a tan futon just behind the boat's galley.

"What do you think?" he asked.

"Does it float, and do the engines work?" I asked.

"Perfectly," he said.

After hearing more details, I responded with a thumbs-up and said, "Let's do this."

My mom flashed me a puzzled look that asked why I'd gone off plan. I couldn't explain it in that moment. It just made sense to snag the opportunity.

She gave me a supportive nod, and the two of us needed only a few minutes to wrap up negotiations.

After hopping back in our car to confer privately for a few minutes and enjoy the heated seats, my mom wrote a check. The owners had prepaid storage through April. They agreed to accept all but the final one dollar of the purchase price. I would pay the balance mid-April when the marina would put the boat back in the water to bring upriver. That kept the boat on their insurance until we picked it up. On the way home, we left a message for my dad and called my grandparents.

"I guess now we know the answer to the riddle," my great-grandmother said.

"What's that?" I asked.

"Which came first—the island or the boat?" she laughed.

The joke might have been on me. I now needed to add a houseboat manual and *Nautical Rules of the Road* to my reading list.

10

Yard Sign

With gentle, precise strokes, I ran the brush through Wyatt's long hair. The routine was being scrutinized by several other Angoras that were waiting their turn. Our living room had been transformed for the day into a hare salon, but the appointments were interrupted when Noah knocked on the door. I apologized to Wyatt and slipped into my snow gear in record time.

"I'm going to Noah's," I yelled to my mom.

"Remember to knock the snow off your boots before you go in their entryway," she said.

Duly noted. For the next few hours, I played video games with Noah and Markus, who was feeling well enough for a gaming marathon. I told them about the houseboat, and they were as excited as I was. Neither of them asked why I would get a boat before I had an island. Perhaps it just made sense, as it might to any teenage boy. Or maybe it made sense because it was me.

When I noticed it was getting dark, I realized I had to go back home and finish my homework. Outside, I saw my mom talking with Ms. Deb at the end of their driveway.

Mom waved. "Homework, right?"

"Right," I said.

The snowdrifts on our roof reminded me that I needed to attack that problem with my snow rake—one of my favorite chores. I liked the way the snow fell off in mini avalanches and crashed to the ground in soft explosions. Too bad Fudge was at the barn—he loved the snow as much as I did. I figured I could take Pax out instead. He liked to dig holes, and the snowy obstacle course of tunnels and bridges Noah and I had built in our front yard was his version of Disney World.

Later, my mom and I caught up inside.

"I have some news about the Bachmans," she said.

That got my attention. I'd spent all afternoon at their house and didn't get wind of anything new.

"What's up?" I asked.

"Our family pinkie-swear about not moving needs to be rescinded," she said solemnly. "They need to sell their house."

"What?" I was shocked. "How soon?"

"The open house is Saturday," she said. "Ms. Deb wanted me to tell you when the timing was right."

The Bachmans are moving? I couldn't believe it. It went against the laws of nature—or at least my sense of what made the world right. But when I looked out the window, I saw a "For Sale" sign being jammed into the snow next to their driveway. *So quickly?* This just wasn't the way I saw our future unfolding. Overwhelmed, I went to my room and got out some Hot Wheels cars that I hadn't played with in forever, since Noah and I were little kids.

Pax wandered in and crawled under my legs. When I ignored his invitation to play, he rested his head on my thigh.

"I know," I said. "It's bad."

At dinner, my parents explained that the Bachmans needed a larger home so Mr. Mike's parents could move in with them. Their extended family was an extension of mine, and I knew their Grandpa B. was ailing and needed help. Clearly, they hadn't made this decision on a whim; it must have been the only way. When I was able to get past my initial emotions, I was grateful they were able to help and excited for this next chapter of their lives.

But I realized it meant a new reality for me. When Snickers died, I wondered if it was possible to make a new best friend. Now that I was older, the gravity of the situation hit me with the force of a hammer on an anvil, and I disappeared inside myself. Noah and I had been best friends since he was born. That couldn't be replaced. And Markus was like a brother too.

"Their plan is to buy a house somewhere in the same school district," my dad reassured me. "Of course you'll still be friends, and we'll figure out how to get together."

"Our families will do whatever it takes to stay connected the way we've always been," Mom agreed.

I had no doubt, but I was still upset. As soon as dinner finished, I retreated to my room and laid low until bedtime.

On Saturday morning, my parents let me sleep in—a rare treat. Farm chores could wait until later. When I finally got up, I looked outside by force of habit. It was a mistake. I should have kept the blinds closed all day to shield myself from the steady parade of cars that drove up for the Bachmans' open house. This move was becoming real. At dinner, it got more real.

"Mike said they had forty-two families take a tour," my dad said. "And eleven of them put in an offer."

"It's a good house," my mom said, with a slight catch in her voice.

"It sounds like they already accepted the best offer," my dad continued.

"No offense to our new neighbors," I said. "But it's always going to be Noah and Markus's house." I kicked the table leg, shaking the table.

Like it or not, things were changing. Where I was once allowed in certain places because I was a little kid, like the convent where the nuns booked time with bunnies or the all-girls slumber parties where they requested rabbits at 9:00 p.m. as a late-night surprise, now I was awkwardly asked if I had girl volunteers. I understood. My voice was starting to crack, and I was a few months from needing to buy my own razor—all normal signs that I was growing up. And my best friend and his family were moving. Ouch.

Maybe this was normal too. After all, Jamaal and Qiandre, who had lived in the rental property at the end of the street, had moved several years earlier. The oldest two of the Troubles were in college, and we called them by their real names now. Even the woman with the dogs behind us had warmed up once she understood that our rabbits had pedigrees too. Not all the changes were bad. But I couldn't find any silver linings in this one.

The next day when we came home from church, I saw the sign in front of the Bachmans' had changed. It now said "SOLD."

My parents seemed to already know about this latest development. They said the Bachmans had until May 1 to finalize the sale, which gave them time to find a new house with enough bedrooms.

"What if they don't?" I asked.

"They will," my mom said.

Something drew me to open the door and walk across the street to their house. I threw on my jacket and boots, pulled on my knit cap, and walked into the Bachmans' garage. I looked at where everyone in the neighborhood had marked their heights as we grew from pipsqueaks to teenagers. I liked being a kid. I wished things were the same as when I was little.

But the marks in their garage reminded me of the current reality. As I walked back to my house, I realized that somehow everything would end up okay regardless. It would take time for me to find complete peace about this move, but I knew being a good friend to them also meant it wasn't about what I wanted. It was about what they needed. I kept the focus on them and was reminded that the great gift of life is the anticipation of seeing tomorrow and sharing it with people you love.

We're Going

I always looked forward to February 14, excited to celebrate Valentine's Day and enjoy a few of the candy hearts that seemed to materialize in my lunch. After school, I was making a card for my grandparents and waiting for my parents to get home for a special dinner together. Then I turned on the TV and heard the breaking news about a mass shooting that had happened earlier in the day at Marjory Stoneman Douglas High School in Parkland, Florida. Everything stopped. I pushed the card to the side and felt a piece of my heart break off.

I absorbed the details, then turned off the TV and prayed, especially for the seventeen families with an empty seat at the dinner table that night. When my parents came and picked me up, I informed them that we needed to take the rabbits to Parkland if we got an invitation. It was the easiest pitch I'd ever given—just one sentence.

"I feel compelled to take the Peacebunnies to Florida."

It was a no-brainer. They had already heard the news. The only discussion concerned figuring out logistics and getting an invitation.

By the time dinner was ready, the phone had already rung a dozen times. My mom coordinated with friends from the Dreamcatcher Family and from Rotary clubs in Florida that were arranging places for us to stay. We packed up the SUV the next night carrying Paxton, Fudge, Hobo, and Daisy. When we arrived and began picking people up at the airport, they asked how I'd chosen those particular rabbits. But I didn't choose them; they volunteered. At the farm, I walked into the barn and asked who wanted to go. Those four were literally banging the front of their cages, as if to say, "Hey, I'm all in."

I expected Whatchi to be among those at the front of their cages. He was always social and a pro at interacting with people in groups of any size. But when I walked into the barn, he was in the far back corner of his pen, as far from the door as possible. It was a clear message that he didn't want to go. Once we met up with the other drivers, we proceeded to Florida, caravanning overnight. As solemn as the purpose of the trip was, it felt good to be part of the shared sense of mission.

Unlike at Newtown, I knew a little more what to expect. Over the years, I had taken my rabbits to other communities that had experienced school violence: Marysville, Washington; Benton, Kentucky; and Townville, South Carolina. Through these experiences, I witnessed over and over that the bunnies were able to do things no human could. My role was to bring them to schools, churches, funerals, memorials, and parks and make them available to children, teachers, parents, friends, clergy, police, and rescue workers—whoever was there and desired a visit. It was impossible to know who needed a bunny, and it wasn't my business to ask why. Sometimes they helped people deal with extreme sadness or difficult emotions; other times they helped them reboot so they could do their jobs. And the rabbits always volunteered for each shift.

Outside the funerals and memorial services in Parkland, I put the rabbits in a wagon, making them available to anyone who wanted to step out of line but being careful not to intrude on spaces that were private or sacred. We attended services of many faiths and some that didn't involve any religion, and yet all of them shared profound similarities—particularly sadness, love, and the unanswerable question of *why*.

Everyone we met seemed to grasp for words and answers. The shock and grief were overwhelming, like being knocked down by huge waves. That's where the rabbits were able to shine. They provided a two- or three-minute time-out, like an island people could stand on. It was in Parkland that I realized I didn't need to buy an island to make Peacebunny Island real, although that would make it even better.

The magical place I imagined where fuzzy bunnies provided comfort was also a state of mind. It already existed for those who wanted to see it. When people heard our accents and learned we had driven around the clock from Minnesota so the bunnies could be there, their eyes widened in surprise and gratitude. Our presence served as a reminder that they weren't alone. And even though we'd never met before, they were our neighbors; it just took a while to get there.

One afternoon, between visitations at the same site, we were waiting outside near our car with the bunnies in pens nibbling on the grass. An aunt of one of the students who had died came over and introduced herself, indicating that her family could really use a visit, especially several of the little kids. Their parents thought the bunnies would help the kids pass the time before the service. I packed everyone up, and we wheeled Paxton, Fudge, Hobo, and Daisy into a hotel meeting room.

"Where do the rabbits come from?" one little girl asked.

"From Peacebunny Cottage," I said. "Someday I hope to have an island for the bunnies."

She thought about that for a moment before looking around for her parents. Seeing they were across the room, she turned back to me.

"I want to go there," she said.

"Even if you never get to come to Minnesota, you can always look at rabbits as a reminder that you are loved," I said.

Paxton Peacebunny, Patriot Guard

The next day we found the last available parking spot near a different funeral home. As we unloaded the rabbits, I placed Paxton on top of a pedestal of double-stacked carriers. Our group started walking amid the growing line of motorcycles ridden by the Patriot Guard Riders, an organization of bikers who volunteer as security at services for fallen veterans and first responders. They had come to pay their respects to the student being buried, an Army Junior ROTC member who had made the ultimate sacrifice while holding the door open for other students to escape to safety.

The bikers' bold tribute line of red, white, and blue flags waved in rhythm with the large palm trees at the white tent where people were gathered, waiting to enter the funeral home for the visitation. It was quite a dramatic scene. I spied a biker who wasn't in line yet. He wore a black leather vest covered with mission patches and pins. As we neared each other, I gave a respectful nod but kept walking, knowing the proper etiquette was to wait for him to start a conversation if he wanted to.

Apparently he did. Pax had caught his attention.

"Hey there, young man," he said. "Who have you got there?"

"This is Paxton Peacebunny," I said. "And this big guy is Fudge."

After introducing those two, I moved the blanket out of the way to show him the lower carrier where the two does rested. "The brown one with the lion mane is Hobo, and the white fluffy one is Daisy."

"Those are some seriously amazing rabbits," he said. He bent closer to Paxton and winked at him. "Are you here on a mission too?" he asked Pax.

I watched him pet Paxton and took a mental snapshot. It was a stunning picture, this older biker and Pax, with the line of flags behind them and blue skies with just enough fluffy clouds to give the impression of angels watching from seats above. The sentiment of this February funeral reminded me of the first time I'd stood in line next to the Minnesota Patriot Guard with Paxton in a wagon. We were among thousands of Minneapolis residents who stood with flags, signs, and flowers to honor a fallen police officer. The motorcade of police cars, motorcycles, fire trucks, and ambulances from across the country had stretched nearly eight miles to the cemetery.

Here in Parkland, a young classmate of the fallen freshman sang "Amazing Grace." Under the tent, many of the guests spoke languages other than English, a beautiful chorus of voices all saying the same thing with different sounds, and somehow the bunnies spoke in a way that everyone understood. As we left for another funeral, I passed through the flag line, where the biker who had befriended us stood silently at attention. Seeing us, he broke line and came over to shake my hand. As our hands clasped, he pressed a challenge coin into my palm, and then he slipped one under Paxton's paw.

I knew the significance of the coin; I gave him a head bow of respect and gratitude.

He returned the nod and in a grizzled voice said, "Good job, Pax."

A Lot of Bunnies in the Back

A little more than two weeks later, we returned to Parkland. On our previous trips to sites of school shootings, we had seen the emotional crash that occurred throughout the community after the funerals and memorials ended and the media left town. No one woke up to normal life again. I thought taking the bunnies into elementary and middle schools through my STEMbunnies program would be a natural way to provide comfort, distraction, and science education. The offer was accepted at several schools.

It required a huge group effort to mobilize quickly. My friend Jacob and our ever-resourceful volunteer Milton took care of the rabbits at the farm, freeing my dad to make the trip with us. We were joined by my friends Kaden and Nic and friends from 4-H who flew down separately. We made the trip down Interstate 75 in two carloads, with one vehicle pulling a trailer containing thirty-five rabbits. The drive was long and dark, crossing various state lines. When I was little, I always liked to see the sign for a new state and shout out, "Welcome to Kentucky!" but now I let them pass unannounced in favor of sleep. Grandma Smith said that sleepiness is part of being a teenager, and I was finding out that she was right about a lot of things.

I remember, for some obscure reason, thinking about my canoe as I was falling asleep. The past two Januarys, I'd written essays for the annual contest run by the Optimist Club. I had used the first-place winnings to buy a red canoe we called the Raspberry, a precursor to my houseboat. The essay theme that year was "Chasing Optimism in the Face of Challenges." I had written about the strength my Ojibwa and Lakota friends and their families gained from prayer and faith, as well as the role their dreams played in their lives. I think of dreams as the light we see when everything else is dark. They keep us from getting lost.

I don't think I actually dreamed about the island at night, but I couldn't shake my recurring dream of an island for the bunnies. Although I still didn't know where that island was going to be, I knew that somehow I would get there. That was enough to give me hope, and that led to purposeful action while I waited.

I thought I might have been having another kind of dream when I was awakened by the siren and flashing lights of a Florida state patrol car. I looked over and Kaden was opening his eyes too. This was no dream, unfortunately. We were in the backseat of a truck hauling a trailer full of rabbits, and Kaden's hair looked like it was flashing red and blue.

I saw the officer's silhouette as he approached the truck and suffered a momentary twinge of concern. Our driver on this early-morning shift was an experienced veterinary technician named Barb. She was cool and collected, which made sense; she was the daughter of the first elected black sheriff in Minnesota. I just hoped this officer was equally cool.

He was stern but polite when he leaned in and looked into the second row of the truck cab and saw Kaden and me. I thought I heard Kaden's heart pounding. Or maybe it was the loud clicking and flashing of the truck's hazard lights.

"What can we do for you, sir?" Barb asked confidently, with an air of hospitality.

Hearing her tone made me relax.

"You didn't pull over and stop at the agriculture station back there," he explained.

"Oh, sorry," Barb said. "I didn't know we needed to. We don't have anything to declare."

"I took a quick look inside your trailer just now and didn't see any horses or livestock, so you folks can be on your way," he said, thumping the side of the truck twice with his hand, conveying, *So long, and have a nice trip.*

"Thank you. Have a good night," Barb said.

Then one of our longtime volunteers everyone called Farmer Todd, piped up, "We do have a lot of rabbits back there."

Barb flashed him a fierce you've-got-to-be-kidding-me look. The officer turned around.

"A lot of rabbits, huh?" he said.

Over the next hour, we waited for clearance and explained that the thirty-five rabbits in the back were the stars of a school education program we were taking to Parkland as our contribution to the healing in the community following the shooting. What got us out of this late-night pickle was when my mom texted us a printed copy of the United States Department of Agriculture regulations explaining that the agency didn't regulate the transport or sale of rabbits the way it does dogs, cats, exotic animals, wildlife, and farm animals. Rabbits are unique and special—something I already knew. I soon learned that my parents were in our SUV about thirty miles ahead of us, and I was glad they didn't need to come back for us.

Before the officer bid us good night again, he let down his guard and expressed how heartbroken he was over the tragedy in Parkland. He kept shaking his head in disbelief and sorrow.

"Do the rabbits really help?" he asked.

"I've seen that they do," Barb said.

"How's that?" he asked.

"They know things we don't," she said. "They say things we don't know how to say."

He nodded and said, "Stay safe, folks. And thank you for choosing to come all this way."

Thumbalina

In the meantime, something serious was taking place with my parents in the other vehicle. There, my mom was watching over seven Flemish Giant babies. Born about a week earlier, they were too young and fragile to be left at the farm with volunteers, especially one little doe we named Thumbalina. Smaller than all the other babies, she had trouble nursing and needed to be held up against her mother or hand-fed. Tiny and underdeveloped compared to her brothers and sisters, she was still touch and go when we arrived in Parkland.

A few days later, we opened the doors to the middle school gymnasium after moving half our team there from the elementary school. It was a more spacious, private setting, and it allowed the older students to take their time with the rabbits, some of which were hanging out on tables while others rested in pens. I was talking to two girls, one dressed in blue jeans and flip-flops and the other clad in black from head to toe.

"This one is Alfredo," I said to the girl in blue jeans, who was reaching her hand toward him. "He's about nine months old."

"I get it," she said. "He's white like Alfredo pasta sauce. Can I pet him?"

Alfredo had already come over and gently bonked her chin with his nose.

"Apparently he's eager to say hello," I said.

The girl in black quietly asked if she could go in the pen with Tator Tot. Soon after she sat down, Tator Tot ran around and finished his routine by plopping down on her foot, which nearly drew a smile from her. I continued telling Alfredo's story, how he was a rescue who was in bad shape when we got him, with deep knots in his hair that pulled at his skin. Something at the previous owner's house must have traumatized him, because he hid in our upstairs bathroom and was afraid to come out even to eat unless we were far away from him. This guy had serious baggage.

I was uncomfortable putting him with other rabbits, so I let him stay in the bathroom, and he basically lived behind the toilet. Over time, he moved away from his throne and ventured into the hall, then the bedrooms, and eventually downstairs.

"How did he get his name?" one girl asked.

"At first he was Bunny under the Toilet," I said. "But my dad insisted he deserved a better name. He called him Big Eyes, which seemed silly. I tried the acronym for Bunny under the Toilet—B.U.T.T.—or Bunny Butt."

They laughed.

"I know. It was funny but kind of disrespectful. Then I started calling him Afraido Alfredo."

"He doesn't seem afraid anymore," she said.

I explained how in his own time he'd learned to trust that he was surrounded by people who loved him and would be treated kindly. "I think we're born believing we will be treated with kindness and love," I said. "Alfredo lost this, and it took some time for him to regain it. It's the same way for many of us." I saw the girl in black wipe a tear from her eye.

"But you know what the cool thing is about Alfredo?" I continued.

"What?" the girl in the blue jeans said as she ran her fingers down Alfredo's back the way he liked.

"When I told my rabbits what we were doing and about our trip to visit you, Alfredo ran to the front of his pen and volunteered," I said. "He was sitting there saying with his body language, 'Pick me! Pick me! I want to go!'"

Before the girls left, we all shared in a spur-of-the-moment celebration. My mom came by to check on me, saw me talking to the girls, and flashed a thumbs-up sign. I explained that she was signaling good news about a newborn bunny that had been having trouble. Then I told them about Thumbalina.

"I bet she's going to make it," the girl in black said.

"How do you know?" her friend asked.

She shrugged. "I just have a feeling."

Sure enough, not only did Thumbalina make it through the trip, but over the next year, she grew to be one of our largest rabbits, weighing more than twenty pounds. Maybe that's why her heart is so big too.

Anchors Away

There was something about being in Parkland that intensified my passion for moving forward with the island. I also felt like it was time to talk more openly about my pursuit, as if talking about it and preparing for it would help move the process along. Despite having sent out several dozen queries to the owners of private islands, I had received only one response, and that island was just too far away from us to be feasible. In other words: more disappointment and frustration.

I didn't know how to get people to respond any faster, or at all. Maybe people who owned private islands had a secret pact that they would never respond to messages. When I thought about it, owning a private island was sort of an antisocial statement in and of itself.

I tried not to get down. I knew it was impossible to achieve greatness without trying to achieve something great, and success wasn't guaranteed. But Paxton shared my determination, and the other bunnies constantly reminded me of the "hopportunities" in store if we didn't give up. Of course, giving up was never really an option. At night, I bookended my devotions with a prayer for insight and assistance. I wasn't desperate, but my boat was coming out of dry dock on April 15. I had visions of an inaugural voyage to Peacebunny Island and plans for the best summer ever. In the scope of the universe it didn't matter much, but in mine it did.

I kept praying and doing my part to push forward so I would be prepared if the right opportunity arrived. Starting in March, I pored over the boat manual, learning about the vessel and its operation, the engines, and even the wiring of the electrical system. I often read while sitting in my parents' bed, relying on them for help and a little encouragement.

In early April, I enrolled in the US Coast Guard Auxiliary class. Kaden took it with me, and we spent the weekend learning from expert instructors. We agreed the in-person instruction took the coming adventure to a new level. After the instructor found out I had a forty-three-foot houseboat, he used it for many of his examples. He explained the different types of anchors and how to select which one a larger boat like mine would need on the Mississippi as opposed to on a lake with no current.

I went home and emailed the men who owned my houseboat. An hour later, I got a response. I ran over to high-five my mom.

"What's so exciting?" she asked.

"There are two Danforth anchors already on the boat," I said.

"Very cool," she said. "I don't want you floating away."

I also learned how to calculate the length and diameter of anchor rode (the rope) that would ensure the boat would stay tethered to the anchor against the river's swift current. I had no idea so much math would be required for boating, but it was awesome to work on word problems that related to real life.

Jacob and Nic also signed up for the one-hundred-mile journey. Although

Jacob wasn't able to take the class with Kaden and me, he completed one later. He also had experience sailing with his grandpa. Nic was certified as a lifeguard, so regardless of his boating skills, we felt safer knowing he would be around. All of us took the Safety Afloat course required by the scouts and started looking at river maps.

The best part of all this was envisioning how the four of us would become more than good friends. We were going to make a good team.

Float Plan

"So, what's the plan?"

It was Thursday night, and we were eating with Our Peoples. Kaden's mom had asked the obvious question. Now that we had a boat, where were we going?

"Can I get back to you on that?" I asked.

One of the major lessons I'd learned in the watercraft operator's permit class was the need to file a float plan. I downloaded the Coast Guard form and looked it over with my parents. The easy part was the starting point. We were going to launch from the Winona marina. I also knew the crew would consist of Kaden, Jacob, Nic, and my mom, with the other parents serving as land support. The hard part was filling in the blank next to "Destination." After much thought, I wrote, "Destination optional."

Maybe we would have a destination, and maybe we wouldn't. Maybe we would trek to the Twin Cities, use the boat for the summer, and then migrate back to Winona in the fall. All I knew for sure was that we were going to head toward St. Paul, a journey of roughly one hundred miles.

Once I started contacting marinas and inquiring about the cost of boat slips, I began to realize how expensive everything was. Renting a place to park the boat at the marina would add up to thousands of dollars for the summer, plus utilities. That was my first experience with sticker shock.

Later that night, I received an email from the owner of an island a little south of St. Paul who said he'd received my letter from February and was intrigued about the possibility of renting the island for the summer. In that moment, I saw a glimmer of possibility, and I just needed to hold on to hope that things would work out. The more immediate plan would be to get the houseboat on the river and go. Things in motion stayed in motion. The worst-case scenario was that we would cruise the river with some bunnies for the summer and then I would sell the boat in the fall. Either way, we would have the best summer ever. Did it matter that I didn't yet know where I was going to tie off the boat long-term?

"It was snowing pretty hard on the day I bought the boat," I said one morning at breakfast. "How much more unconventional could things get?"

My mom, who was watching the weather report on the local news, swiveled around and looked at me like I knew nothing at all about living in Minnesota. Then, with a fateful laugh I recognized from when we got stuck in a snowdrift, she uttered a single word:

"More."

Minnesnowda

My family always has at least two months of nonperishable food items and two weeks of bottled water in case of an emergency. When I earned my emergency preparation merit badge, there wasn't much new information. It all boiled down to two tips: Prepare. Prevent the preventable. That's just how my family rolls.

Fill the car's gas tank so the engine block won't freeze.
Have good insurance.
Save up just in case.
Keep jumper cables and a first-aid kit in the car.
Prepare.

We aren't extreme about prepping, and it's not like we have everything in top-notch shape, but we plan ahead for the big stuff, which, as my parents say, gives us the ability to adjust to the little stuff. Speaking of little stuff, on the morning of April 13, my eyes were focused on the small print scrolling across the bottom of the TV screen listing the school closures. The area around the Twin Cities was about to be slammed by a massive blizzard. I was eating a bowl of cereal, hoping to see my school district listed among the closures and thinking a snow day would be an awesome way to start the weekend.

I got up to refill my cereal bowl and waited for the banner to scroll all the way through. Almost all the private schools were listed. Preschools were canceled. *Ah, good, we're getting somewhere,* I thought. What I needed was for some superintendent somewhere to stand in their driveway, decide they didn't want to leave home, and declare the unofficial holiday.

I'd worn shorts the day before, and the marina had scheduled our boat to be put in the water that weekend. This was crazy—but fun.

And then it got more fun. School was canceled!

"Grab your boots," my mom said moments later.

"School's canceled," I announced enthusiastically.

"Gotta get to the farm. Now."

She didn't use that tone often, and I got the message that regardless of what the schools were doing, we had work to do. She took a personal day from work, and we left quickly before the roads became impassable. I ran through the checklist: Hot chocolate to go. Sandwiches and apples. Three boxes of apples for the bunnies. Two boxes of carrots. CDs for the car. Motivation. Double and triple check. All systems were ready. We were in the zone, a finely tuned machine.

Like a hockey game, the storm came in three periods. While we were driving to the farm, the first part hit: torrential rain that eventually changed to sleet. We were nearly done with the chores at the farm when the sleet turned to freezing rain. By the time the third-period drama started—the humongous snow dump—we were safely back home, having tucked in the bunnies and arranged with a friend who lived close to the farm to check on them daily while we waited out the rest of the storm.

By Saturday morning, the entire Twin Cities metro area was shut down. The National Weather Service sent out blizzard warnings, reminding everyone of the historic Halloween storm of 1991 that had blanketed Minneapolis–St. Paul with twenty-eight inches of snow. Flights were canceled, and the highways were littered with more than six hundred accidents, including twenty jackknifed semitrailers. The Twins even postponed three home games for the first time since moving from the Metrodome to Target Field.

Those aren't the only statistics I recall. April 2018 became the snowiest on record, and the sustained below-freezing temperatures delayed the melt. Why do I know this? Because I learned that an inch of average snow on one acre of ground is the equivalent of 2,715 gallons of water. This translated to an extraordinary high-water mark on the river. Water sloshed over the shoreline.

Although we didn't personally know anyone who lived along the banks of the Minnesota or Mississippi Rivers, we were aware of how the water spills into communities and fills up basements. We learned that while lakes rise, the water in rivers rises *and* flows over everything in its way, including islands.

Like at the End of a Hockey Game

The late snowstorm changed our plans to get the boat in the water by April 15. After the snow dump would come the melt and flooding. Beyond that it was anybody's guess as to when we could take the boat out. I just hoped it would be soon. I was eager for school to end and my summer adventure to start. If there's a term like *senioritis* for middle schoolers with a pending houseboat trek up the Mississippi, my picture was next to the term in the dictionary.

I took advantage of the extra time to work on additional details. Although Jacob and Kaden had passed the watercraft operator's test and Nic was fully competent in any water-related situation, their parents were still waffling because of all the unknowns and the nature of our adventure. We were teenagers planning a one-hundred-mile excursion on the mighty Mississippi to an unknown destination. To me, the lack of a landing spot was the biggest issue, even though there were any number of potential issues along the way. There was no getting around the fact that this trip was best described as Huck Finn meets "Are you kidding me?"

Each day I checked the calendar, read up on the river, talked with my crew, and wondered when this great adventure was going to happen. All I knew for sure was that the boat needed to leave the marina at some point. It's like at the end of a hockey game. At a certain point, the clock is going to run out. In my head I heard the announcer saying as the lights turned out at the arena, "Thanks for coming. You don't need to go home, but you can't stay here."

They say timing is everything. I think *they* are people who are no longer waiting. For me, the wait was excruciating. I snacked endlessly on crackers. I paced my bedroom. I even cleaned my bedroom, and then, just as I was thinking about straightening up the rest of the house, something happened.

And I realized timing was indeed everything.

Underwater Island

"Wait! Wait just one amazing, incredible, holy-cow minute!" Kaden exclaimed. "You're serious? It's happening?"

We were having dinner with Our Peoples. It started out like an ordinary Thursday. Only that day, April 26, turned out to be anything but routine. After several emails and a couple of phone calls over the past few weeks, I was notified by a family foundation that they had come to an agreement. I could rent their island for the summer.

Woohoo!

There should have been a bump on top of my head from jumping up and hitting the ceiling. Okay, I'm exaggerating, but only slightly. If I'd heard this news while I was at school, the day would have been a wash. I would have had to go to the nurse's office and ask to be sent home on account of feeling too good to stay at school. As it was, I danced around the kitchen with my mom, then Whatchi, then Paxton, and then both rabbits at the same time. We put the hop in hop, skip, and jump.

At dinner, Our Peoples were ecstatic to hear about this new development. I'd learned from experience that until the papers were signed, nothing was real, so I tried to remain cool and calm. But you know what? That was a total system fail.

"Peacebunny Island is happening!" The words flew out of my mouth. "It's actually two islands, but the main one is really long, and if you count the smaller one to the north, there's approximately twenty-two acres for us to explore."

"Seriously?"

Everyone at the table was looking at me. My whole body had turned into a smile.

"Here's how I'm thinking it will work," I said. "We'll bring the boat up and park it off the island, not at a marina. Then we'll hang out on the boat and the island for the entire summer. And you guys can come as much as you want to."

"And I'm going fishing, right?" Kaden asked.

"Yes, Kaden, you can fish," I said, rolling my eyes as if that were all he could think about. "Just like our plan, except that instead of needing to sleep on the boat every night, we can pitch a tent, go hiking, have campfires . . . all that stuff."

"Unbelievable," he said. "Everything is perfect."

There are friends who are there for you when times are tough, not just when times are good, and I was blessed to have a core group of good friends. They'd been with me through the plummeting low of losing the first island. They were invested in and committed to helping me and the bunnies and the dream. Our energy ricocheted off the walls.

"There's just one glitch," I said.

Everything stopped. Eyes turned toward me.

I gave everyone a painful wince.

"What is it?"

"With the huge snowmelt these past few weeks, the island is currently underwater," I said.

"Well, of course you did, Caleb," Kaden's mom said. "Why wouldn't you rent an island that's underwater?"

I laughed as she mimicked my great-grandma.

"You see what no one else sees," she continued. "You take things no one else values and somehow bring out the best. You're the guy who bought a boat in a snowstorm, so who here is really surprised?"

My mom was nodding her head. "I know. In a Caleb way, it all makes perfect sense."

I told them about having taken Paxton to the shore the past weekend to check it out and meet the family whose foundation owned the island. I described speaking with the neighbors on the shore and how they were furiously pumping water or stacking sandbags.

"They said this section of the river floods every year, but this flood was an outlier, a fifty-year phenomenon," I explained. "The land dries out long before school gets out for the summer. Which is perfect for me. They already have a great home at Peacebunny Cottage. I want a *summer camp* for the rabbits."

"But it's underwater—like, completely flooded," Kaden said, as if I didn't get it.

"You can see the trees," I said. "They're sticking up above the water. It's just that the dirt is underwater. And it will let me see the island at its worst, so it's a real test before making a decision. This is a gift."

A few days later, I repeated the Q&A at scouts with Nic and Jacob.

By the time I told the Bachmans, they had already heard the good news and congratulated me with high fives.

"Well, farm boy," Mr. Mike said, "I guess you're about to have quite an adventure."

"Best summer ever," I said convincingly.

Noah was waiting to tell me something, and it turned out he had some good news of his own. He and his family weren't moving after all. They had exercised their option to back out of the sale before May 1.

"Yes!" I said, with a celebratory fist pump in the air.

This piece of good news far exceeded my acquisition of an island—another prayer answered. Only this time I didn't jump around and dance; it was more like I could start breathing again.

Noah and Markus and I had made a pact that they wouldn't visit the island until they could both go. Markus was the wild card, of course. We were like the Three Musketeers in that way. *All for one, one for all!* For the rest of our lives.

X Marks the Spot

After school on May 3, we had a signing party at the foundation's lawyer's office. Because I was a minor, we structured the purchase—and the Peacebunny business in general—in a way that gave me certain rights and responsibilities, with my parents acting in trust until I came of legal age. At that point, I would assume full control of the business. Everyone agreed, and all of us put our signatures on the documents.

By "all of us," I mean everyone in the office. Before the drafts were printed,

I had made a last-minute stipulation. It was nonnegotiable, too. I insisted that Paxton Peacebunny also had to leave his mark on the formal documents. At first the lawyer thought I was kidding, and everyone laughed on the phone. *Sure, kid. Whatever.* Then, when I showed up at the lawyer's office with a rabbit, they saw that I was serious—and they laughed even harder.

"Well, now. Who do you have here?" the lawyer asked.

"This is Paxton Peacebunny," I replied.

"He's a big boy, huh?"

"Yes, sir."

"I've never seen a rabbit like him running through my backyard."

"No, sir. And you probably won't. He's a rare one, inside and out."

After the foundation's representative signed the lease agreement, he handed the pen to me and I signed on the line with my name, Caleb B. Smith, CEO/founder. Then my parents signed to make it official for the government.

The lawyer thought we were finished, but I looked at Paxton and said, "To make this right, we still need to acknowledge how all this came to be."

I reached into my pocket, pulled out a sponge cut into the shape of an X, and dipped it in some ink, making Paxton a cosigner on the documents. With his footmark officially imprinted on the papers, the deal was sealed.

We toasted each other with sparkling apple juice my mother had brought, along with the glasses she and my dad had used at their wedding, and we shared carrot cake. Pax nibbled a carrot top. I closed my eyes and said a heartfelt thank-you to God for everything—the boat, the island, the fact that the Bachmans were staying, the summer ahead of us, and everything that had led up to this moment.

I was so lost in thought I almost didn't hear the lawyer talking to me.

"What are you going to do with the island?" the lawyer asked again.

"I'm going to figure out how to make something wonderful even better," I said.

11

Radio Check

The boat's name was *Channel Surfer*, at least for now, and from bow to stern, it was beautiful. It was the first time I'd seen the boat in the water, and it was even bigger than I remembered. As I stepped on board, feeling the gentle bob, I headed straight toward the brass bell at the bow. I double-checked that the clapper was there and then gave it a good, loud ring, after which I formally bent over and signed the ship's new logbook.

My mom applauded. I smiled. At that precise moment, I made what I saw as the formal shift from boat owner to captain.

I wasn't the only one getting my sea legs. I held up Huckleberry, officially my first mate (no disrespect to Nic or Jacob, whose only titles would come from our ongoing cribbage competition), so he could ring the bell too. I had hoped to bring Paxton, but he declined and wanted to stay at Peacebunny Cottage. I knew that sooner or later he would agree to head to the island with us. For now, he gave every indication that he preferred land to water, whereas Huck, in his eagerness to participate, exhibited all the best qualities I needed in a first mate—primarily, keeping the crew in good spirits.

Huck loved being on the boat and immediately took off down the deck to explore. In a flash, he went from *aye aye* to *bye-bye*. His reaction confirmed my decision to promote him to first mate. It was a perfect role for this next generation of Peacebunny. I made a rule that all guests who came aboard the boat for the first time needed to step on the front deck and ring the bell as a rite of passage before signing the official ship log. The bell rang three more times that day as Nic, Jacob, and my mom all came aboard.

It was early May, a couple of weeks from the start of the one-hundred-mile journey. I paid the boat owners the last dollar, finalizing our deal and transferring ownership. The insurance paperwork had to be processed before we could take it out for a drive. The flooded river currents were still running fast and high, so waiting a few more weeks would mean less stress on untested motors.

But we decided to spend the night on the boat. We might not have been going anywhere, but my imagination was free to roam, and it did. Without even shutting my eyes, my mind soared, eagle-like, above the island. I saw the potential for creating a special place where kindness was the rule of law, and the boat was an extension of that.

I'd assembled a three-inch blue binder containing all the registration, documentation, navigation rules, state requirements, and maps, along with our official float plan to Peacebunny Island. Every time I said that name to myself, I felt my heart speed up.

The three of us guys reviewed the information and practiced walking through the checklist. With six years of scout camping under our belts, we followed scout policies without thinking twice. Jacob and I were both First Class, and Nic was finishing the design for his Eagle project. Creating packing lists and checklists were second nature. Inviting the Coast Guard Auxiliary to come aboard for a safety check felt like the right next step. Inspection was voluntary, but the preparation leading up to it provided the opportunity to make sure we were capable and ready.

In our inventory of the boat (translation: we enthusiastically flung open every cabinet and drawer), we found random items like screwdrivers and touch-up paint, twenty-five bright-orange personal flotation devices in the cuddy, and some Polaroid photos of the boat when it was brand-new. Those were great, like looking at pictures of my parents back in the day and seeing how different their hair was when they were in high school.

Jacob made the best find of the moment: the switch for the horn, and he gave it a playful *beep-beep* that caused both Huck and me to jump. The horn clearly delighted Jacob, who pushed it several more times while flashing a toothy smile. Although I was the captain, he would be sharing much of the driving. I saw that he was already enjoying himself at the helm. He pushed every button, checked every knob, and then turned on the VHF marine radio.

"Radio check! Radio check!" he called out, pressing the handheld mic as he spoke.

We heard crackles. Then silence.

"We'll need to try that again later," I said.

"Aye aye, Captain." He nodded.

Later came sooner than I expected. As I peeked over at Huck, now perched comfortably beside the air-conditioning unit, no doubt practicing his lookout duties, I heard Jacob confirming radio checks on some of the recreational channels, not the "big three" that are used for distress, calling the Coast Guard, or talking with commercial vessels. Everyone who had a radio within twenty miles could hear him talking, and that was fine with me.

Eau de Diesel

As part of our mission to be as informed about the houseboat as possible, we headed to the stern of the boat to take another look at the engines. Jacob grabbed the cords from one side while I pulled up the other, lifting the heavy deck covers that sat over the bilge—the large, open space where the twin Mercury engines sat, eager for the coming adventure.

Huck came right to the edge and peered down on the deck as Jacob and I ducked inside the hole, making sure we didn't step on the glass fuel filter, as the previous owners had warned us. I took the opportunity to give some instructions to my first mate.

"This is the bilge, and you aren't allowed down here," I instructed Huck. "It's pretty dirty. The boat is getting old, you know. It was built in 1973."

"Hey now, I heard that!" my mom said from where she sat above on the flybridge. "Nothing wrong with a little life experience."

After allowing the area to air out, I checked for the smell of diesel fumes, inhaling a long, deep sniff of the bilge.

"How does it smell?" Nic asked.

"Exactly as it should." I nodded. "All clear to safely start the engines. Just the faintest hint of my new favorite manly perfume, Eau de Diesel." I fake coughed.

I yelled up to Jacob, who was at the steering wheel, eager to turn the key. "Ready on starboard!"

A moment later, the starboard engine purred. The port engine, by contrast, gave a small, slightly less confident sputter but started up too. Together the engines were so loud and powerful that we found ourselves yelling to hear each other until we closed the covers. The owner had said it was important to lower the lids slowly and make sure the rope loop handles stuck out a little so it would be easier to lift them again the next time.

I stepped between the covers and looked toward the outboard portion of the motors. The water was bubbling up, and with it came my smile. If only today were our departure date instead of two weeks from now. The engines were clearly ready for an adventure up the river. I gave everyone a thumbs-up as I joined them on the flybridge, where we would do most of the driving. But our check-off wasn't complete yet. We practiced unknotting the mooring lines and tossing the anchor on the count of three. It sounds simple, but do you throw on "three" or say "three" and then throw? Lastly, all of us learned how to fill up the one-hundred-gallon fuel tanks and use the dipstick to measure the fluid levels.

Then we were finished. But to my dismay, we learned that the inspector was still a few hours away. It was agonizing for us to be on the boat and have to sit and wait. It didn't help that this was our first vessel-safety check. Each step was exciting in its own way, but only after passing inspection could we relax and look forward to beginning our journey.

As we passed the time, my mom unveiled what she'd been working on that afternoon while we were focused on the boat: a river's-edge scavenger hunt.

No Pooling

At my request, my mom had planned a team-building challenge, and although it took a while for the guys to understand the deeper motivation behind it, it didn't matter, because we were having such a great time together. Our hunt took us on a ninety-minute hike around the marina and then along the shifting shoreline of the Mississippi River.

We saw families on the beach, some kids building sandcastles, and other kids throwing rocks and sticks into the water. Then someone spotted a small nonpoisonous snake, which disappeared into the water as the current took it away. I've never wanted anything to do with snakes, so I felt no disappointment to see it drift off.

Nic was already running to explore the sandy ridges, completely off track from the scavenger hunt, but his glee was contagious. The three of us took turns running and tumbling down the sandy hills, stopping just short of the river's edge, where there was only a light current. Nic, who loves to snowboard, took full advantage of the moment, doing a flip off the highest peak and landing feetfirst in the water. I marveled at his athleticism and confidence, but I wasn't about to risk getting hurt before our adventure truly began.

When we finally decided to return to our hunt, we started to understand and appreciate each other's strengths and weaknesses: each one of us had different skills and superpowers (as evidenced by Nic's running flip into the water), and it was important for all of us to recognize those differences and how we could be stronger, better, and more capable as a group.

Nic was an experienced camper as well as a lifeguard, and he had a wide variety of experiences that included tall-ship sailing at Sea Base. But he also ran after shiny objects. Jacob was a master of lists and details, and his organizational skills were exceptional. He had tons of sailing experience. But he also was very strong-minded, and he let you know exactly what he was thinking. Kaden, who would also join us for the journey, was a thought engineer—grounded, focused, and creative. He was more of a wild card because we didn't know him as well, but I sensed that if our journey ever spiraled into an Apollo 13 mess, he would somehow figure out how to get the round plug firmly fixed in the square adapter. And Huckleberry, who had opted to stay back in the cabin during the hunt, somehow made everything more fun.

The first major clue in our scavenger hunt instructed us to search for an assembled pile of rocks in the sand.

"Should be easy to find," Nic said. "So are we walking or running? Sticking together or doing this treasure hunt as fast as we can?"

"Let's stick together," Jacob said.

"Off we go!" I cheered.

When we finally located the rock pile, we all dug into the sand, unearthing a buried plastic bag with a map of the Mississippi River and a yellow sticky note with the question, "Which pool are you in?" None of us knew that the term *pool* referred to areas on the river between each lock and dam. Each pool was numbered for the dam located farthest downstream. As I later learned, Peacebunny Island was located in Pool 2 above Dam 2. But at the time, as we stared at the note, we all began making random guesses.

"Looks like a code," I suggested.

"Are we supposed to find a swimming pool?" Jacob asked.

"Is there a pool party?" Nic wondered.

"I don't think there is a pool anywhere nearby, or we would have seen it."

"We're pool-less."

"Come on, guys, stop pooling around. Let's get serious."

Eventually the bad puns stopped, and we realized we were stumped. We sat in the sand for quite a while, thinking and bouncing ideas off each other, before Jacob noticed that the title of the map, written in large, bold letters, said, **UPPER MISSISSIPPI RIVER**. And below it, the subtitle said, **Pools 5A and 6**. We finally got it. There was nothing tricky about it. The answer had been in front of us the whole time.

"And the lesson is?" I asked.

"What?" the guys said.

"Drumroll, please," I said. After Nic and Jacob rapped their fingers against a nearby bench, I added, "Don't overthink things."

"No pooling."

Aye Aye, Captain

The inspector arrived early that evening and, after a thorough review, wished us a good adventure, along with fair winds and safety on Lake Pepin. He sighed, adding that he wished he were our age and going with us. At dusk, the three of us sat outside in brown stackable lawn chairs, with Huck rubbing against my feet, waiting for a pizza to be delivered. That had to be one of the coolest things ever to a bunch of teens: to have the pizza guy come to your boat. Huck munched on some veggie treats. Several men who were my new neighbors in the marina gave me a few tips as a boat owner.

"Treat her with respect," one man said.

"Talk gently and do a lot of listening," another said.

It sounded like they were giving me relationship advice. I couldn't even drive a car yet, and I certainly wasn't thinking about being tied down. But that clearly didn't matter to the gentlemen who felt obliged to share their wisdom.

"Don't let her catch you making eyes at other boats, or you'll be hearing about it," another said with a laugh.

"Yes, sir."

One wrinkled, bronzed man at the marina said, "Young man, there are only two days that will be equally amazing and joyful. The first is the day you buy your boat. The second is the day you sell it."

I nodded, and he laughed. "Beer?"

"No, thank you," I said, refraining from explaining the obvious: I was underage and didn't drink anything stronger than smoothies.

"Just kidding," he said. "Got a girlfriend?"

"Nope."

"You're gonna do okay."

After dinner we filmed portions of our meeting for Kaden, who was staying at his dad's that weekend. As the sun disappeared, I kicked back and reflected on how the boat's previous owner had held out the two floater key chains with the boat key while I'd held out my dollar. With a firm handshake, the transaction was complete and the huge vessel was my responsibility. I still needed to pinch myself—to ring the bell and listen to the water lap against the hull—to remind myself that this whole experience was real.

With all that came a subtle but definite change in my perspective. I now owned this boat. We were going to drive it to the island I was leasing. In telling my friends to close the refrigerator door so we didn't waste battery charge, to take off their shoes before they came inside, to shut the doors, and to throw their trash away, I had taken charge, accepted responsibility, and stepped into my new role as captain and owner.

On a scale of one to ten, with ten being the coolest thing possible, this was currently somewhere above eleven. The only trade-off? I was beginning to sound more and more like an adult. I was saying things my grandparents and scout leaders and teachers would say. Maybe that comes with being responsible for stuff. But as we laid out our sleeping bags, I couldn't have been any happier.

"Good night, Huck," I heard Nic say with a yawn.

"Good night, guys," Jacob answered.

Then I added, "Good night, moon."

Cast Off the Lines

We were roused early in the morning by a storm that battered us with rain, lightning, and big winds, rocking the boat quite a bit even in the harbor. That let me check off another box on my list of fears. It also gave us one last story to share with Kaden when we filled him in on our initial weekend on the boat.

Before returning home, we dropped off a canoe at a nearby landing for when we arrived at Peacebunny Island. We also stopped by Peacebunny Cottage to feed the rabbits and tackle the other chores. With all of us working together, we finished relatively fast. Huck went back to the colony to rest up for the coming adventure and share some stories with Pax and the others.

The next two weeks of school dragged on slowly until finally Memorial Day weekend was upon us.

Yes!

I was thrilled that the fog had lifted and our insurance paperwork had finally arrived, allowing us to make the trip back to the Winona marina. The river was still fast, but I felt safer knowing we were covered, just in case.

Huck took to exploring the boat again, and I loaded our food into the refrigerator and stowed a Peacebunny Island banner in the galley. I planned to unfurl it once we landed. Jacob was prepping for the final safety check before we cast off, and Kaden hoped to meet up with us along the way. Nic wasn't able to join us for the trek, although he and his sister, Maggie, still planned to help host events that summer. I'd learned by now to hold plans loosely. I was reminded of that saying: "If you want to make God laugh, tell him about your plans."

Jacob and I completed the final morning safety checklist. For the first shift, my mom was on board in the event that a trained adult boater needed to step in. Jacob's mom was paralleling us in an escort vehicle. I checked the skies, which were blue above us; the radar showed the same to the north.

"Let's start up the motors," I called to Jacob.

"Starting the motors, check," he responded crisply.

I turned to the first mate. "Huck, it's time to head to your station," I said.

I picked him up from the floor where he'd been stretched out and placed him on the shelf by the AC unit, allowing him to enjoy the same view of the water as we had. I leaned in and touched foreheads with him.

"Keep an eye out for barges," I instructed. "We need an extra set of eyes today."

After we said a final prayer asking for safety, alertness, and joy, plus two strong motors and plenty of space between us and other boats, it was finally, unbelievably, gleefully go time! The purring motors added to our excitement, as if the rumble were a roaring crowd celebrating our departure. We called ahead to Lock and Dam 5A, confirming that they had an opening to "lock through" heading upriver if we could be at the gate in less than thirty minutes. I checked the clock and thought that seemed reasonable. I took a moment to write the entry in my logbook, the first such extended entry of this long-awaited journey.

June 2, 2018, 10:35 a.m. Mile marker 726 upstream from the Ohio River. Location: Dick's Marine on Mississippi River Island #72. Latitude 44°03'20", Longitude 91°38'15", Winona County, Minnesota.

Boat: Batteries at 12.6 volts, motors at 10,000 RPM starboard and 8,000 RPM portside.

Weather: 61 degrees Fahrenheit/16 degrees Celsius, 77% humidity, 29.9 barometer, winds out of the east, southeast at 15 miles per hour. Fog lifted. Partly cloudy and very promising sky. Radar clear to the north.

I closed the blue logbook.

"Ready to launch?" Jacob called.

I untied each of the dock lines from the cleats, flipping the well-worn white fenders back to the cabin side of the railings.

"Ready!" I answered.

My response was equal parts statement, question, and aspiration. It was time. This was actually happening. I said to myself, *Full dream ahead.*

Amen

"Preparing for reverse!" Jacob shouted.

"Ready for reverse," I responded.

The vessel lurched as the gears shifted, and then we slowly pulled away from the dock. Jacob cautiously maneuvered to get us turned around and headed out of the marina. Only when I saw clear water ahead of us did I let the air out of my lungs. I wondered how long I'd been holding my breath. Along with the mere idea of unannounced snakes, my fear of hitting another boat in the harbor was way up on my list. Now I felt most of the nerves and stress wash over the deck and disappear into the wake behind us.

We turned the boat north, heading into the main channel, where a few other boaters were zipping around. I guessed they saw the same forecast we did. I returned a head nod from a few fishermen we'd met on the beach two weekends before. Everyone we met seemed to be rooting for us, many of them sharing how they wished they'd done something like this at our age. We were frequently asked about the island and the meaning behind its name, and the response was usually something like "Wow, that's pretty special," followed by a solemn warning about entering Lake Pepin. Everyone cautioned us to only enter Pepin on a day we knew our vessel was dependable, the waves were calm, and the winds were fair.

The first lock passage would reveal much about the condition of the boat and our teamwork. I felt my heart beating faster as we headed toward the lock entrance on the left ascending bank, which was the Minnesota side of the river. The steering was responsive and smooth. Jacob kept it in low; we both thought it would be smart to get through the first lock before finding out what kind of power it had.

We arrived faster than expected, and the marine traffic light was still glowing red. Rather than shifting gears into idle in an untested boat, Jacob made a few small loops while I glanced ahead at the tall, woodsy bluffs flanking the river.

At last the large metal doors opened wide, inviting us into the water elevator. Thankfully, there were no barges in the area and only one other recreation boat headed into the lock, so we were able to enter the holding area by ourselves. That took off a lot of pressure. Classroom training is great, but nothing compares to actually doing something.

The dam was on our right, closest to the Wisconsin side. It spanned three-fourths of the river's width, looking like a bridge to nowhere. The final fourth of the river was taken up by the lock, which was outlined by the huge yellow concrete walls. We had rehearsed our approach to the lock with maps and reviewed our respective roles, but it felt different now that the wind was pushing back the brim of my hat.

I grabbed the frontmost fender and tossed it over the railing, where it was attached. Then I made my way back to the stern, flipping each fender on the way so they would provide a buffer for the boat as we drove in.

"Please keep us safe as we go through our first lock," I said out loud. "Amen."

"Amen," Jacob echoed from the helm.

My mom added another amen. I didn't realize anyone had heard me. But after the chorus of amens, I began singing, "A—men, A—men," and soon everyone joined me for several rousing choruses. We knew that as much as we had planned and prepared, we still needed divine protection, especially at these stops.

The locks are a series of water elevators that open at the next level. After this one, 5A, we had four more to go. Jacob was steering from the flybridge to see better. I was down below in his blind spot.

"Fenders out!" I called as I put the bumpers out on the port side, where the lock worker held a line for me to grab.

He was outgoing and chatty, offering encouragement to us the whole time. We headed into the lock perfectly straight, in textbook fashion, but the wind kept pushing us closer to the wall, making the long concrete pool suddenly seem very small. Another worker walked toward me. He told Jacob to cut the motor, but we didn't slow down fast enough.

"Engines off. Put her in reverse!" the man called down.

The first guy I'd spoken to told me to let go of the line. He tossed another one to me farther in front. It splashed in the water. I picked it up and held on. I wished I were wearing gloves. Despite the burn, my firm grip kept us in place while the doors closed behind us and Jacob cut the motor.

Rising Water

Another boat eased in behind us just before the lockmaster closed the gate. Together we watched the water slowly begin to rise.

"How are you folks doing?" one of the workers called down to us from the lock.

"Awesome," Jacob replied. "It's our first time locking through."

"That's what I heard." He nodded and grinned.

Over the next ten minutes, I watched the painted notches on the concrete wall get swallowed by the rising water that filled the bay. Soon the light would turn yellow, then green, and then there would be a horn that signaled we could proceed.

"Can we do a VHF test with you?" Jacob asked one of the lock workers.

Our radio hadn't worked earlier that morning, and we'd only reached the lockmaster by calling on Jacob's cell phone. A radio would be preferable and more dependable. After getting a thumbs-up, Jacob turned the radio to channel 14.

"Lock and Dam 5A, this is *Channel Surfer Peacebunny*. Over."

I heard Jacob's voice bellowing in stereo from inside the cabin and from the lock's speakers, which broadcast his voice like a rock concert so everyone in the lock and beyond could hear.

"Roger that. Heard you loud and clear," the lockmaster responded.

"Ten-four," Jacob said confidently. "*Peacebunny* out."

He clipped the VHF mic back on its stand behind the steering wheel and looked at me. "Captain Caleb, the radio's working fine."

The worker congratulated us for making it through our inaugural lock, then told us to have fun and, above all, respect the river.

"Starting the engines!" Jacob announced with a wave.

A moment later, I heard Jacob shout from the helm. "I can't get the port engine to start!" That meant we were about to go solo on the starboard motor.

I felt a slight jerk, then a pull forward to the right, forcing the stern side of the boat to fly out toward the concrete wall as we fishtailed. I winced as I heard a small crunch coming from the back corner. I didn't look.

"More starboard!" I shouted as one of the workers looked on from the lock with a smile on his face. I could see him thinking, *Boys, this is how you learn.* "We need more throttle to get us away from the wall!"

Jacob tried the port-side ignition key again, and this time the motor decided to run. With both motors running, we slowly but steadily headed away from the dam. We weren't going to be sucked down into the churning water and crushed in the spin cycle. Another fear of mine abated!

I checked the trip log and clock, shaking my head in disbelief. The whole encounter had taken only about fifteen minutes. But in that short time, I think I grew a chest hair or two.

"Nice job, Jacob!" I shouted.

"You, too, Captain!"

True Friends

The stretch of the Mississippi riverfront near Wabasha was especially quiet that night. Only one other pleasure craft was near us. Even the railroad tracks alongside the river were empty. The lack of other noises amplified the sound of the river and the gentle creaking of the old rope lines that were keeping us in place.

In my mind, I replayed the day's events since we'd motored out of Winona earlier that morning. My soul felt at rest.

I realized that all journeys, large and small, start and end in the same place—inside us. We need to look there as often as we do at the scenery outside.

I thought about how bringing a pet home is the start of a journey of its own. Most people don't think about it that way when they take guardianship of a pet. In our fostering application, we always asked people to describe the kind of bunny personality and breed they preferred. Did they want a docile companion content to sit in their lap and watch TV? A playful pal? A runner like Little John? An explorer like Hobo or Amelia Earhart? A mischievous buddy like Tator Tot? A friendly first mate like Huckleberry?

Those were the easy questions. Two others often stumped people: "What do you want to give to the bunny?" and "What do you think the rabbit will want when it comes to live with you?" More often than not, people wrote, "Good question!" Pets ask us to think in new and unexpected ways.

Long after the fireflies had come out along the shore, I told Jacob the story of "prom bunny." Toward the end of the school year, a girl in high school who was seeking rabbit advice called our number. She explained that her boyfriend had taken her out to dinner and, as part of asking her to go to the senior prom, surprised her with a pet rabbit. She was all gaga at first because the bunny was cute, but once she took it home and showed it to her parents, reality set in.

"How long had she had the bunny at that point?" Jacob asked.

"About four hours total," I said, laughing.

She wanted to drop the rabbit off with us that night. I politely explained that we weren't running a bunny rescue. "I felt so bad for her," I told Jacob. "I tried to help. I gave her the number of a rescue and invited her to Bunny Bootcamp. I also suggested that she could give the bunny back to her boyfriend and make him figure out the next steps."

"Seriously?"

"I was trying to help. But I had another idea," I said. "Maybe she should give up the boyfriend and keep the bunny to help her get over any heartache."

"What'd she decide?"

"I don't know. But it sounded like she was going to follow at least one of my suggestions."

"Did you ever hear from her again?" Jacob asked.

I shook my head. "Nope."

We talked late into the night. The stories I told led me to see how far the business had come, as well as how far I had come. I hadn't realized how much we'd done. After tossing the snacks toward me, Jacob asked, "So which rabbit is your favorite? Is it Huck?"

"Why do I need to have a favorite? Look at the rabbits: they love whoever they're with in that moment. They aren't busy looking around, wishing for someone else to walk in the room or checking what was just posted online. They aren't distracted. They give their full attention. That's a true friend."

Under the moon that night, my closest friends were Jacob and Huck. Of course we appreciated the other friends who had helped us get to this point on the journey. But for now, we were savoring this moment right in front of us. We were the team that was going to cross Lake Pepin the next day. Two of us were about to fall asleep, and the other one, already snoozing, would open his eyes at 2:00 a.m. and wake me up by licking his water bottle.

Wait for It

I was glad Huck couldn't read a map or the nearby signs and therefore wouldn't know we were moored in Wabasha next to the National Eagle Center. Bunnies and eagles will never be found trading friendly chatter at the same party. But with the eagles safely inside the building, neither of us needed to be concerned.

Lake Pepin was another matter. I knew the lake was treacherous and we needed to be alert and smart when we crossed. It was a serious safety challenge . . . unless the breeze was minimal and the water calm.

We asked for both—and plenty of wisdom—in our morning prayer. Throughout the trip, Huck often looked like he was bowing his head, so either he was fervent about his prayer life or fastidious about giving himself a bath. I didn't bother to investigate—we would take all the help we could get.

About fifteen minutes after pulling away from Wabasha, we crossed under a fifty-foot-high bridge that spanned half a mile, which was impressive, especially because I was getting to look at it from the underside. I've always been fascinated by engineering and bridges, and this angle offered a whole new perspective.

"Hey, Jacob, ready for some tunes?" I shouted as I looked through our stack of CDs.

"Roger that." He beeped the horn twice because he was driving the boat and . . . well, he was Jacob.

While I got out a CD, the Eagles classic "Peaceful Easy Feeling" came on the radio, and it was more than appropriate as we left the Eagle Center. It also fully addressed my mood. An hour later, as the river opened wide into Pepin, we met the change with healthy appreciation. Until then, the channel depth was a minimum of nine feet, as maintained by the Army Corps of Engineers. However, parts of Lake Pepin went down more than fifty feet, as deep as the bridge was high, with strong currents keeping the deep water moving and unsettled.

The lake was enormous and immediately commanded our respect. We had a mile of water on either side of us and twenty-one miles ahead of us before we would reach the safety beyond the northern edge. Forty square miles is a big tub that made our boat and all the others look like little toys.

The current pushed forcefully against the boat as we danced across the waves. The front of the boat was a bumpy ride, but it was pretty smooth sailing in the back. Although Huck didn't seem to mind the waves, I moved him to the main cabin floor, and he went back to chewing the carrot top he'd started earlier. Eventually, he lay down for an afternoon nap. Seeing him relax made me more relaxed too.

As the town of Pepin came into view, the wind picked up again, and the waves became choppier and laced with whitecaps. My legs felt a little rubbery from standing at the wheel for so long, not to mention the added tension of paying such strict attention to everything. My mom came up from the cabin to check on me and make sure I was staying hydrated. When I complained about my legs, she pointed to the sign we'd brought and taped to the boat's dashboard—a small index card that said, "Whatever doesn't kill you makes you stronger." It was true, but also a joke, because both of us knew the other side said: "Except for bears. Bears will kill you." She always did this silly growling-bear impersonation when we said it.

But Pepin wasn't a joke. Four days later, we would learn from other boaters that Lake Pepin had claimed yet another life when a fishing boat capsized due to high winds and rough water. We were fortunate the conditions didn't get worse than the light chop when we were crossing.

As we passed Deer Island, the lake curved to the right and we matched it with the map. Soon I spied the huge rock face indicating the approach to Stockholm, Wisconsin. The sky was reassuringly clear and bright. Jacob switched tunes, and I started to sing along: "Look all around, there's nothing but blue skies." I held Huck as we started to sway to the music.

At the three-hour mark, I spotted the outline of Maiden Rock, a small city named after a cliff where, according to legend, the daughter of Dakota Chief Red Wing jumped because her love was killed under orders from her father. I was glad we'd looked up lots of history before the trip, because it made me appreciate different spots along the way.

One of our biggest challenges of the trip to that point came when we overtook and properly passed a northbound barge. We made contact on the radio, advised them of our plan, then held our collective breath during the maneuver. As soon as we were clear, we let out a triumphant whoop.

It was a long, challenging afternoon, so when we hit the channel opening at mile 783 near Greene Point, everyone got high fives, including Huck. We were moving past Lake Pepin intact and with more confidence.

The next stop was Lock 3. We called ahead to ask about expected traffic. The lockmaster indicated it was wide open, a perk of locking through in the late afternoon. By the time we entered Lock 3, which was near Pickerel Slough, we'd been driving on the river for nearly six and a half straight hours, but it felt even longer. We got through the lock easily, and the only giveaway that we were novice sailors was our self-congratulatory cheering.

Not everything was smooth sailing, however. The lock was barely out of sight when we heard a horrible clanging from the back hatch. Jacob and I immediately made eye contact.

"Uh-oh," I said.

"That didn't sound good," he agreed.

"Jacob, go take a peek," I said.

He was already on his way.

"The port engine is sputtering," he reported from the back. "It's still running, but it sounds horrible."

"Is it pushing any water?" I asked.

"Nope."

"I'm turning it off just to be cautious," I said. "Let's hope the starboard engine doesn't decide to act up too."

The starboard engine was carrying the full load, so I decided to take a last-minute turn into a side channel that opened into Sturgeon Lake. The chart showed there was a marina on the Minnesota side . . . and hopefully a mechanic who made dock calls.

Our arrival in Red Wing wasn't pretty. We came in hot and would have created a mess if not for the extra-long dock. I was relieved to be there and filled with gratitude despite the uncertainty about the engine. It's interesting how two conflicting emotions can exist simultaneously.

I was glad we had extra cash to pay the unexpected slip fee at the marina. I hoped the motor just needed a rest, not a lengthy or expensive repair.

Then I heard Jacob cheer, "Hey, look at this!"

"What?" I asked, finding him just in time to see him plug the boat's electrical cords into shore power and turn on the galley lights.

"Ta-da!" He beamed. "We have permission to use electricity, so we can see when we play cards tonight, and . . . wait for it . . . take hot showers!"

Countdown to Peacebunny Island

The detour also turned out to be a godsend. A serious thunderstorm was forecast to roll in, and it was safer and more sensible to spend the night tied down at the marina. Within a few hours, the unrelenting rain, the howling wind, and the rolling waves accentuated how small—and blessed—we were.

By dawn, the skies bore no trace of the nighttime ruckus. It was as if the storm had never happened. We left a message for a local boat mechanic, but he couldn't make it until the next day. We were only thirty-two miles from Peacebunny Island. We had a choice: we could chance the rest of the trip on one engine or we could wait for the mechanic. I saw more water accumulating in the bilge and opted to wait and enjoy another full day together.

Late the next morning we rose from deep sleeps and welcomed Kaden onboard. He was ready for adventure, and that's exactly what we were serving that day, provided the mechanic showed up on time. He did, to a chorus of whispered amens. He replaced a cracked belt (the source of the noise) and spent some time fine-tuning both engines. Jacob and Kaden were thrilled to get a little dirty helping him, and all of us learned a ton about the engines. It was time to let the cribbage games begin!

Early the next morning, we began the final leg of our journey to Peacebunny Island. I kept a detailed record of the day in my logbook:

6:00 a.m.: Woke up, downed breakfast, stowed sleeping gear, and did a weather check. Called our parents to let them know we were back on the river.

6:45 a.m.: Went back south on Sturgeon Lake nearly two miles until we could reenter the main river channel, turn, and head north again.

7:45 a.m.: Near mile 802, saw lots of cute coves and great beaches to camp on in the future.

8:45 a.m.: The highway that parallels the main river channel on the Minnesota side is far away, so the parents aren't available for this stretch. The plan is to meet them in Hastings so they can take pictures. Without a land support crew, I feel like we're on the dark side of the moon. We passed a super cool boat moored on an island but didn't see anyone. Lots of birds humming along the water surface. Beautiful, peaceful morning.

9:10 a.m.: At mile 813.5, the train lift bridge looked too low. We called ahead and asked if they were going to raise it. They told us to take down our flybridge, estimating that we could pass underneath safely or we could wait fifteen minutes for a train to pass. We chose to wait, causing us to miss a rendezvous with the Sea Scouts vessel. Saw Dad getting a few photos from the shore.

10:15 a.m.: Entered Lock 2 at Hastings. Final stage!

11:45 a.m.: We passed by Grey Cloud Island. The channel was tricky but well marked. We stayed between buoys. Saw a few fishing boats as we got closer to the Twin Cities.

12:30 p.m.: Excited to see the historic swing bridge in the distance and two small islands in its shadow, one with a tall rope swing dangling from the tallest tree around. We must go back there sometime.

12:45 p.m.: After being on the river for six hours, we got our first glimpse of Peacebunny Island!!! Twenty-two whole acres! We weren't sure where to land at first, but then we saw a beach area leading to the knoll on the south side. Drove past it, then turned around and headed straight toward the island!

I put Huck up on the console so he could watch as we pulled onto the shore.

Jacob declared, "Peacebunny Island straight ahead!"

The next sound we heard was the hull of the boat crushing the sand as we pulled ashore and the *Channel Surfer Peacebunny* came to a blissful rest.

12.

One Giant Step

Looking out at the shoreline of Peacebunny Island through the pilot house window, I struggled to find words for the moment. Majestic cottonwood trees were swaying in the breeze. The sky was a warm blue, dotted by puffs of clouds; the trees were in full leaf; and the water lapped against the shore with a gentle gurgle that might as well have been the excited chatter of a new friend full of things to say. All I could voice was "Wow!" and "Thank you."

The island was so much more than I expected. Its twenty-two acres stretched as far as I could see in every direction. The river water had receded to a near-normal level since the spring flood, exposing acres of glorious sand and soil, along with the heads of tiny white wildflowers. The houseboat fit like a puzzle piece onto the natural rise of the beach.

Kaden heaved the heavy Danforth anchor onto the beach and gave the line a hearty yank, catching it in the sand. Jacob moved the wooden ladder to the front of the bow and prepared us to disembark onto dry land. I let that sink in. Dry land! Then he swung a leg over and climbed down, followed by

Kaden, and they waited for me on the shore. I heard the flutter of small birds and the loud honk of a blue heron as my friends interrupted their solitude.

"How does it feel?" I asked.

"Amazing," Jacob said.

"Better than amazing," Kaden said. "But the soil feels a little squishy, so watch your step."

I took a deep breath and held it in my lungs for a moment. This is what I'd dreamed of and worked to make a reality over the past three years—from when I first declared that we needed an island to now, as we prepared to explore the twenty-two-acre rustic sanctuary on the Mississippi River.

I was filled with awe and gratitude. I tried to hold on to the moment. *Remember everything,* I told myself.

I ducked back inside the pilot house for a moment and grabbed the rolled-up banner we'd made to mark this as Peacebunny Island. I glanced around the gallery area and out the back window at the river. *Well,* Channel Surfer, *my blue-moon beauty, you helped get us here safely. Thank you.* It was time to formally christen her with a new name, the SS *Peacebunny,* acknowledging her transformation too.

I stooped low to pick up Huckleberry, whispering some words in his ear intended for only the two of us. He whispered back and leaped into my arms, his powerful back legs launching him up onto my chest as if confirming that he was ready to go ashore too.

I rang the bell just before we stepped down the ladder.

"I'm going slow, Huck," I said. "I want these first steps burned into my hard drive."

Huck seemed to understand. I set him down in the dry sand and watched him take in the moment, as I had done, until he gleefully hopped toward Kaden and Jacob.

"That's one small step for man, and one giant leap for bunny kind," I said, just as I'd rehearsed in my head so many times.

Although there was much to do, I first took time to kneel and recognize the Provider of all good things. The guys joined me in giving thanks, and afterward I gave what can only be described as a barbaric yawp as we unfurled the Peacebunny Island banner, tied the ends to the nearest of the shoreline trees, and declared our intentions. For one hundred days of summer, until the houseboat was taken out of the water in the fall, this would be Peacebunny Island.

Huck darted up the hill toward the knoll, and the three of us followed behind him. It seemed appropriate for him to lead the way in our first few minutes of exploring the island. He was digging beneath a cottonwood tree when we caught up to him. We walked east across the island, and then we spontaneously broke into a run as each of us headed in different directions, yelling, "Look at this!" and "Over here!" and "You've gotta see this!"

We wanted to do and see everything at once. But we had time. I'd leased the island until the end of October, allowing us plenty of time to camp out and explore, and ultimately figure out whether the rabbit sanctuary idea would work.

We hiked over to the small islet off the northern tip. I wanted to compare it to the map now that the river level had gone down to the ordinary high-water mark. On our way back to the knoll, Jacob's phone alert went off and reality intruded. He and Kaden needed to get back home. It was a school night—the weekend was almost over.

"I can't believe it's time to go," Jacob said.

"How do we go back to normal life after this?" Kaden added.

We met my dad at the agreed-upon rendezvous point, where he was waiting with a canoe to shuttle them back to our car and take them home.

Jacob stepped close to the edge to pull the canoe closer to the shoreline. But before you could say "dangers of the fire swamp" (à la *The Princess Bride*), he started to sink into the mud. The recent floodwaters had softened the normally marshy shore. It wasn't quicksand, but it was close. Struggling only made Jacob sink deeper. Kaden and I dug into the mud with our hands and then with a paddle, trying to free his legs.

"Oh no! I lost my water shoe in the mud," Jacob said.

"First get your one leg free," my dad instructed. "Then we'll help work on trying to get your shoe back."

A few minutes of wiggling ensued, buoyed by lots of laughter (sorry, Jacob), until my friend finally freed his leg, found his balance, and inelegantly pulled himself into the canoe before scrambling back onto dry ground.

Having skipped dinner in an effort to extend our time on the island, we all sat on the shoreline and devoured huge chunks of cheese, summer sausage, and apple slices. Then Dad and the guys took off, leaving Mom and me on the island, where we spent the evening on the SS *Peacebunny* instead of heading home. It would have been anticlimactic to finish this incredible first day by going home and sleeping in my own bed.

Because I didn't want the guys to miss out on a lot of the firsts of exploring the island, I basically hung out on the boat and the nearby shoreline for the rest of the evening. Huckleberry sat next to me while I worked on casting my fishing line into the main channel, instinctively watching the bobber even though I didn't bring any hooks. It was such a quiet, peaceful sunset, and at last my heartbeat started to slow down.

Without solar panels, we didn't have an electricity source, so once it became dark, we turned in relatively early. The water lulled us to sleep.

It felt different out on the island—a good different. I'd reached a long-awaited destination, but I had also arrived at a new beginning. And it wasn't formally summer vacation yet. After four more days of school, I'd still have one hundred days to explore and experiment. It was a school night, but there I was: Sleeping on a houseboat. On the Mississippi River. Tied to a river island. With my bunny. It was definitely the best school night ever.

Purple Pixie

A few days later, Kaden, my mom, and I were canoeing round the northern tip of the island. He was very skilled at steering from the back, and I was happy to paddle along as we turned the corner and caught the main channel current. Kaden and I noticed a group of fallen trees that made a precarious bridge from the smaller island to the mainland and noted that we needed to go back to try crossing there.

We were making good time on our first day trek back to the island. We planned to wait until everyone was together before heading to the main campsite knoll or taking the houseboat out for another cruise. But that didn't rule out a quick mini-adventure like this. I was excited that Kaden's mom was able to drop him off so he could go with me to take advantage of this gorgeous

June evening for a few hours. Jacob wouldn't be able to join us again until school was out the following Thursday and Nic was scheduled to work, but I wanted to check on the boat lines and maybe get in a little exploring on the north end of the island.

That was when Kaden and I spotted a canoe, tied to a branch near the small cove (which I later named Carrot Cake Bay). I also spied a small tent between the trees and a couple of brightly colored towels draped over some bushes. As we floated downriver, we had only a few seconds before the view of the campsite disappeared behind the row of bushes.

"Hello!" I called out. "Hello!"

Silence.

I tried again as we got closer to the shoreline and floated past.

"Anyone here?"

We heard a rustling in the woods.

"Just a minute," a female voice called back. "Let me get my clothes on."

Kaden and I looked at each other and froze. Thankfully my mom was there and took over the situation. At her direction, we steered our canoe into the little bay. I wanted to avoid a confrontation. I didn't know how many people were at the campsite. We had only heard the voice of a female, and she admittedly was not dressed. This was a private island, but I wasn't ready to see anything private.

I hopped out of the canoe and pulled ashore, making way so she could get out.

"Mom, regardless of who they are, I feel a responsibility to the island's owners because I signed the paperwork."

"Let's assume the best," she said, climbing out of the canoe. "I'll go over and talk to them."

A few minutes later, Mom waved us over. We weaved through the bushes to the tent site. Next to Mom was a woman in her twenties with purple hair in a short pixie cut. We sat down on the log next to her tent and learned that she was a proud, bubbly Minnesota native and a former wilderness canoe instructor who had canoed the entire Mississippi River to the Gulf a few years before. Earlier that day, she'd started out on a solo journey starting from the Hidden Falls boat launch in St. Paul on her way to St. Louis.

"Wow, you're going by yourself?" I was surprised she didn't have a support crew or someone to help her paddle.

"Well, how did you guys end up on this island?" she asked, changing the subject.

"I'm leasing it for the summer," I said.

She did a double take and zeroed in on my T-shirt.

"Peacebunny Island?" she said. "Where's that located?"

I pointed to the ground where we were sitting. "This is it," I said.

"I'm so sorry," she said. "I had no idea this was private. What do you do here on Peacebunny Island?"

I gave her the short summary about how I planned to use the island to train comfort rabbits so they could help people through grief and loss and explained that this was our first week. She shook her head and then crumpled over and started to sob.

"Of all the islands," she wept. "Of all the places to land and camp. Peacebunny Island. You can't make this up."

Through her tears, she explained that she and her dad had planned a long canoe trip together but that she had come straight from his funeral. She'd cut and colored her hair and packed up her supplies and then hastily set out on the river just a few hours earlier. Overcome with grief, she couldn't see where she was paddling anymore. She pulled over to clear her head on the first shoreline she came to. Then, feeling weighed down by the heaviness of her sadness, she tossed all her supplies onto the shore, and somewhere in all the emotion, tossed off her clothes, too.

"I've been sitting here questioning everything," she said. "Why did he die now? What should I do? Should I go on with the trip and honor him? Should I call someone to meet me and take me home?"

She wiped her eyes and looked at me. "I can pack up and leave if you want," she offered.

Ordinarily I would have taken some time before deciding, but that wasn't necessary. The answer was obvious. She needed a night to herself on Peacebunny Island. In the quiet and solitude, maybe she would find some of the answers she sought. Or maybe she would find the strength she needed to continue her search. Even though she wasn't able to visit with one of our comfort bunnies, it seemed to me that the island itself could provide what she needed.

"No, please stay the night," I said.

After well wishes for her journey, we got back in our canoe and shoved off, paddling downstream toward the SS *Peacebunny*. I told Kaden and my mom that I wanted to cut our plans short rather than explore the island. Instead, we would allow our new friend to have the whole place to herself.

As we continued to paddle, I knew it was the right decision. I also knew it wasn't a mistake that she'd landed there.

Summer

I went into the summer wondering if the reality would be able to live up to the expectations I'd built up in my dreams. It was better.

It really was the best summer ever.

And it wasn't just the time I spent on Peacebunny Island that made it amazing. That honor, in my opinion, belonged to my neighbor Markus, who had just graduated from high school. My friend, whom doctors had predicted would never come home from the hospital and had outlived almost everyone born with his conditions, earned his diploma and was looking ahead to continuing his education and his life. The Bachman family threw a celebration that spilled across the entire block with people eager to share in this miraculous milestone.

Our street was filled with so many cars that people had to park around the corner. The Bachmans' house and yard overflowed with people who shared pictures and memories and tears of gratitude and love—the perfect way to kick off summer vacation.

"He is our remarkable reminder of God's goodness," Ms. Deb said. "He's been in and out of hospitals his entire life."

Mr. Mike added, "And yet here he is, nineteen years old, and he just graduated from high school. He starts college full-time in the fall—as a junior, with all the classes he's already taken. This is quite a moment."

I wove my way between the guests to the backyard and chatted with Markus's rabbit, Captain Phil. Along with their dog, Champagne, he was one of the unofficial greeters. Then I headed back into the garage for a reunion photo with the neighborhood kids who were now in high school and college, some even starting careers.

"Remember your rabbit Snickers?" one guy asked.

I nodded.

"He was cool," another guy said. "Always out there with us."

Each of us stood next to the lines that marked our progression in height over the years. We were all a bit awestruck by how much we had grown up since the last time we'd seen each other. The older boys tousled my hair and challenged Noah and me to play some hoops later that evening once the street cleared out again. Although not everyone was able to come, it was such a gift for us to be back together. Everything felt right in the world as we played in the street again, like old times.

Markus and Noah wanted to hear all about the island, so after the party wound down and we helped clean up, we sat and talked about Peacebunny Island. The sun ducked behind their fence, leaving a cozy sky and warm early evening air. Even though the three of us had made a pact that they wouldn't visit unless we all went together, I knew they shared my vision for what I was trying to establish there.

We wanted Peacebunny Island to be a place that people could believe in and hope to visit one day. Even if they never actually stepped foot there, somehow the world could be a little better—and so could they—just knowing it existed.

In the days after Markus's party, Huckleberry seemed eager to head out with me on another adventure to the island. Every time we packed up the carrier, I checked in with Paxton, but he exhibited no interest in exploring his namesake island. He had seen it from the shoreline the night we signed the lease in May, but after that he was content to stay at the cottage and leave the sailing and hiking to others. I longed for the day he would join me out there.

Most of my campouts with Huck were short—two or three days at most. Once we got there, I always checked the island for uninvited guests. I didn't want any more purple pixie–style surprises, though I was relieved to learn the woman had had a successful journey.

I had two main questions to answer over the summer: (1) Would the bunny-island concept really work? and (2) Could the island be adapted in a way that would sustain me and the bunnies and eventually some guests? Those questions led to more questions.

One day as I was canoeing to the island, I realized I was being watched. As I rounded the northern tip, I was startled by a loud slapping against the surface of the water. I nearly dropped my paddle.

Reflexively, I turned around and saw ripples in the water heading away from me. They disappeared close to the opposite shore. It was the first of many interactions with a beaver I began to call Xarol.

He slapped his tail every time he saw me before diving under the surface and swimming away. The noise he created usually alerted a loud bird of some type, which sounded its own squawking alarm, causing other little birds to take flight and scatter.

I also uncovered plenty of fresh tracks, some from deer, others that looked like raccoon and beaver, as well as some made by muskrats. Every night, a gaggle of geese relaxed on the western sandbar.

The shoreline was always dotted with little treasures, like feathers, shells, and sometimes the occasional flip-flop, plastic cup, or discarded can. One day I found more than thirty golf balls, so clearly someone was having some fun.

Following a few weeks of cleanup, which included eleven Hefty bags of bottles, cans, glass shards, and plastic everything, the island was completely rustic and restored. I got an approving flyover from the family of ducks that stopped by every evening on their trip to Carrot Cake Bay, and a great blue heron I named Chester began to come by for a daily nap and fishing expedition, as if my efforts had been solely for his benefit.

I took it as a compliment.

I'm Only a Rabbit Person

The next few weeks were spent identifying birds, plants, and trees, taking soil and water samples, and learning everything I could about the river and the island. I wanted to be sure it would be safe for the rabbits, so I began working through the checklist that I would turn in to our environmental advisers. The most important thing I confirmed was that yes, of course there were predator birds in the area—mainly eagles, but also some hawks, all of which tended to avoid humans. Over several weeks, we tracked the birds, identified where nests were located, and noted the scat piles left behind as we figured out the animals' patterns.

The bottom line was that the birds of prey stayed away from our island, and they were too busy nabbing fish out of the river to bother with what was happening near us. Plus, they had telltale calls, which helped us know where they were heading. Observing and tracking their habits would never make the entire island completely safe, but our advisers agreed that if we kept to our plan and stayed nearby, it would serve as a strong deterrent.

That opened the door for the next phase: bringing out some bunnies of the same sex for short-term visits while we were there supervising. This was the moment everything else had been leading up to, and I couldn't wait to discover how the rabbits would respond to the new environment.

On the first trial run, I brought a Silver Marten named Harley Jo, who chose to do four back-to-back trips. Of the four original Peacebunnies, only Casper showed a strong interest in returning to the island multiple times. He always seemed ready to explore the pasture at the cottage or go on a vacation. On the island, he enjoyed hiding and relaxing on the sand, looking like he wanted to order some carrot juice with a tiny umbrella.

I eventually ramped up the logistics to bring ten mature does at a time. They were great-granddaughters of the first four Peacebunnies—six white, two black, and two agouti (shades of brown). We spent time observing how they reacted to the relaxing river life. The younger kinderbunnies in the pilot project responded well to the training, especially when they came with the older rabbits that knew the drill. I decided that age would be my focus the next summer—if I had another summer on the island.

Tator Tot was clearly in heaven. He couldn't climb or jump or scamper or dig enough. He chased the waves the way dogs do at the ocean, running to tag the edges of the white water and then springing back up the shore, turning around, and doing it all over again. One weekend I took him camping with Jacob, Kaden, Nic, and me. It was clear he didn't understand that people get tired and need sleep.

Whatchi was at the other extreme. He acted like the friend who arrives at a campout wearing neatly pressed clothes and a bow tie, preferring more refined ways to socialize. With his long, carefully smoothed coif, he preferred to avoid the sand or the rugged outdoors. Periwinkle sat in the hammock with the wind blowing through her luxurious mane, but she also enjoyed digging in the sand. When she'd had enough of the camping life, she jumped into my arms, letting me know she was ready to go home.

Fudge acted like he owned the island and was quick to show everyone around. Bandit, our black-and-white-striped beauty, treated the island the way a foodie might enjoy a trip to Paris, nibbling clumps of grasses and white flowers with a connoisseur's bottomless appetite. She always wanted to sit on the helm of the houseboat when we were driving and pretend she was calling the shots.

I wished Paxton showed more interest in going, but I also understood that some rabbits, like some people, are homebodies, especially as they age, and Pax was advancing in rabbit years. Maybe he would change one day—my own family was proof that change was possible.

One day my dad and I were watching Xarol and his family of beavers construct their wooden lodge along the north shoreline, and I wished they would eat buckthorn rather than the tender young trees.

"That would really help prevent erosion ten years from now," I said.

"I can see that," my dad said.

"If I had full control of the island, I'd bring goats out to eat the invasive plants like buckthorn and clear out the shoreline before planting more native seedlings," I said.

"Goats?" He winced.

"Yeah," I said.

He shook his head and looked as if he had bitten into a green apple.

"No goats," he said. "I'm only a rabbit person."

Don't Stop Believing

I wish I could say my summer visiting the island ended with a sign that this specific island was always meant to be Peacebunny Island, like maybe if a Snickers chocolate bar had washed ashore.

That didn't happen.

Instead, we made a trip to the island and removed all traces of our main campsite, including the Peacebunny Island banner.

The day was bittersweet, but we promised to return for a final trek at the end of October, when our lease formally ran out, and say goodbye to Xarol and his beaver family, our blue heron neighbor, and all the other creatures we'd come to know as our friends.

I didn't want to think that far ahead. From the day the houseboat first dropped anchor on the sandy beach, I knew I was right where I should be, and I wanted to buy the island if given the opportunity. I had leased it knowing the owners weren't sure if they wanted to sell it, so I didn't let myself think about it too often. At that point, I hadn't even known if this island idea would work. But it did. The Peacebunny Island banner looked like it belonged.

I had to stay in the moment.

Meanwhile, the Minnesota State Fair served as a welcome distraction. At the end of the Labor Day weekend, the Peacebunny crew brought home thirty-two ribbons in the open competition, including ten for best of breed. It was a satisfying button to the summer and an upbeat way to transition to the new school year.

Then, without any warning, the representative from the family foundation that owned the island called. My dad and I had just returned home from Peacebunny Cottage. He answered the phone and quickly put me on speaker.

"This is going to sound crazy," the man said, "but do you really want to buy the island?"

"No question," I said, trying to remain calm and make sure my voice didn't crack.

"We've talked about this at length, and we've decided to give you one month to raise the funds. If you can't raise the funds, we have another interested party."

After that call, everything went into hyperspeed. Thirty days wasn't very long to secure the financing I would need to purchase the island. Acting quickly, I did some research and came up with a counteroffer based on the sales of other undeveloped properties along the river. But that was just the tip of all the work that needed to be done. Fortunately, we had a great team— a Realtor, someone to run the title search, someone to help with insurance, and someone to draft up the formal purchase agreement. We never would have pulled this deal together so quickly without them.

Next, I needed an investor. I got out all the business cards I'd collected over the years—professors, Realtors, lawyers, bank officers, business owners—and laid them across the living room floor. On the back of each card, I'd written where we met and notes about our conversation. It was one of the best tips I'd ever received.

I also added my LinkedIn contacts. Then I arranged the stack of cards the way I organized my hockey cards, with a separate pile for all-stars. These were my first calls. Because there were no completely cold calls, everyone I spoke with was nice and encouraging. They already knew about the bunnies and were supportive of me. But with a purchase this large, the talks quickly got down to business. The investors didn't need to hear more stories about comfort rabbits. They wanted to hear how I was going to make monthly mortgage payments on a twenty-two-acre island and not lose their money.

After several phone calls, I had a breakthrough. A family member had introduced me to a woman several years earlier who was savvy about real estate. She thought buying land is always a great investment, and from her perspective, the intended purpose only made the investment better. After hearing some of the details of my business plan, the woman crunched the numbers on her own and let me know that my proposal added up. My proposal made sense to her, and she was in—but only up to a certain price. The only remaining requirement would be to justify the price-per-acre value.

However, within hours of receiving that support and feeling like I was going to be able to make a strong offer, something happened that made the island dream seem remarkably insignificant. Grandpa Tractor underwent emergency open-heart surgery and then developed MRSA in the intensive-care unit. It was one of those events that doesn't just change your perspective. It creates the only perspective.

My mom immediately caught a flight to Missouri and kept an around-the-clock vigil at Grandpa's hospital bedside for the next ten days. Somehow, while Grandpa was being prepped for a follow-up surgery, she fielded a call from the foundation rep with an update. "No offense," he started.

But as my mom later explained, she couldn't handle whatever it was he had to say. She told him to call the home office number and leave a message for me. I got home from school a short time later and shuddered with disbelief when I played the message and heard him say the family was leaning toward selling to the other party, who he said was "very interested and persuasive."

As if I wasn't?

"No offense," the rep reiterated on the message, but they'd decided to sell to whichever party offered the most money and could close the deal the quickest. "I hate that it has to be this way . . ."

If I was going to make an offer, I needed to get it in ASAP. I had to remember the advice I got a while ago: It's personal. But it's not *personal*. They had no idea that one of the most important people on my team (and the bunnies' team, for that matter) was currently fighting for his next heartbeat.

All I wanted was for my grandpa to get better, and I'm sure people would have understood if I asked to put things on hold or dropped out altogether while we waited to see what happened to him. But I hung in there. I don't know how, but I did. With my dad working extra hours and my mom several states away and our lawyer out of town, I entered this final phase of negotiations for the island largely on my own.

I was okay with that. I accepted the fact that I was a fourteen-year-old in a property bidding war for an island. Ultimately this was my decision and my offer to make.

It was Friday afternoon, and I had gone to Grandma and Grandpa Smith's after school. After my dad took me home, Paxton and I stepped into our backyard just as the sun delivered its last hurrah of warmth. I sat on the blue swing set, my legs now so long they dragged in the dirt, while Pax dodged and dipped between my feet before finally lying down in the grass near the lilacs, which had been Snickers's favorite place too.

Eventually I lay down next to him and looked up at a sky that suddenly seemed chillier and more distant. Several stars appeared with a comforting twinkle.

There are times when you pray specifically for guidance. This time I didn't know what to pray for, and after a bit, I found myself simply praying for peace.

I took a deep breath and got up. It was time to call the foundation rep. I went back inside, dialed the number, and submitted my offer. I believed it was a fair value per acre. After that, I chose to trust that I would get the island if it was meant to happen. Beyond that, in terms of how the decision would be made, it was out of my control. I had to let it go.

I laid down the heaviness and focused solely on praying for Grandpa Tractor, whose heart had been opened, cleaned, repaired, and prepped to heal.

As I prayed, the words just flowed. I prayed for my heart too. I asked God to prevent the buildup of emotional sludge that often accumulates over a lifetime. I prayed that my heart would stay open and beat with the optimism that had led me to buy a houseboat in the middle of a February snowstorm and lease an island that was underwater. I wanted to keep the ability to dream and see people through eyes of kindness. I wanted to always feel hopeful.

When I was my grandpa's age, I wanted to be able to look back and hold up a few simple measuring sticks for whether I'd been a success.

Did my journey and its lessons lead me to become a better version of myself?

Did I genuinely care for and bring out the best in the people who were on the journey with me?

Did my work help make the world better in some significant way?

Did I take good care of what God entrusted to me, and did I follow His instructions for how things work?

Did I help create a kinder and more loving world?

That whole week, it felt like time stood still as Grandpa Tractor started his slow road to recovery and as I waited for a response from the foundation rep. There were no emails, no phone calls, no hint of what direction they were leaning. However, somewhere in those painfully long days and nights, my prayers were answered.

No, I didn't hear a booming voice telling me what to do.

No, my grandpa didn't suddenly get better and walk out of the hospital.

And no, I didn't hear from the foundation rep.

But I did find peace.

I had no doubt that God had heard the words I said, plus those I only thought. I didn't walk alone. Neither did I wait alone. It wasn't just about arriving; it was about each step of the journey. And I was reminded of how sometimes you get grace—more than you could ever hope for or deserve—and this was one of those moments.

On Sunday evening, after picking Mom up at the airport and getting the update on my grandpa (miraculously, he was on the mend), the three of us went to Peacebunny Cottage to feed and water the bunnies, and to give them all a little extra love. They were eager to give us plenty of love too.

Somehow the rabbits sensed the uncertainty about our collective future. Little John acted a bit restless, but he settled down once my dad stopped to say hello. Taffy and Oreo, the two rabbits who had first opened my heart to rescues, heard me coming and thought it might be time for a party. A quick rub behind their ears settled them down—and me as well. Mom had a visit with Fudge, and I caught up with my business associate, Whatchi. When I told him the latest about the island, he licked my cheek, tickling me with his angel tufts. I took that as a vote of confidence.

Just across the way, Huck looked ready for the next adventure. I sat down next to him, and he put his paws on my chest. That meant he wanted news.

"I don't know what's going to happen," I said. "They said I would hear from them soon."

Monday Morning

It was almost ten o'clock, and I was in my room when the phone rang. I'd stayed home from school to have some family time after my mom got back. I didn't know where my parents were or why they weren't picking up the phone. I walked into the living room and got it right before it went to voice mail.

"May I speak with Caleb, please?"

"Speaking," I said, immediately recognizing the voice of the foundation representative and feeling my body temperature rise a thousand degrees.

"Congratulations," he said.

The foundation was accepting my bid!

"Check your email. We sent a signed purchase agreement. It's done."

I know we said a few more words to each other, and it was all very professional. But I didn't hear anything after "congratulations." I was jumping up and down and ready to scream.

God was good.

Life was amazing.

Peacebunny Island was coming true!

"Mom! Dad!" I yelled, as I raced through the house to find them. "Guess who's buying an island?"

Epilogue

We've Come a Long Way

For Paxton, it was better late than never—late autumn, that is. My handsome American Blue rabbit was making his first trip to Peacebunny Island. Though he had declined boat trips for six months, Pax finally let me know that he was ready to see it for himself. This time when I asked who wanted to go, he gave me that look and enthusiastically stepped to the front of his pen.

Now, on a crisp October day, we were cruising toward Carrot Cake Bay on the SS *Peacebunny*. Paxton sat up high in Huckleberry's spot, where he could oversee my steering and enjoy the wind blowing through his fur.

"That's it, up ahead," I told him. "The island named after you and your family."

He bowed his head to clean his paws. I took that as a sign of approval.

Unlike most river outings, it was just the two of us that day. As we traveled down the long side of the island, we heard a splash in the water, and Pax turned his head in every direction, alert and curious.

"Oh, those are the beavers," I explained. "When I first got the island, it was just Xarol and his wife. But the two you heard are the youngest of their family of busy builders. I named them Frank and Lloyd."

As we glided to a stop, I pointed out the statue-like bird poised perfectly still about twenty yards up the shore, ready to announce our arrival.

"That's Chester, our friend the blue heron," I said. "He's here all the time."

For me, this day was a chance to thank my original Peacebunny for all he had inspired. I showed him my favorite trail on the island, the view from the two highest points, the spot where I hunted for golf balls, and the patch at Carrot Cake Bay where the wildflowers were most plentiful. In the afternoon, I built a fire and we enjoyed the crackling warmth, accompanied by the nonstop symphony of gurgles, chirps, and rustles.

"Pretty relaxing, don't you think?" I said.

As he nodded off, I described the two small neighboring islands that I'd recently purchased. "I named the one by the bridge with the rope swing Hope Island," I said. "And I called the other one Hoppiness Island."

As he rested in my lap, I felt Paxton's pleasure and pride. I stroked his soft blue fur, and after a while I got down on the ground with him so I could press my forehead against his.

"Remember everything," I told him silently.

I could almost hear Paxton reply, "We've come a long way together, you and me."

It Looks Magical

Since his first trip to the island, Paxton has been content to stay at our house or out at Peacebunny Cottage and listen to the stories we bring back from our adventures. Pax has heard all about Oreo snacking on wildflowers, Fudge nibbling the tall grass, Tator Tot zipping around the ever-changing natural agility course, and of course the first training session I did with his great-great-grandbabies, the young kinderbunnies.

Since then, I've lost track of the number of times I've taken kinderbunnies and rescues to the island to train with our youth volunteers. They learn to sit in wagons while we pull them around, and we take note of which ones are the best cuddlers. I have to say Oreo, Taffy, and Harley Jo are excellent at showing the young ones the way things are done. It's like they can whisper instructions on the ancient ways of kindness.

Even at just a couple of months old, the kinderbunnies are receptive and trusting. They enjoy the interaction and seem naturally drawn to us, most of them coming close to give a whisker kiss or a nose bonk to say hello. Nothing is more joyous than watching a litter of young rabbits come to the island for the first time and scamper, sniff, and hop around the outdoors in total freedom. I never tire of seeing the way bunnies know exactly how to be bunnies and comparing that to the way people are constantly trying to be something different from what they actually are.

During my second summer at Peacebunny Island, I investigated whether it would be possible to have guests beyond immediate family and Jacob, Kaden, and Nic and a handful of volunteers. I ran several contests, with the prize being a visit to the island for the winner and up to three guests. Contest categories ranged from guessing Oreo's favorite snack (grapes) to suggesting names for newborns (Snowdrop and Moonblink were the winners) to finishing the sentence "If I were a bunny . . ." Entries came from as far as New York and even Spain. A middle schooler from Ohio wrote the winning essay on why she wanted to visit Peacebunny Island.

> The little things in these furry creatures are the things that make them so lovable. The soft fur, the cute way they chew, the energy in their springy hop. These magical creatures have perfected the love potion. I particularly enjoy sleeping with my stuffed rabbit, Caesar, because he is fluffy and the perfect stuffed animal. That's why I want to come. Spending time with the Peacebunnies will help me to reconnect with myself and break from my crazy life.

It turned out others felt the same way. Word of Peacebunny Island spread, and my email in-box was flooded with requests to visit. "I don't mean to be a crazy stalker person, but the bunnies have stolen my mind," one woman wrote, attaching a silly photo. "I must meet Tator Tot!"

Another woman wrote, "I am at a complete loss. I just suffered a miscarriage, and no one knows what to say to me or how to help, and I don't know what to ask for, exactly. Then I thought about you and the bunnies, and I finally figured out what would help. Would you please let me come for a visit, just to sit on the shore like you do and watch the bunnies play?"

For every request, there was a different reason. I received notes from cancer survivors, caregivers, tourists, and newlyweds ("Nothing says love like a honeymoon with bunnies! Please, please, please, let us come and stay for a few hours!"). There was even a note from a man who knew his days were numbered and wanted to spend at least one or two of them on Peacebunny Island. "I am terminally ill," he wrote. "I always wanted to take a float trip on the Mississippi River and camp on an island. I can't believe a place like this exists in the world. Or is it heaven already?"

Of course, not everyone can visit Peacebunny Island in person. But I've developed a website and posted videos on social media to share the love with people, even if they can only get there in their imagination. "It looks magical," one woman wrote from Australia. "And even more so in my head!"

Hope, Hugs, and Hoppiness

The recent challenges posed by the coronavirus have tested the Peacebunnies in new and unforeseen ways. Like everyone, we have had to adjust financially and emotionally. All our annual Easter events, parties, and school visits were canceled, and we hunkered down at home. Then a local assisted-living home for seniors reached out to me; they were looking for a way to celebrate Easter while their residents were in lockdown.

Enter Lionardo da Vinci, Fudge, Willow, Tator Tot, Morris, Thumbalina, and a few of the youngsters from the Peacebunny unit. We made videos, including a special one for those in hospice, and shared them with the residents on the facility's closed-circuit television channel. Then, with the help of our volunteer teams, we cradled at least one bunny in our arms and made hundreds of window visits to seniors who were completely cut off from their loved ones.

All the training on the island paid off—the bunnies were as charming and soothing as ever, eagerly greeting the residents, who waved and blew kisses through the glass.

"The bunnies brightened our day," one of the directors said in a message to me.

When don't bunnies brighten the day?

I've relied on their cheerful dispositions myself. As disappointed as I was about the changes and cancellations brought about by COVID-19, it also meant more time with the bunnies, more campouts on the island with friends, and more time to pause and reflect. It gave us a chance to rest, regroup, and reinvent the ways the Peacebunnies can provide comfort to those going through difficult times.

We visited more senior homes. We mobilized teams of bunnies to bring relief to frontline health-care workers. And we bolstered our biosecurity plan to guard against the outbreak of RHDV2, the deadly rabbit hemorrhagic disease that has devastated so many animals across the Southwest.

Life hasn't slowed down as much as it has changed, which I suppose is the way it has always been for us two-legged creatures. Change is inevitable. I think that's what makes our memories so important. No matter what, we can return to them again and again, and they only seem to get better and more precious with the passage of time. I often think of the day I spent with Paxton on Peacebunny Island.

That afternoon, we climbed into the hammock under the cottonwood tree. With a warm breeze rocking us back and forth, I thought about the sweet furry creatures that were no longer with us, the volunteers who found us through a shared passion for bunnies, and all the amazing people we've met along the way.

"Hey, Pax. Are you thinking what I'm thinking?" I said.

His eyes sparkled in a way that said, "Go on, tell me what you're thinking."

I whispered in his ear, "Amazing things happen when you choose to open your heart."

His expression said, *I'm glad I was sent here to train you.*

He reached his head up and licked my face. I laughed and massaged his back. The island's stillness provided a reassuring sense of calm. Clouds floated above us. The wind hummed through the treetops, and birds serenaded us like background singers.

Funny how we can get so busy working and living that we overlook all the blessings that are right in front of us.

All that after only three summers on the island.

And I still have a lifetime ahead of me. But who's counting?

When my great-grandma learned I was writing this book, she asked what it was going to be about. I told her it's a story about a boy who sets out to get a new furry best friend and along the way finds himself working to save endangered rabbits—and training the calmest among them to comfort humans in need of help and healing. And how he eventually does it from a twenty-two-acre Mississippi River sanctuary named Peacebunny Island.

"It's a story that I hope will inspire even more hugs, hope, and hoppiness," I said.

With a full-belly laugh, she said, "You know, only a true visionary or an idiot would lease a river island that's underwater."

I smiled and gave her a gentle, loving nudge.

Grandma laughed again. "Well, Caleb, everyone likes a good idiot story. But I think they're going to love your true story even more."

Acknowledgments

My life story is made possible by the love and support of my four amazing grand-parents and my great-grandma, who have modeled service, integrity, purpose, tenacity, stewardship, and faith. What a blessing!

Thank you to my parents, who have given me the best gifts ever: a loving home filled with lots of laughter, joy, and time together, and the stuff that is helping me to become a man who chases after God's heart. Thank you for honoring your promise to support me that first year and going so far beyond that—immersing yourself in my dreams, providing guidance both to me and to the business, and figuring out how to keep them separate. Thanks, too, for not taking over or trying to fix everything, because the struggles are when I may have learned the most.

Thanks to the rest of my large extended family, especially Uncle Kris. Together with my close friends, we share a lifetime of memories and private jokes.

Thanks to my four-legged furry friends for letting me inside your world and making me part of your legacy.

I am especially grateful to the extended Peacebunny family of volunteers, farmers, leaders, donors, supporters, advisers, boaters, and business experts who have shown up at just the right time. What a gift to work together! I cherish you, not just for what you do, but for our growing friendships.

Thanks to my mentors, teachers, and leaders, with special thanks to the elders in my life whose stories provide so many lessons and much inspiration. (A huge thank-you to *all* those who choose to invest their time, wisdom, and resources in the next generations.) I'd also like to acknowledge the educators, city leaders, and specifically the Rotarians, who are people of action to open doors in our community.

Thanks to the members of the Dreamcatcher Family, who have taught me the importance of speaking and showing love and sharing hugs, starting with Ms. Debbie Gutowski. I have such fond memories of host families who have graciously welcomed us into their homes. To those who have given so much of themselves to travel with therapy animals and the Peacebunny Unit, you each filled a role that was perfectly matched to your heart and your skills. Thank you for choosing to serve. Special love to those who have been grafted together through these times together: *Ba Ma Pee.*

With respect and gratitude to Chief Arvol Looking Horse, Ms. Paula Horne-Mullen, Ms. Lisa Bellanger, and other elders: it is important to acknowledge that the Peacebunny Islands are located in Mni Sóta Maķoce (Minnesota)—the traditional, ancestral, and contemporary lands of indigenous people. The islands are within the Mississippi River, or Wakpá Tháŋka, downriver from Bdoté, where the Mississippi River meets the Minnesota River, near Inyan Sa (Red Rock), Taku Wakan Tipi (Carver's Cave), and Eháŋna Wičháhapi (Indian Mounds Park burial mounds). I invite readers to join me in learning about the history and first peoples of the places we live and learn how to best protect the environment for future generations. *Mitákuye Oyás'iŋ* (We are all related).

Thanks to all those who see potential and choose to take a risk, to open doors, and to share their expertise. A special thank-you to Todd Gold, Dan Strone, Sarah Atkinson, Stephanie Rische, and everyone engaged in bringing this book together or in sharing the larger story. Thank you also to government leaders who have embraced a youth-run business and helped us navigate your world successfully. Special credit to Bruce. I appreciate Barbara O'Brien and Henry Schneider from Open Window Production for sharing their skills behind the camera and in the studio, and to our media friends who have helped preserve memories.

Thanks to all the students involved in starting and running the nonprofit organization. Special kudos to those trailblazers, especially in the St. Paul Lego League, for your leadership and observational research on animal-assisted

learning and behavior intervention. Your Animal Allies project led to the Reading PALs (Pet Assisted Learning) program for improving literacy and to the Bunny Relaxation Rooms for promoting self-regulation and trauma-sensitive learning. Your hard work to get grants, implement programs, and conduct assessments led to a proven model for other schools to follow. This is what happens when youth lead with their own ideas and adults support their vision!

Thanks to all those who care for animals and the environment. I deeply appreciate the countless experts who have taken time to share insights, wisdom, research, and even differing perspectives. Rather than simply making assumptions or dismissing a kid on a mission, you have helped shape our programming and improve the way we care for the rabbits and the island. (Good motives are a starting point, but we aim for highest standards, too, so come join us to make our organization even better!)

Thanks to all the big dreamers, the fire starters, the entrepreneurs out there who are creating the change they hope to see in the world.

Thanks to all the committed worker bees behind the scenes: you make the world better and sweeter and kinder, whether or not you get noticed and acknowledged. The world needs you!

Thanks to all those who show courage as they go through big challenges right now and especially all those who have an empty chair at their dinner table.

And finally, thanks to *you* for sharing this journey. You are hereby officially invited to be ambassadors of hugs, hope, and hoppiness.

Ephesians 3:20

About the Author

Caleb Smith is the 16-year-old visionary behind Peacebunny Island, an animal sanctuary where he trains rescued and rare heritage-breed rabbits to become comfort animals. His business includes a fostering program that has involved nearly 500 families; a Peacebunny Unit, which brings therapy rabbits to visit seniors at assisted-living homes and hospices; and a responder program that helps people who are dealing with loneliness, trauma, and grief, including those in crisis situations and juvenile justice facilities.

Caleb launched the Peacebunny Foundation, which hosts rabbit-themed STEM educational programs to excite youth about science, technology, engineering, and math and to mobilize them for community service. He is the recipient of the Gold Congressional Award and the Duke of Edinburgh's International Award. He lives in Minneapolis, Minnesota, with his mom and dad, and he cares for a colony of rabbits at Peacebunny Cottage.

Peacebunny Island

Follow our adventures at
Peacebunny Island!

Visit

WWW.PEACEBUNNYISLAND.COM

Find us on social media

@PEACEBUNNYISLAND

Meet the bunnies by watching the

"JOURNEY TO PEACEBUNNY ISLAND"

video on our YouTube channel.

Proceeds from the sale of this book will support
Peacebunny Islands, Inc., and Peacebunny Foundation.

CP1651